Tales and Trails Of KrispyKritter

Adventures of a Long Distance Hiker

By

wayne p. petrovich

i

Disclaimer:

There is a saying in the hiking community that each individual should "hike their own hike". The foundation of this statement is based on the premise that each hiker has a different hiking style, stride and most importantly, different levels of knowledge, competency, and gear. What works for one, may not work for another. Take this concept and expand it to include any form of outdoor recreation.

The advice, tips and rules found within this book are only suggestions to make backpacking and outdoor recreation easier and to give an individual a better chance in surviving unexpected emergencies. Each situation is unique and should be approached on a case by case scenario. A successful conclusion may be achieved through the application of different techniques. So far, those mentioned in the book by KrispyKritter have worked for him, but they may not work for you. They are suggestions that you may, or may not use. Injury or a fatal incident may unfortunately still occur even when all resources are successfully deployed. What you take with you, how you implement a plan, and the judgment used to put the plan into action, is your responsibility, and in no way makes Wayne Petrovich aka KrispyKritter responsible.

Cover Design by: Zack Turco
Editing by: Richard Gretsky

Front cover photograph taken by Greyhound on the John Muir Trail near Carson Pass, Ca.
Back cover photograph taken by KrispyKritter on Little Hump, Appalachian Trail

ISBN-13: 978-0615810980
ISBN-10: 0615810985

Printed in the United States

DEDICATION

This book is dedicated to Valaria Petrovich, my mother. No longer able to walk through nature due to illness, Mom encouraged, supported and vicariously found another way to enjoy the benefits of nature through my adventure journals, phone calls from various trail towns, and long hours of discussion each time I returned from the trail. Thank you for being my number one fan.

CONTENTS

ACKNOWLEDGMENTS

My hiking adventures would never have happened if it were not for my childhood experiences with my family. I owe a great deal to the two people who were instrumental in bringing the world of nature into my life, so from the bottom of my happy feet to the top of a spirit that soars with the eagles, thank you mom and dad.

A special thank you needs to be expressed to another part of my life. Even though we do not see eye to eye on the merits of backpacking long distances, my wife Jacquie (Lady Kritter) has still supported my hikes, helped write my journals and kept our nest safe for my return. Thank you my love.

Sincere gratitude goes out to several individuals who helped me in the final stages of writing this book. David Miller (trail name AWOL) has been a tremendous help in getting this manuscript to print, Kathy Moyer (Kat) for proofreading my stories, Zack Turco for art direction and Richard Gretsky for editing the manuscript. You guys rock!

I am also deeply indebted to Greyhound, a great friend and hiking partner. Together, we have learned to respect each other's hiking style and developed a common bond of reverence for the land. I hope our trails continue until the stop sign at journey's end.

Any book written about hiking is deeply indebted to the people who spend countless hours of manual labor maintaining the trails. My experiences (and this book!) would not have been possible without the hard work of these trail maintainers. High five, folks!

Lastly, my family - my mom, dad and everyone else whom I love and care for deeply, thank you for putting up with my ramblings. In addition, a family is not always defined as a group of individuals who are genetically related, but also as a group brought together by common bond. Over the years and miles of trail, I have found a second family that consists of hikers and trail angels. I thank you from the depths of my heart and to the center of my Vibram soles, for you are truly brothers and sisters walking with me on the bosom of Mother Nature.

.

INTRODUCTION

My first memory of Mother Nature is from the age of four. My parents, as they always did, saved stale bread in the oven for the weekend when my dad was off. They put the bread into a brown paper bag and drove my sister and me to the Tarrytown Reservoir to feed the ducks. It was sunny and a slight wind rippled the water as it broke onto the rocky shore. I broke apart the hard bread, threw the broken pieces into the water and watched one duck, then two, and then a whole flock, swim to the floating food and scoop it up with their bills. Green trees stood tall around the lake, the wind blew through my hair, the sun warmed my young face, and there, I found nature.

Growing up in a family of five, mom would regularly wrangle us up in the evening, sit us down, and tell us stories of how she traveled out west in wagon trains; stories of sleeping at night on plateaus surrounded by mountains, songs, dancing and storytelling around campfires, crossing mighty rivers and learning how to survive the environment of the west with the help of the Native Americans. As I grew up, we would have family outings in nature with boat rides on the ocean and frequent weekend camping trips into the interior of Florida. During my teenage years the family took long summer trips to the mountains out west to live out those wagon train adventures. The Boy Scouts further developed my interest for the outdoors through education, survival techniques, and caring for the environment.

As an adult, I discovered that nature gave me a sense of well being and a calming teacher of how things work in the world. I began to understand what John Muir said when he penned:

"Climb the mountains and get their good tidings. Nature's peace will flow into you as sunshine flows into trees. The

winds will blow their own freshness into you and the storms their energy, while cares will drop away from you like the leaves of Autumn."

After venturing out more and more, I realized that I was a true Gemini, living in two worlds: the civilized and that of Mother Nature. The first contains man-made objects, family and friends, a house on the edge of a forest with developers waiting to destroy its trees. The second is the natural one, filled with an assortment of landscapes, living plants and animals, and people like me who understand the importance of living life immersed within this world. My senses are more and more awakened as I spend time in the beauty of that second world, gently earth-touching Mother Nature's trails.

When I return from my trips into the wild and step back onto the concrete and asphalt of the cities, I am frequently asked some form of 'What is it like to be out there?' Sometimes I tell them that it's like being one with nature. Other times, that it's like seeing the earth as the hunters and gathers did hundreds of years ago. It really depends on the story they're asking about or the particular person I'm talking to, but the stories of adventure persist; those of landscapes, animals, and unique journeys that have made a significant impact on who I am.

I first started writing in a private journal to remember the different experiences I was having in nature. Then those journals slowly became a sizeable amount of short stories, and one day my wife, Lady Kritter, said, "Why don't you write a book of your stories and call it The Tales and Trails of KrispyKritter?"

So, that's what I did. Because I love telling the stories, and in the hope that through my writings, I could encourage others to get up off the couch, get away from the electronics of civilization and experience the same feelings, have the same wonderment - simply by going outdoors.

"I only went out for a walk and finally concluded to stay out till sundown, for going out, I found, was really going in." -John Muir

I've adopted this mantra, and stay in nature for long periods of time - enjoying the mountains, the valleys, and wherever the paths take me, using the same method of transportation that the cavemen used, slowly earth-touching the land. With only food, shelter and water on my back, I leave behind the concrete jungles and Mount Trashmores of the cities for a simplistic way of life. I feel more alive, better connected to the heartbeat of life. There, alone with Mother Nature, I become not just a visitor, but another living being engaging with its environment.

I sincerely hope you enjoy my stories, but, more importantly, that you create your own.

Krispykritter

CHAPTER 1
A Newbie in the Woods

It is amazing to me how events in one's life can have a direct effect on the outcome of the character of the person. For me it began during my childhood with early memories of me being outdoors with my parents. Throughout the years of my youth, weekend family camping trips were taken to different flora and fauna of the wilds of Florida. The big camping trip was planned during the summer vacation from school. This trip involved 3 to 4 weeks on the road, visiting national, state and historic sites, between Florida and the Rocky Mountains, in a camper. By the time I hit my teenage years I found what John Muir calls, "the wonderment of nature". I was the oldest of five children and my parents would inspire each of us to love and respect nature, as well as one another. Ever since that first family camping trip out west, I have had a connection with Mother Nature's mountains and forests.

The mountains were calling. When I graduated from high school I left the high humidity and flat as pancake lands of South Florida for a college in the Appalachians of West Virginia, hoping never to return. I think that more than anything else, being 19 and naïve was the reason I came back home. I still had a lot of growing up to do. It was family at first that kept me in Florida. I grew up in a family enriched environment and learned valuable lessons from family members.

Then, a realization hit me when I read a book called *Appalachian Trail* by Ronald M. Fisher that was published by the National Geographic Society in 1972. The content was amazing; it challenged me in such deep ways that spoke to some of the dreams and desires of my very being. I knew at that moment that I was going to be a backpacker! But, how was I going to do it? Where would I go? What equipment would I take? It took me several years to get the nerve to put those thoughts into action. Most men my age had their baptism into manhood through military service in Vietnam. I got mine with the City of Hollywood (FL) Fire Department, and was becoming a seasoned firefighter/medic. I thought I could do no wrong - so, I bought a small department store A-frame pup tent, an external frame backpack, food for three people and set off with my girlfriend and five year old son for a weekend adventure in the wilderness. It was that trip, and those that followed soon after that set the stage for later long-distance ones. I learned much in them, and those lessons have contributed to a journey that has not yet ended.

Baptism into Backpacking 101 – Myakka River State Park
On a hot and humid day in late August 1979 - at the age of twenty-nine years old - I took my first steps on a dusty Florida trail.

I had decided that the first foray into the wilderness would be in my home state of Florida. Myakka River State Park was the site of the jaunt; a the three mile hike with my girlfriend and 5 year old son to a place called Bee Island Primitive Camp Area. We followed a slow moving creek and crossed over hot, open areas of palmetto prairies. The green colored grass fields ran into the horizon, meeting blue skies that were spotted with floating cotton ball clouds. The park was beautiful: clumps of dark green oak hammocks resembled islands in an ocean, dotting the landscape and providing shade from the merciless summer sun. The calm was only temporary, as those same oases were home to squadrons of ferocious blood sucking vampire-like mosquitoes. This tranquil, yet irritating, backdrop helped me learn one of my first lessons from Mother Earth – that there is a balance in everything, and though it is good, it isn't always pleasant.

Two hours later we arrived at the primitive campsite nestled in an oak hammock. And then it happened, I quickly was taught the second of many lessons taught to me by Mother Nature.

In the cool of the shade as the sun was going down, I started a small fire from wood I'd gathered around the hammock. In between the hoards of flying mosquitoes, I attempted cooking for three famished hikers with a Boy Scout Mess Kit for one. What...was I thinking?! I eventually gave up; it was too much trouble. If Lesson 1 was 'Balance', Lesson 2 was definitely 'Always be prepared'. I hadn't been on that day, with pots not large enough to cook for more than one person. Undaunted by the day's events, I made that night tea for everybody and handed out nuts and dried fruit for dinner. I set up the single-walled pup tent as more squadrons of the mosquitoes dive bombed any skin left exposed. Lesson 3, 'Mosquitoes suck'. Needless to say we took refuge inside the steamy pup tent for the remainder of the night. By the morning, condensation inside the tent created its own wet-weather system, causing the tent roof to sag and soak everything inside: people, clothes and sleeping bags. Lesson 4 - 'Tents with ventilation are a necessity'. I remember waking the next morning and though there were greetings, none of them were "Good morning".

I thought four quarts of water would be sufficient for all of us to drink on this overnight hike. I was so wrong. We used at least half that amount on the hike into the campsite. I now know, on days like that day, four quarts would be the required minimum to take per person, per day, without water re-supply. I cooked oatmeal in the morning and let everyone drink the remainder of the water to rehydrate. Lesson 5 'Everybody carries their own water and enough of it'.

We still had to break camp and head back to the car. I slowed the pace to conserve energy. Mother Nature had taught me to temper my cockiness (Lesson 6 - 'Realize healthy limitations' was already learned from pushing myself too hard and getting exhausted). Some of the things that I had learned in the civilized world did not necessarily translate to life in the wilderness. Critical items important for survival in the wilds are water, shelter and food (Lesson 7). Oh yeah, and *bug spray*. Thirsty, tired and hungry we arrived at the car, threw the gear into the back and they companions dragged me to the nearest water spigot in the park and then the closest fast food restaurant. Lesson 8 'Know the limitations and needs of the people in your group'. Each person is different. A child's needs are greater than an adult and each adult can be different from another. It's possible that their expectations of that trip were a little different than mine.

Days after coming home I went to the local thrift shop and bought a 2 quart aluminum sauce pot with a lid. Aluminum, I thought, was a better choice because it was lighter than stainless steel or cast iron and just as good as a heat conductor as other pot metals. The versatility of using the pot over a cooking fire, or a stove, gave the pot dual purposes. Lesson 9 - 'Dual purpose equipment eliminates redundant gear and weight from the pack'.

Next, I went to a backpacking store in Dade County with the goal of buying some sort of backpacking stove instead of building a fire every time I wanted to eat (Lesson 10 - 'Fire is vital'). I finally decided on a Seva 123 white gas stove. When I took the stove home and placed it next to the sauce pot, I realized the stove fit very nicely inside the pot, saving space. I was immediately at ease with the simplicity of the stove's instruction and operation during test runs in the backyard. The cooking combination of pot and stove became standard pieces of backpacking gear for me. The same pot and stove has remained a reliable constant in my equipment inventory to this day, thirty years later.

My next purchase was a rainfly (a tarp used for rain protection) to cover the pup tent, hoping to eliminate the awful condensation.

A Rookie Still In Training – Long Pine Key Campground, Everglades National Park

A month later I was sitting in the A-frame tent with my girlfriend in a campsite at Long Pine Key Campground, Everglades National Park. The heat and humidity were oppressive and the mosquitoes were even worse than we'd experienced at Myakka River State Park. In the Everglades, I learned what an unknown pioneer meant when he wrote, "You could swing a pint cup and catch a quart of mosquitoes." I guessed that was the main reason the campground was almost deserted, except for a small, but dedicated, Boy Scout troop and a gal from Miami.

By that trip, my hiking prowess was already making progress. I had plenty of water, a stove that was working great and bug juice to keep the insects at bay (the only disappointment was that the rainfly did not stop the condensation at night).

This taught me a major lesson: when you're properly prepared for a trip, you're the most open to experience the beauty that's around you.

In the Everglades, we explored the Anhinga Trail overlooking Taylor Slough (a channel of slow moving water that stays wet year round) slowly drifting through buttonwood, willows and cypress trees. We spent countless hours listening to and watching the slough come to life on the trail's boardwalk. The tea-colored water contained an ecosystem that maintained the balance of life during the dry season. Rosettes of light green leaves of water lettuce floated on the slough's surface, intermingled with water hyacinth. Rooted in the shallow watery floor of the slough, and extending out of the water, were arrow shaped leaves of the arrowhead, cattails, floating yellow water lily blossoms and the spikes of violet blue flowers of the pickerel weed. A menagerie of animals could be seen from the boardwalk: alligators, gar, bream, frogs, turtles, ducks and gallinules entertained us with their various activities. Birds with long skinny legs-the great white heron, the great blue heron, and the American (common) egret - were scattered throughout the landscape and stood motionless, waiting for their dinner below. The *Anhinga* (how the trail got its name - commonly called the "water turkey", or "snake bird") could be seen dive bombing with folded wings into the water for their food. The Anhingas then swam with only their head and long neck above water (resembling a snake), sometimes with a small fish between its bill. Other Anhingas were perched on a tree limbs with their wings stretched out to dry after their swim. And at the end the day, nature's grand finale was a merging of brilliant colors into a sunset slowly dipping over the sawgrass. When the bright orange ball fell below the horizon, I knew I was truly hooked with the outdoors.

Learning to Adapt, Improvise and Overcome – Highland Hammocks State Park

Many men have lived by the concept "adapt, improvise, overcome" - and I, too, have adopted it to live in a spirit of harmony with nature; but I feel this concept has been lost in the throw-away, mechanical, concrete jungle of modern man.

Those three simple words have been tools of survival in the wild, as well as, useful in the civilized world - and on more than one occasion, remembering them saved my life.

One particular weekend camping trip I used those three words in a survival situation in a primitive area (no water, electricity or bathrooms) located at Highland Hammocks State Park. I was still not happy with the department store A-frame pup tent. A new problem developed as the tent's fabric started to stretch, causing the middle to droop. No matter how tightly I secured the center, it was sagging down into my face by morning. Thus, the tent was always filled with condensation.

The weather for the weekend was predicted to be a light rain with a few thunder showers. I wanted to experience Mother Nature in all conditions, not just bright sunny days like everyone else. On Saturday and Sunday, a light rain had fallen throughout the day. Hikes along the Cypress Swamp Trail out into Charley Bowleg's Creek, Fern Garden Trail and the Ancient Hammock Trail released the musky, earthy smells of the hammocks. The civilized world had retreated indoors, protected from the soggy elements of nature-while I had the whole place to myself.

On Sunday night, my peaceful world of wetness became a world of survival. As the day was losing light, an ominous dark-blue gray cloud, exploding with lightning and thunder, approached from the northwest. As a warning, the wind picked up, the temperature dropped and the smell of rain was in the air. This was not going to be a fun night. Suddenly, a great gust of wind blew through the camp swaying the pine trees! "Oh, my God!" I knew that if it could move pine trees, it could hurt me. I had set up camp in a grove of trees and looked up to see if any dead tree limbs (called widow-makers) might be prepped to fall my way - based on wind and distance from myself to the trees. I couldn't be sure.

Within minutes fierce lightning bolts were striking, closely followed by the immediate clap of the loudest thunder I had ever heard. Heavy drops were pelting the tent. Without a vestibule (an antechamber between the tent and the outside) on the tent, the nylon fabric on the tent door was barely keeping the rain out. I had to put together something quickly to keep water out of the tent's entrance. Using extra stakes, rope and a space blanket as a tarp, I set up a makeshift canopy over the entrance. Waves of heavy wind, rain and lightning continued throughout the night. I would hear every once in awhile the heavy thump of a tree limb hitting the ground somewhere close to my tent. I thought for sure I was going to die, either by a lightning strike, or crushed by a limb.

Fearful as I was, I slept during minor lulls in the storm. It reminded me of being in a weak, yet dangerous, hurricane - while in a tent. As the overcast morning light came shown through the soggy wet walls of my tent, I poked my head out: large tree limbs laid all around me on the ground and the space blanket I'd set up was in tatters. Looking back inside the tent: puddles of water and everything that could absorb moisture were saturated.

Everything was wet and some of my equipment ruined, but boy was it good to be alive! To this day, this was one of the most powerful storms I have ever encountered, anywhere. That trip really taught me, through that storm, how powerful and awesome nature really is.

And on the hike back to the car, nature showed how balanced it is by displaying its beauty as the earth 'came back to life' after the storm.

Sunshine revived the landscape and cool, moist air filled my lungs. Beads of water were quietly bursting on the ground after rolled off their leaves. All over the forest, water droplets looked like tiny crystals dangling off magnificent spider webs. Steam rose from the hammock's floor where rays of sunlight penetrated the trees' canopy, reaching the vegetation on forest floor. I encountered a young buck grazing in an old orange grove, a leftover picture of what the earlier Florida pioneers would have often seen. Quietly, at a respectful distance, I stopped my progress to watch the movements of the deer. His head popped up from his meal and I could feel his energy as he gazed at me. We casually nodded at one another and parted ways, more as friends than enemies.

Back in my car, as I played out the experience in my mind, I realized that - as delightful as some of it had been - I had to make a change. Riding out storms in a pup tent was not acceptable in the future. It was time to upgrade. I researched, talked with other backpackers, and armed with information, went back to the camping store where I bought my stove. I came home with a better quality tent that was popular with the hiking community. The tent was pricey but I was learning that good quality gear typically had better durability and could last much longer with proper care.

Go West Young Man, Go West – Rocky Mountains of Colorado

I continued to challenge my abilities to live in nature (and the quality of my gear), each time I went out. I felt like my basic backpacking skills had been getting pretty solid and I was also building a trust in my gear - by spending money to get proper gear, and by using that gear over and over, learning how each piece performed and what its limitations were.

It was time to take it to the mountains.

I picked up my sister and her husband in Greeley and set out for the northern terminus of the Colorado's Front Range west of Fort Collins. It was early autumn and the aspen leaves were already turning their famous golden color. We headed for the West Branch Trail, located in the Rawah Lakes Wilderness, a trail that I knew was littered with glacier-carved valleys, granite peaks and an abundance of ridges dotted with mountain lakes. The beginning of the trail was fairly level and followed a dirt road with some gentle climbs as it paralleled the West Branch of the Laramie River. The trail crossed a creek and traveled through aspen and spruce groves. I got my first introduction of a mountain switchback (a trail that zigzags up the side of a mountain at a reasonable angle to climb a steep grade). Between the elevation and the climb, I was breathless within a matter of minutes. A photographer at the time, I was also burdened with a pack weight that included two large body 35mm SLR cameras, assorted telephoto lenses and accessories. In addition, the trail did not get any easier: it narrowed, became very rough and then traveled over rocks of assorted sizes. And, it was also a pack trail. So, as I was climbing, (most of the time out of breath and looking out to not trip on rocks), I also had to lookout for another type of nugget (aka, horse shit). After crossing a large stream on a log bridge I heard the most beautiful word for that day, "camp". Within minutes my new tent was up next to the stream with the hopes that the sound of the cascading water would lull me to sleep. I spent the remainder of the day exploring up and down the creek until the late afternoon thunder showers moved in. Cold air rode in with the approaching darkness of night, chilling me to the bone.

I had not expected the brisk temperatures throughout the night. I was unbelievable, hypothermic-shaking type of cold. I couldn't stand it any longer. I got up before the light of day and used my flashlight to hunt for any type of firewood I could find. I gathered enough wood to start a small fire until the warmth of the morning sun came to my rescue. I sat down by the flickering flames and radiant heat to ponder where I failed, what I could have done differently to avoid similar problems in the future. I wandered around camp to build up more body heat. I turned to head back towards the stream when it hit me. THE STREAM! I was too close to the stream. The cold moist air from the stream was creating an atmosphere like a three ton air conditioner; great for hot summer days, but horrible for cold weather.

Soon after, I moved the tent to an area of boulders facing east. My plan was to catch the morning sun heating the rocks that, in turn, would act like a convection oven and give me a cozy wake up in the warmth. The plan worked. I improvised, adapted and overcame my situation. The remainder of the hike we passed through spectacular scenery of high elevation meadows and parks surrounded by rugged mountain peaks, some with crystal clear mountain streams running through. During rest breaks I closed my eyes and pictured individuals from a time long past, walking through the grassy meadows, gazing at abundant wildlife and being in balance with nature. I knew that I, too, was entering into a harmonic relationship with Mother Nature.

My sister and her husband had to get back to work, so I dropped them off in Greeley and headed back into the mountains. I'd decided to take a five day road trip while I waited to pick them back up and we headed back into the wilderness together.

I drove westward and visited the ghost towns of Cripple Creek, Victor and Central City. Years ago, these towns didn't have the lights and action of the gambling casinos that are there today. I visited the Portland and Independence Mines that made Cripple Creek and Victor rich and famous for gold. Everywhere, you could see the remains of foundations of where buildings once stood. The whole area was littered with holes dug in the ground by men searching for that one big mother lode, and finding nothing, they abandoned the holes (foot sized to cavernous) to start another - creating gaps in the ground concealed by years of vegetation growth. Creating a potentially hazardous place to hike around and explore. I'd had enough, and quietly headed back to the car.

Towards the end of my road trip I found a campsite on a mesa overlooking a canyon below at Black Canyon National Park. The canyon is carved out by the relentless flow of the Gunnison River with sheer vertical cliffs on the northern rim and a steep sloping southern rim. I learned from a ranger that there was a particularly hard trail that went down into the canyon to campsites on the river. "Why not?" I rhetorically asked myself, as I tightened the shoulder straps to my backpack and headed down the trail descending gently through low growing evergreens. The path steepened further into the canyon and started into switchbacks. Twenty minutes from the trailhead the degree of descent steepened and each step had to be taken with extreme care. The degree of decline became so severe that rangers attached a chain to a tree that worked like an extended handrail for 200 feet of descent. Beyond the chain, the trail was blazed by yellow ribbons tied to the limbs of small bushes. It was very easy to lose the trail, so when I got to the first ribbon I started looking for the next one down below. I leapfrogged the ribbons until I reached a field of scree (loose gravel). Rocks and boulders of all sizes and shapes were everywhere, held loosely together by one another. Each step I took dislodged a rock, causing it to cartwheel below. I set up little cairns of rocks so I could follow my path back up when I decided to return from the canyon floor.

Finally, I stood on a large boulder jetting out into the river on the canyon floor. It was hard to describe the raw, natural energy I found there. Swift clear water of the mountain river swirled around boulders on its shore. Water cascaded over large sections of fallen rock that broke away from the canyon walls. The water's activity never stopped: thousands and thousands of gallons of water constantly pushed downstream searching for a river and the ocean.

Once I got use to the wild river, I looked up and received a visual overload: the canyon wall was so close it felt like I could reach out and touch the other side, yet it shot to the sky majestically in front of me. Tiny reflections of cars passing above were barely visible at the rim. My first thought was, "If there was a large magnitude earthquake, I would be buried by the fallen rock. Maybe...my remains would be discovered thousands of years later. I would represent what future man would think about mankind in the twentieth century." Playfully, my mind ran with the scenario. I could see the archeology report in my mind, "During our excavation of the campsite we found the crushed bones of a slender male, with primitive clothing and footwear made from a plant fiber called cotton. Next to the body was a metal framed piece of equipment with fabric remnants that we believe was used to carry his essentials on his back. Carbon testing indicates this individual lived around 1900-2000 A.D. We can tell by the bone structure that he was probably quite attractive." I laughed to myself the remainder of the evening as I thought about the scenario, almost as a defense mechanism so that I didn't worry about the looming rocks. And luckily, no earthquake came. I left my site the next morning and followed my cairn blazes, the yellow ribbon, the chain and finally the footpath out of the canyon (and my would-be-tomb).

I left the arid, dust and dirt of the western range of the Rockies and headed back to Greeley to pick up my sister and her husband for another round of adventure backpacking. I spent the night in a campground along Blue Mesa Reservoir on the way back. Being the only occupant of the campground, I had the pleasure of being serenaded by the howls of a pack of coyotes throughout the night. I believe this was the first time I felt in complete harmony with nature. I was losing my status as a visitor and gaining my residence. I found my drug and I was hooked.

My next Colorado backpacking exploit took place in Rocky Mountain National Park on the Fern Lake Trail. It was here that I came face to face for the first time with the lurking, wild beasts of the night.

I knew unusual events were about to take place when my sister, her husband and I registered at the ranger station and was told an early September snowfall was expected above 8,000 feet. Our campsite was at 9500 ft which meant this could very well be my first experience in snow. We parked the car at the trailhead in Moraine Park and began our hike. The trail initially followed a relatively flat terrain that paralleled the Big Thompson River through a valley full of golden aspen. It took almost two hours to hike along the Big Thompson because I stopped every hundred feet or so to stand on a boulder alongside the river and scan the mountain scenery, breathe in the mountain air and take pictures. The trail started its climb into the mountains with sheer walls on either side, and then the trail wove through a series of huge boulders called Arch Rocks (cottage-sized rock monoliths). Shortly after leaving Arch Rocks we entered a small canyon of steep walls where the force of the combined waters of the Big Thompson River, Fern Creek and Spruce Creek created a large eroded pool of churning water as well as several smaller pools. An area appropriately named The Pool. We crossed the river on a wooden log bridge and found that our campground for the night was high above the river on one side and Fern Creek on the other - with scenic views of mountains and forests surrounding us. I had learned my lesson by camping next to the water in cold weather, so I set up my tent as far away from the water as possible. The temperature was quickly falling as a beautiful sunset indicated the close of the day. I strung my food bag on a tree limb that hung over my tent as the last rays of daylight faded. We then settled into our warm sleeping bags for what I had hoped would be a cozy peaceful night in the mountains.

Little did I know, the creatures of the night had other plans for us. Around midnight I was awakened by the soft sound of something lightly hitting the roof of my tent. Not fully awake, I assumed the sound was large snowflakes alighting on my tent. But then it happened. I heard something else: the unmistakable sound of footsteps. I was immediately fully awake and all my senses were on alert. I tried to identify the sound. My first thought was that my sister or her husband was outside their tent on a nature call. I called out to them.

"Are you guys outside?" The reply was, "No!" I then asked, "Did you hear the footsteps?"

Quickly I heard both of them say, "Yes!" "Then what is outside?" No one knew because we were inside our tents with the flaps down. "Maybe the footsteps will go away," I said. Fat chance, as moments later more steps were heard. I tried to distinguish the sound as man or beast. At one point I even asked if someone was outside, foolishly thinking someone would reply. I could still hear the footsteps along with the soft pelting sound hitting my tent. I finally had enough and decided to face the unknown with a flashlight in one hand and my Buck knife in the other. I quickly unzipped the screening of the tent, opened the flap and jumped up in a defiant stance ready to do battle. Thinking it was either man or bear; I looked at eye level and found my high intensity beam vanishing into the forest. Lowering the beam, I looked down and found myself surrounded by a pack of full-size raccoons. I then realized I was being hit by falling matter. I focused my eyes up with the beam of light to the food bag hanging in the tree and saw another raccoon eating the bag of puffed wheat that had been in my food bag. The same puffed wheat that was gently falling on my tent like fresh snow.

I had placed the food bag too close to the trunk of the tree and tree limb (another lesson learned through experience). The crafty critters unzipped my food bag and found an all-you-can-eat buffet. The eating frenzy was on and no matter what I tried to do, I could not get the four legged piranhas to leave. My sister's husband came out and between the two of us we scattered them with our saber swords of light. However, they didn't leave. Those pesky good-for-nothing varmints stood on the periphery of our lights waiting for us to go back to the warmth of our sleeping bags. The remainder of the night we stood guard over our precious cache of food.

The raccoons apparently decided that they'd had enough food and fun for one night and went home at first light. We took an inventory of our food supply and it was not good. Outside of a few snacks all our meals were eaten or damaged by the marauding animals. It was senseless for us to continue on our journey without sustenance. The views of Little Matterhorn, Knobtop Mountain and Notchtop reflecting off the lake's water would have to wait for another time.

My First Long Distance Hike - Learning Skills in the Wilderness

What constitutes a "long distance hike" in the outdoor world has been a debate for years with no clear definition. Most people will agree a long distance hike involves an individual hiking multiple days and nights in the outdoors. The conflict comes into play when mileage is placed on the definition. Does it begin at 20, 50, 75, or even for some 100 miles? There is no right or wrong answer. I believe each individual should make up his or her own definition according to their particular hiking style.

My long distance hiking, up to this point (August 1986) consisted of several weekend backpacking trips under my waist belt. I felt backpacking in the wilderness charged me with positive energy experiences. I had no problem leaving behind civilization's hectic pace of life and finding solitude in the woods. Most of all, through stamina and fortitude, my backpacking was building within me a determined individual who could overcome any type of adversity. So, I decided my first real long distance hike would test my endurance and strength on a ten day trek through the Great Smoky Mountain National Park (three times longer than any stay I had had in the woods so far). The hike would start at the southern boundary of the park on the Appalachian Trail (AT) at Fontana Dam, extend northward on the AT across the national park, and reach the northern boundary at Davenport Gap - a total of 72 miles.

This feat by itself was to be a major accomplishment. However, to further challenge my abilities, I decided to invite four diverse and unique individuals to join me: My first choice was my girlfriend at the time, who on our first backpacking trip together, sneaked an electric hairdryer and curling iron into her backpack. She brought them she said, "just in case an electrical outlet was found". I gained confidence with her as a hiking partner after several backpacking trip together. Next was my athletic and goal-oriented, twelve year old daughter, Alison. Recently crowned a state champion in gymnastic, she wanted to conquer yet another arena of mental and physical challenges. I also thought this would be a good time for a father and daughter to spend quality-time bonding. My third choice was my younger brother Dereck, whose culinary talents as a chef - I was hoping - could teach me how to turn cardboard tasting beef jerky, noodles and dehydrated foods into delightful outdoor cuisine. A late addition to our group was a lady by the name of Debbie who worked for the local county fire department. Debbie never backpacked before in her life and needed some time away from the department to decompress and do something completely different in her life – seek adventure. Together, we pushed each other, and I was challenged to push my limits in leadership as well.

The hike had to be carefully planned and organized before the first foot fell on the Appalachian Trail. Road maps were studied to find a route that led us out of the flat lands of Florida and into the mountains of North Carolina and Tennessee. Next to the road maps were the topographical and trail maps of the national park. Food was prepared, dehydrated and packed into meals, then divided into five groups. Each of us had to carry his or her share of the food. We would not have the convenience of running to the store on the trail. I was taking these tasks very seriously; four people were counting on me to safely get them through seventy plus miles of wilderness.

The planned date of departure arrived and we loaded hikers and gear into two vehicles, and drove for many hours. We arrived safely in Gatlinburg, Tennessee after leaving one of the vehicles at the Davenport Gap trailhead, and spent our last night in civilization double checking our backpacks and contents. The backpacks were packed and re-packed until each one was a comfortable fit and I was satisfied. That night, giddy with excitement, we all cherished our last ice cold drinks and then slipped into our last indoor beds.

Early the next morning we were crossing Fontana Dam when someone showed up who has since been my constant companion:

Murphy's Law – "Anything that can go wrong will go wrong". The girls were in front of me walking the road on top of the dam and getting acquainted with the weight on their backs, and Dereck was somewhere behind me, when suddenly, I heard a faint, unfamiliar sound that quickly grabbed my attention. My auditory receptors were hearing foot falls, but a flapping sound accompanied each step. I turned around and it was Dereck. He stopped walking, looked up at me while holding his right boot in the air and said, "Check this out, I got a blowout!" At the same time the sole of his boot separated from the bottom of the boot and with the snapped back loosely into place, causing the previously-heard flapping sound. He placed his foot back down on the road with another flap. I looked at this separated sole and got the impression of a tongue doing a raspberry at me and started to laugh - but it really wasn't funny, because footwear is such an important part of staying healthy and safe while on trail. I asked Dereck if he had brought any other shoes, but I already knew the answer; I was only hoping that I was wrong. "Nope." he said. Ten minutes later we were on the move, the flap sound was gone and Dereck was wearing a new pair of boots courtesy of the #1 tool in any wilderness survival kit – duct tape.

The climb up Shuckstack Mountain on that first day was strenuous for us Florida flatlanders. Each individual developed a particular handicap that demanded strength and words of encouragement from me. I knew that, as the leader, it was vital that I help in any way that I could. If I failed in front of the others, then I failed myself. Alison, from the onset, was having second thoughts. The backpack was heavy. Her muscles were beginning to ache from the weight. Emotionally, Alison was drained, and we'd just started a couple hours ago. The faces of the others also showed signs of "What in the hell are we doing here?" At this point I called for a rest stop.

The stop did two things. It got the backpacks off our shoulders to give our bodies a rest, and it gave us the opportunity to discuss with everyone the goals of this hike. I told them we were not there to beat ourselves to death. We were there to take our time and enjoy the sights and sounds of nature. Forty-five minutes later, rested and hydrated, we were back on the trail refreshed and pushing onward. After several more rest stops we had hiked six miles and climbed to an altitude of forty-eight hundred feet, reaching our first destination.

The next unexpected event tested my first aid abilities. Alison and Debbie were on the trail, and in the lead, when they walked past a ground hornet's nest, unintentionally stirring them up. I could see from my vantage point, the cloud of flying stingers rose up and engulfed the girls. Dereck was in front of me and heading straight for the cloud. My shouts of warning were too late. Dereck woke up from la-la-land at the first sting. Alison was hit 6 times on her legs and was initially in great pain. Debbie, my fiancé, and I escape the stingers of pain. Quick reaction and medicine from my first aid kit reduced Alison's suffering. Dereck however, became allergic to the stings, causing his right ankle and knee to swell. The medical problem, anaphylaxis, was becoming a real emergency. I treated Dereck with antihistamines and monitored his vitals for possible shock. Thirty minutes later Dereck assured me he was ok to continue, but I still had concerns for the swollen ankle. The swelling could weaken the ankle and cause it to twist on the rocky path. That crisis was alleviated by making Dereck's backpack lighter and sharing the weight with all. Several days later, after careful treatment and assistance, the medical problem disappeared.

The single most significant factor that drove the group to the limits of their endurance was the weather. There was a heavy downpour for days. Dry clothing was only a memory. I had to watch each individual carefully throughout the day for signs of hypothermia. Putting on cold, wet clothing and hiking through the rain became a tormented odyssey for even me. When the rain did stop temporarily, the clouds were so low they covered the trail in a blanket of fog. Beautiful views of the mountain range, ordinarily seen on a good day, were covered by sheets of white mist. We learned from a passing hiker that all the bad weather was due to Hurricane Charley hitting the North and South Carolina coastlines.

Three notable events occurred at the height of the inclement weather. The first one happened at the Newfound Gap parking area. Instead of just me making the decision to call off the remainder of the hike (after several days of rain); I thought it best that it would be a group decision. We talked about the positive and negative aspects of continuing; however no one wanted to make a commitment one way or the other. Abruptly, twelve year old Alison looked over at the drenched adults, slung her backpack onto her shoulders and headed north towards the AT. She turned to look back to see what we were doing then stated in her energetic cheerleader voice, "We came here to hike, so let's GO!" All four adults looked at each other and, one by one, without saying a word, picked up our backpacks and followed Alison up the trail.

During the night at Ice Water Springs Shelter, in the pouring rain, the second event occurred. We heard a commotion in front of the chain link fence. Dereck shined his flashlight into the darkness and lit up a confrontation between a shelter rat and a skunk.

Daughter and brother having a miserable day as well as the camera at Newfound Gap, Appalachian Trail

"Please Mr. Skunk, don't spray the rat and our gear hanging on the chain-link fence," I thought. Dereck quickly turned off the light with the hope skunk spray odor did not hit our nostrils. The next morning we woke up to find the skunk inside the fence foraging for dropped food on the shelter's dirt floor. I told everyone to be still and let the skunk leave when he is ready. I slowly got up opened the gate and when the rain stopped the critter left. Just like us, he had wanted to stay dry.

The third event happened north of Charlie's Bunion at Laurel Top. The group got separated in the fog. Dereck and I were behind the girls and slowed down to pick and eat blueberries. We had found a gold mine of juicy, plump berries off the side of the trail, and couldn't figure out why they had not been picked. We leaned over into the cloud of whiteness and grabbed the berries. At one point Dereck was my anchor as he held my left arm and with my right I reached out to pick an exceptional group of the blue delights. Full from our taste bud orgy, we picked a container full for the others and continued up the trail. Suddenly, we heard the shrill noise of a whistle blasting three times: our group's pre-described signal for distress. My mind raced for answers. Who was hurt? What was happening? Who was lost? Fear and adrenaline began to surge through my body. Dereck and I quickened our pace towards the sound of the whistle blasts as I gave two whistle blasts as a response. Once again three blasts of the whistle. My heart was pounding as I ran closer and closer to the sound. I came to a turn in the trail and found my fiancé sitting on a rock, disoriented. I approached and observed signs of relief on her face. She explained that she became separated from the group and felt all of a sudden alone in the wilderness, miles from the nearest town, surrounded by fog and not knowing if she was still on the trail. Keeping calm and not letting panic take over, she remembered my instructions to everyone in case of an emergency, or getting lost. "Stay put, use your whistle and we will find you. Do not try to find us."

Then, we heard a loud noise of something crashing through the bushes. "Now what?" I thought. A sigh of relief came over me when I saw that it was Debbie and Alison also responding to the distress whistle. At last the group was a single unit again, trekking onward towards Davenport Gap.

A park ranger later that night stayed with us in the shelter. After supper, Dereck and I offered everyone the large container of berries for dessert. The ranger was impressed with the berries and asked where we found such good looking fruit. The ranger's face went blank when we told him where on the trail we found the berries and how we got them. He said we wouldn't be so jovial about our find if we knew what was on the other side of the fog-covered berry plants. Before we could ask what he was talking about he continued on and told us we had been on a steep ridge and one slip while picking the berries would have been a 500-foot fall to the ground below. I made a note to myself later that night, "Berries that look too good to be true late in the season are there for a reason. Leave them alone."

Glad to still be alive and unscathed, we went to bed soaked by several days of rain and expected more of the same in the morning. Daylight broke the next morning and a refreshing beam of sunlight burst into the shelter. But Mother Nature sometimes likes to play jokes on you, and as our clothes were just about dry, darker clouds quickly moved in over the mountains. By the time we reached our afternoon shelter, everyone was soaking wet, *again*. Dereck collected firewood and started a fire in the next shelter's fireplace to take the chill off. Thick smoke was going up the chimney and outside the fireplace into the shelter.

Alison and Dereck at one of the shelters on the Appalachian Trail in the Great Smoky National Park

Dereck was blowing into the wet wood trying to get better flames when I heard a thud and saw Dereck trying to back pedal as fast as possible, his arms and legs getting tangled up. "Dereck what's up?" I said. It took a few seconds to comprehend his reply through his quick breathed response. He pointed to the wood in the fireplace and repeated, clearly, "A snake fell out of the chimney and landed inches from my face!" Sure enough, there on top of the wet wood was Sammy the Snake, also trying to get out of harm's way.

We faced many obstacles on that trip to the Smokies, and as we neared the end of the trip, our resolve was strengthened and our group became hard, stout hearted individuals whose will to succeed could not be shattered. On the tenth and final day, not a cloud was visible in the sky. We beheld grand mountain vistas in splendid grandeur. Overlooking the green valley below, we closed in on the northern boundary of the park and I thought back to what the trip had meant to me.

I had learned that by using fortitude and stamina I could persevere through the difficulties of the unexpected. An added bonus was I could take these experiences of the wilderness and apply them back in the city. I now knew that whatever obstacle I faced, whether it is in the city or the wilderness, would not dampen my spirit to survive.

CHAPTER 2
Six Months on the Appalachian Trail

My first contact with the Appalachian Trail didn't involve a backpack, or even stepping on the trail. I was in the school library during high school when I found an article about it. The story talked about a vision that a man, named Benton MacKaye, had had. He wanted to create a "wilderness long trail" through the Appalachian Mountains so a great number of people in the heavily populated eastern region of the United States could escape into nature. The trail was planned, constructed, and the idea grew up until the Appalachian Trail became the first National Long Distance Trail, established by the 1968 National Trail System Act. I was mesmerized by the words and pictures describing this ribbon of dirt extending into 14 states, from the mountains of northern Georgia to Mt. Katahdin in Maine. This path rode the ridges of the Appalachian Mountains connecting summits, forests, valleys, rivers and towns for over 2100 miles. By the time I finished the article, I knew that one day I would hike the entirety of this long distance path.

Yet every time I planned a thru-hike on the Appalachian Trail it was blocked by an event in life. I got married, began my own family and supported them throughout my career as a firefighter. I swore that, when the kids were old enough and on their own, the AT would be my reward. The children became adults and were on their own, but then work was my barrier to the AT. I could not give up 20 years of work and not have some type of retirement plan. So, I continued to be employed as a public servant, protecting lives. Time after time I would feel the magnetic draw of the AT and hoped to quench this thirst by backpacking different sections for days, weeks at a time. I even went to Vermont one year to section hike the trail. I thought maybe this compulsive attitude would wane. The problem was that every time I came off the trail, I wanted more.

Towards the end of my career as a firefighter, I received a small gift from a co-worker who was retiring. On his wall was a picture of a wise old owl with the following quote below it:

"There are three kinds of people: Those who make things happen, those who watch things happen and those who wonder what happened."

As he took down the picture from the wall he handed it to me and said, "One day you may need this." I took the picture, not knowing that, in four months, these words would be coming down from my office wall.

I began a career working for a system of values that protected the lives and property of individuals. I was a dedicated employee who gave blood, sweat, and tears - sacrificing countless hours away from my personal and family life. I watched things happen as the same system I was working for turned on me through politics and deceit (it is amazing how those two words often flow together) that left a scar in my belief of the system.

I then realized that it was time to "make things happen", to get back my lost personal time, to get back to the things that were truly important: The love and support of my wife and family, to feel the wind in my hair, the rain on my face, sunbeams dancing alongside me and to watch, in a continuous interval of time, Mother Nature at work. I wanted to, once again, become the student and learn the fundamental, simplistic way of life with Mother Nature.

It is said that the Appalachian Trail is a gentle and patient teacher that will teach you what you need to learn. I took that boyhood dream of hiking the Appalachian Trail, and in March 2004, I began my AT journey to "make things happen". I was no longer one of "those who watch things happen".

"And those who wondered what happened?" They are still working in the system waiting for the ax to fall...

Spring was just around the corner during the last months of 2003. I was retired and sitting at the dining room table planning another section hike. All of a sudden it hit me. I actually had an opportunity to thru-hike the Appalachian Trail! The timing was perfect and the excuses of why I couldn't attempt it were evaporating as quickly as they came to mind, I looked into the window of opportunity and said, "Let's go!"

But that...that was the easy part.

The hard part was telling my wife. Once I realized what I was about to do, I approached my wife, Lady Kritter, with the, 'I have some good news and I have some bad news', routine. "The good news," I said "is that I am going to hike the Appalachian Trail." "And the bad news?" Lady Kritter asked. "I'll be gone for six months." I replied.

Amazingly, she supported my dream, though it would have an impact on us both.

Once the decision was made to walk over 5 millions steps northward, a whole new world emerged of schedules and questions. Having a dream that turned into a reality, set off a tidal wave of emotions and thoughts. Ideas, views and images rapidly entered my head and were quickly replaced others. I was stumbling down the trail and I wasn't even on the AT yet. "STOP!" I yelled to myself. I placed my mental walking stick firmly on the ground, halting my forward slide. I took several deep breaths, meditated and cleared my mind.

Emerging from the calm, I realized my simplistic needs for survival: mental attitude, shelter, food and water, needed to be coordinated. I could hear my wife saying to me, "Be organized and write everything down; that way you won't forget." I carried a spiral notebook, writing notes of "things-to-do" to myself as well as writing and rewriting the gear lists to meet my survival needs. All I had to do was remember where I placed the damn notebook.

My final days before March 15 were full of preparing equipment and supplies to fulfill my needs. I spent a week sewing and cursing a tarp-tent together. Lady Kritter would approach and ask how things were going, I would invariably mumble something insane about my work and she would quietly back pedal to leave me to my turmoil. I constructed, tested and re-tested my cooking stove and wind screen. I tried to not shut out my wife amidst all the preparations, because she was - and still is - a very important part of my life. March 15th (the scheduled departure date for the AT) was fast approaching. Time was becoming precious and I wanted to spend as much time as possible with Lady Kritter. It was a task maintaining the balance, but overall, I think we managed it fairly well.

I was asked why I wanted to hike 2,172 miles on the Appalachian Trail all in one shot - leaving behind friends, family, and all I'd known. I had two answers.

First, I wanted to awaken my dormant five senses. To see the hue of colors within each day's grandeur, to smell the musty and fragrant aroma of Mother Nature, to hear her sing, to taste the harmony of continually living with nature, to feel her warmth. I wanted to experience Mother Nature in all her fury and to be caressed by her beauty.

The second answer for me is simply described by Colin Fletcher in his book *The Secret Worlds of Colin Fletcher.* I wanted to "just muck about." Just go. Leave with no idea what would happen. I wanted adventure.

I said good-bye to family and friends, loaded up the car, and with Lady Kritter and her brother Dale we headed north towards Georgia and the very first white blaze (markers that hikers follow designating the AT). The following passage is taken from Lady Kritter's journal and best describes that very first day.

"March 15:

Morning dawned hazy, overcast, and drizzling – It was a GREAT day to start the trail. Hikers and families all met for breakfast, the hikers with elation, and some family members with trepidation. It is here I feel the need to share this little piece of wisdom: So few people have dreams today, even fewer act on them. Whether these thru-hikers make it to Katahdin, or not, they have acted on their dream, they have tried, and THAT's what counts!

Breakfast broke abruptly as the predetermined hour neared. It was time to check out, load up and head down to the Amicolola Park office for the official weigh in and the all important Signing in the Log. There were another three hikers waiting in the parking lot who were welcomed into the roiling mass, the sixth addition being Shaun "Beatbox". Families and hikers collected within after jokingly taunting one another over pack weights and luxury items. A few moments of silence as each penned their names in the Logbook - their name, the date they began their journey, and where they intended to complete it. Wayne P. –

"KrispyKritter", 3/15/04, to Mt. Katahdin, Maine. Well, now it was official.

Documentation is the proof of any occasion of this magnitude. Pictures had to be taken of each hiker signing the Logbook, pictures with their packs on, then more pictures individually AND collectively at the Arch which marked the beginning of their Appalachian Trail adventures – the approach trail.

Dale, my brother and I had promised to hike the first mile of the Trail with Wayne. As the hikers loosely assembled, we joined in just as though we belonged, and began climbing the switchback ascent to the top of the falls and a little beyond. The mood was buoyant and infectious. Although it had begun to drizzle, no one's spirits were dampened. They all took turns in taunting one another as the zig-zag trail grew steeper. The awareness that THIS WAS THE BEGINNING breezed through the assemblage. Early on, quite naturally and seamlessly, the hikers fell into two groups. We were in the first group of three hikers, and two tag-alongs. This seemed the faster group, the cheerful rogues. Camaraderie swelled. Expectations were light, like the banter; brief histories of former lives were shared, and the promise of a consistent repertoire of "digs" at one another wove the experience together."

"All too quickly the end of the first mile broke at the road. This is where KrispyKritter and I would say goodbye. We had previously decided not to turn around once parted, for there was no telling how well our emotions could be held in check. I felt a lump in my throat, my eyes began to fill and I had to breathe very deeply to take control. I can only imagine how KrispyKritter felt. If it had not been for the jovial new friends, this could have been a messy good-bye. We looked into one another's eyes but we had already said all the words. I could feel the sheer joy! One last picture and they were off to unknown adventures drawn by the lure of the Trail. As Dale and I walked away he mentioned that KrispyKritter was good to his word, he had not turned around after our goodbye. The drizzle had ended. Parting was bittersweet."

My last look at Lady Kritter before turning and hiking north on the AT into the unknown

"Life is not a journey to the grave with the intention of arriving safely in a pretty and well preserved body, but rather to skid in broadside, thoroughly used up, totally worn out, and loudly proclaiming 'WOW – what a ride!'"

From this point on, Lady Kritter considered herself a 'trail widow' during my six month hike. At one point she wanted this to be her trail name; I think just to make a point. In my opinion the trail name Lady Kritter better describes her personality, classy, but not afraid to rub noses with the animals.

The AT in Georgia and North Carolina is a dark brown path anywhere from 18 inches to 24 inches in width. This ribbon of earth winds around the sides of mountains, passes directly over cliffs, rides along ridges and slopes, travels downward into the gaps, all within the forestry of the mountains. The trail is marked by a 2 inch by 6 inch white blaze painted on tree trunks, rocks, buildings, telephone poles, or any other surface that might be in the line of sight of the hikers. It is a constant battle trying to keep your footing on the trail. Hikers encounter a mixture of rocks, boulders and roots of every size imaginable camouflaged by the autumn leaves of the past. Trees that are alive and trees that are dead can be blown over, or fallen across the trail from mountain storms. Every day the AT challenges you and in order to make it you must win the challenge. The confrontations could be the next mountain ascent or descent, the elements of nature, planning for food and water, keeping your body temperature regulated, having the confidence of a solid foot step on uneven ground, and the list goes on. The bottom line is to have a positive attitude towards whatever obstacle comes against you: get it done, put it behind you, learn from it and plant the next foot forward down the trail.

KrispyKritter's very first hiking family at the beginning of the Approach Trail (starting from left to right Peek-A-Boo, Boo-Boo, KrispyKritter, Cuppa Joe, Fire Marshal and, front row by himself, Beat Box)

I found other hikers who had the same hiking speed as me and we adopted each other as a nomadic hiking family. I hiked alone in solitude most of the time. Other times, I would catch up with fellow hikers at a predetermined spot, like a shelter, a mountain top, a gap, a stream or a town. There was another family pod just ahead of me and another hiker family unit behind me. Moving from shelter to shelter, to campsite and once in awhile into a trail town, I would leapfrog these other members from these family pods and learned to recognize their backpack or - from a distance - their walk. We took care of each other; making sure mind, body and the homes we carried on our backs were safe. Since we started in Georgia and went north we called ourselves "northbounders". A few "southbounders" began later in the summer in Maine. Whether northbound or southbound, we all had the common goal of finding the last white blaze.

Two weeks into my hike I wondered what the difference was between thru-hikers that made it to Katahdin and those hikers who went off trail (quit their hike). The word that came to my mind was drive. Even though each member of the 2004 AT hiker family had a common bond (going to Maine), each had a different drive, a different reason to hike the 2100 miles to achieve their goal. I have always been a person with drive, to push the challenge, to succeed in any endeavor through improvising, adapting or overcoming obstacles. It was at that moment, during that conversation with myself, when I realized that I had the power to decide the fate of my hike. I shouted with gusto, "I'm going to Maine"!

Even though I walked through mountain forests and wilderness areas, I was constantly reminded that mankind had been there before me. Garbage littered the trail. Most hikers try to do their part by picking up the small pieces of trash they see and carry it out. Trees big and small are cut down with stumps left as reminders of their existence. And then, as myself and fellow hikers descended from the mountains and approached the small human communities nestled in the valleys, we noticed the increased debris of man, assorted plastic and paper items carelessly thrown away, manufactured goods no longer in working order discarded and dumped. As a society, we American's are so wasteful and careless that it is no wonder visitors from other countries think of us as opulent and pretentious. History labeled the Native Americans as savages in the wild that needed to be civilized. However, they believed in and respected Mother Earth with reverence and kept the balance. So who is really the savage? As one person, I try to do my part. If everyone took the time to do their part, just maybe we could also begin to see the balance. Living in harmony with Mother Earth is a worthwhile endeavor for a healthy today and our children's tomorrow.

Communication on the trail in was similar to that found in any primitive nomadic community. The main source of information is passed on by word of mouth. On the trail we call it trail mail. Hikers passing each other will stop, discuss trail conditions, what's up ahead, what hiker is doing what, and of course the latest trail gossip. You could actually pass a message, or become a messenger that someone is looking for a particular person. And, if that particular person was within a hundred miles, they would get that message. Sometimes you would get the message faster than if you were to use 'snail mail'.

Another source of information was the trail register found in shelters, hostels, cabins and some hotels. Written by hikers for hikers, the registers, besides information, contain literary and artistic entertainment, usually read before hiker midnight (after sundown).

Computer and cell phone technology is gaining popularity as a source of communication. Hikers can sit on a mountaintop, download or upload information and let family members back in the civilized world know that they are safe, as long as there is a signal. Hikers are even calling each other miles apart to gather trail information and get the latest trail gossip concerning other thru-hikers. In trail towns hikers gather around computers to read and write web journals.

This can be very beneficial, in moderation, but that's often not the reality. Way too many electronics are on the trail and are plugged into hiker's ears in the form of iPods and cell phones, ruining the very experience sought when hiking; to be in Mother Nature. Too many times I have been hiking high on the mountain ridges and had my tranquil solitude shattered by the piercing ringing of a cell phone. "TURN THE DAMN THINGS OFF!"

In today's modern technological world I believe a cell phone can be a valuable survival tool if it is used as an emergency signaling device. But keep it off and easily accessible in your backpack. Learn to communicate with the Earth Mother; she will teach you an awareness of the natural world you did not know existed.

On the trail, instead of using real names, almost everyone gets a nickname as their trail identity. The hiking community calls it a trail name. (And to this day I still don't even know the real name of the majority of the hikers I have met on the trails). Names like Boo Boo, Paddler, Pegasus, Luna, Bear Tracks, Mad Scientist, Gaia and the list goes on. A trail name is usually earned during the first month of your

There are a variety of shelters on the AT. This shelter, called Walnut Mountain Shelter is located in northern North Carolina

Bryant Ridge Shelter, a three story shelter in Central Virginia, is one of the newer shelters on the AT

hike or, can be carried over from a previous hike. Some hikers even pick their own name, knowing if they didn't you might get stuck with a name you didn't like. That's what happened to Fire Marshal. Grant was part of our hiking pod that didn't have a trail name for a while. A bunch of us were hiking in the mountains south of the Great Smoky National Park when we started to see a heavy white haze riding the wind currents. Ash particles floated back and forth towards the ground. My professional nose told me the forest was burning nearby. Grant and I came up to a ridge and could see in the far distance a forest fire burning on the mountain ridge. He got out his cell phone and called the Department of Forestry to report the fire and to see if there was an evacuation. The person on the other end had no idea what Grant was talking about and asked his location. Grant replied, "On the AT". "Where on the AT?" the information officer wanted to know. "Northbound," Grant replied. Frustrated, Grant called another number he copied on one of the trailhead bulletin boards and finally got the information he needed. All was safe, but I already knew that. Grant let every hiker he came in contact with throughout the afternoon know about the fire. The next morning, during A.Y.C.E. (all you can eat) breakfast in Fontana Village, 23 hikers were sitting around the table talking about the previous day's events. The fire was brought up and someone mentioned about Grant's heroic efforts on the telephone and how he acted like a Fire Marshal. "WAIT A MINUTE!" somebody (me) yelled. "Grant you don't have a trail name yet, do you?" Grant looked at me inquisitively and said "NO! I don't want....". I interrupted and yelled, "All in favor of Grant's new trail name being Fire Marshal raise your hand. The count was 22. All those oppose? One hand went up. Someone yelled, "Hey Grant, put your hand down, you are now Fire Marshal. Getting a trail name happens that quick and when you least expect it.

Then there was Boo Boo. His original trail name was Weather Man. Every morning during the first five days on the trail Boo Boo would come out of his tent and give us the weather report. He would stick his finger in his mouth, hold it up into the air and tell us wind direction and speed with a lot of theatrical drama. He would tell us if it was going to rain, or not. What was amazing is that he was always right. All the hikers thought it was brilliant that he could predict the weather accurately. Someone said, "Your trail name should be Weather Man". And so it was. Then one morning a hiker was passing

Weather Man's tent and heard him listening to a NOAA weather report. The word was out that the Weather Man's talent only had to do with remembering a radio report. In a democratic vote he was stripped of his name and no longer called Weather Man. Instead, he was renamed Boo Boo as a tribute to the cartoon character Yogi Bear's sidekick. They both had a knack for talking people out of their food. Boo-Boo was always conning food off someone else.

Bear Tracks got his name because he kept finding bear tracks on the trail. Paddler, because he likes to paddle whitewater rafting. Cuppa Joe, because he likes his cups of coffee. KrispyKritter was born around a campfire one night when I was talking about the job (firefighting) and mentioned the word "crispy critters". My story was stopped in mid sentence and all of a sudden I heard "ALL THOSE IN FAVOR!" Nobody told me how the name could be spelled, so I replaced the c's with k's and the trail name KrispyKritter was born.

Hikers come from all walks of life and countries. Spoon is from New Zealand, Simone is from Canada, St. Rick is from England and Sauerkraut is from Germany. There are hikers who bring their dogs, which I envy because they have a companion and a warm body to sleep with at night.

At first, I was leery with all the dogs I came across, but they had each been well behaved and their handlers courteous to fellow hikers, so I lightened up considerably. I will say long distance hiking can punish an animal just as well as hiker. Care should be given to look for signs of fatigue and injury, for oneself and for any pets.

There are senior hikers in their 60's and 70's: Joanne, a seventy-something year old woman who I met the first night out, Sarge, a 72 yr. old black man, retired from the military who first thru-hiked in 1997, Grizzly Dave, a 68 yr. old former state senator from Iowa. However, the majority of the hikers are young adults who quit their jobs, are in between jobs, or school and decided to go on this adventure. Each year more and more females join the ranks of thru-hikers with the same drive and determination as the males. All in all, the nomads of the AT are a diverse group of individuals with their own reasons and stories for being on the trail.

One of the most bizarre and strangest individuals I met on the AT, or on any other trail, occurred on a rainy evening at the Bearfence Mountain Hut in the Shenandoah National Park. I had had one of those days when you wake up and just know that the day had a special energy, a day extraordinary events were going to happen. On this particular day I got up early to do a 20-plus mile day. I wanted to enjoy the coolness of the morning, escape the heat of midday, and arrive at the shelter before the afternoon rains. I left the Pinefield Shelter and was immediately greeted by a good omen, a deer walking down the trail. The deer did not flinch at seeing me and continued to stroll in my direction. People say that animals can smell, some say sense the fear from other animals. It's hard to explain, but I was feeling I was becoming a part of Mother Nature and not just a visitor. This animal had no fear of me. I could, if I wanted, reach out and touch the deer's coat as it walked right passed me. It was a great experience to see the deer's movements up close without the hypersensitive flight syndrome usually associate with the presence of a predator nearby. We looked at each other, nodded and continued in our separate directions.

Krispykritter on the AT in Grayson Highland State Park, Virginia

I had several good climbs over Weaver, Hightop, Saddleback, and Baldface Mountains, Virginia. The whole day was cloudy, which made the ascents almost enjoyable. The humidity was terrible from all the heavy rains we had the last three days. It drizzled off and on throughout the morning into early afternoon. Then, around 2:30, the skies opened up and let out a downpour. During a lull in the rain, as I was going over Baldface Mountain, I discovered a huge pile of fresh bear scat right on the trail. I knew it was fresh because I could see the vapor rising off the top of the heap as the heat met with the coolness of the air. The size and amount of the scat indicated to me that this was a sizable animal. Not far from the scat, I found fresh bear tracks in the trail mud, and the distinct musky odor of an animal hung in the air. I could feel the presence of eyes staring at me - which, literally, had the hair on the back of my neck standing at attention. I knew the bear was near. I began talking out loud and repeating over and over, "Hey Mr. Bear, I know you're out there. Here bear-here bear," I repeated to let the bear know I was in the area. My senses were on high alert for the tiniest movement or sound. Nothing else happened, so I cautiously continued down the path. Soon after passing the pile of goo, the heavy rains started again. I finally made it to my day's destination, Bearfence Mountain Hut for the night. Already in the shelter were Epiphanies, Pegasus, Wooly and Mountain Dew, drying out gear and preparing supper.

Thirty minutes after I arrived at the shelter the weirdest person I ever met entered my hiking world. I first noticed this person when I saw movement outside the shelter. The figure was a dripping wet, middle aged woman without a backpack. In both hands were numerous loaded K-Mart plastic bags. She came in from the rain, and began to take over a large section of the hut by placing the plastic bags on the sleeping deck of the shelter, a section next to my sleeping bag and gear. Trying to make conversation, I asked, "What's your name?" In a low, nervous monotone voice I heard, Bev. I then asked, "Are you northbound or southbound?" In the same monotone voice see immediately snapped, "It's none of your business." "Wow!" I thought. I didn't need to be told twice, not thankful for the cold response.

Meanwhile, this woman was constantly going in and out of her K-Mart bags, over and over again. Clothes were thrown into a corner of the shelter. Quest stepped into the hut and noticed the "new addition" to our current hiking family. He asked the woman her name. Already blasted by the chill from this woman, I was eagerly anticipating the look on Quest's face as she replied. I was not disappointed. He was told, without her looking up from fidgeting with the plastic bags, that it was none of his business, she doesn't give out her name to people she doesn't know, and she then went back to fidgeting with the plastic bags. A short time passed and she blurted out "…and names to strangers." Quest made eye contact with me, giving me a puzzling look and I could tell he was ready to retort back. I quickly shook my head and at the same time mouthed the word, "DON'T." Mountain Dew, an 18-year old kid, stopped writing in his journal and asks the woman what shelter she came from. Her reply was quick and snappy, "None of your business. Are you putting that in your book?" She did not eat and spent all her time preparing her bed by lying on top of the clothes and putting more clothes on top of her as a blanket. Everyone was nervous to go to sleep, not knowing what may trigger this person. I think we would all have put up our tents, if it weren't for the rain. The antics of the strange lady continued. I had the dubious distinction of being the closest person sleeping next to her. Once the woman made her bed, she shuffled over, quickly grabbed the shelter broom and laid it between us. The bristles next to my head. I really don't know how she did it, but she constructed some type of tarp covering that went over her from head to waist shielding her from the rest of us. As darkness fell she entered her cocoon of clothing and turned on a flashlight. The light remained on throughout the night and everyone had trouble sleeping as we were hearing the constant guttural noises emitting from her corner. At one point, I fell asleep and had a dream of waking up in the middle of the night with this woman standing over me. Her "wicked witch of the north" face was illuminated by the flashlight placed under her chin. I woke up and for the remainder of the night I stayed in a semi-conscious state, sleeping with one eye open. The next morning everyone left the shelter early and left the woman by herself. Quest asked me as we were walking away from the shelter if I had put the broom between her and I. "No," I said. "She put it there as her get-away vehicle." I never heard about this woman through trail mail, or saw her again. It had been truly one of my most eerie nights ever.

Throughout my hike, I was asked so many questions by day hikers and town people. I figured out that there were ten questions that occurred more than any others:

"Did you start with someone, or are you hiking alone?", "Have you see any bears?", "Do you carry a gun?", "How long does it take to hike the whole thing?", "How many miles have you hiked?", "Where do you sleep?", "Are you afraid?", "Do you ever think about quitting?", "How do you get your food?", "What has been your worst day?"

Most of these questions are easily answered (in order): "I have both started hiking alone and with someone", "Yes, sometimes I see bears", "No gun", "It depends on how fast you go", "Thousands" "On the ground, or in a tent, shelter, hostel and sometimes as a luxury in hotels", "I'm rarely scared, but it happens". "I never thought about quitting." "There are numerous ways, but mostly I pack it and replenish in the cities".

And the last question, "What has been your worst day?"I can quickly answer.

The day I completed my thru-hike on Katahdin and left the trail. In fact, I was seriously contemplating doing a yo-yo (a long distance hiker word used to describe the completion of one segment from start to end then turning around and going back to the start.) In my case, I was turning around and heading back to Springer Mt. in Georgia. I was talking to Lady Kritter about this over the telephone just before she left to meet me in Maine. I wanted to feel her out to see what her thoughts were. Since I had to hike back down Katahdin 5.2 miles anyway, my rational was that I technically already started my yo-yo. Lady Kritter was all in agreement with the idea and that really surprised me. I knew somewhere in the next sentence there would be a catch. Lady Kritter continued, "Oh, by the way, when you finish (What'd you call it? A yo-yo?) And you come home, knock on the door, and strangers answer it asking 'Can I help you?' you'll know what happened." "OK. OK. I get the message. Meet me as we originally planned." I didn't want to lose my house and woman.

And if they were to have asked me if I had any days when my mental attitude was low, I would have told them that there were two time periods that stood out in my mind, the first in Tennessee and the other towards the end of my hike in August and September.

The first low occurred after completing the KrispyKritter Challenge - a series of difficult hikes I developed to mirror some more traditional challenges hikers attempt while on trail. There are two sections of trail where hikers challenge themselves and do what is called a marathon hike. One is called the Damascus Marathon where the hiker travels over 26 miles into Damascus Virginia in one day. The other one is called the Three State Challenge. This marathon encompasses hiking through the states of West Virginia, Maryland and into Pennsylvania for a total of 40 plus miles in a 24 hour period. I know I told some folks that I would not do a marathon, but things have a habit of changing constantly on the trail, including personal opinions.

Instead of following others and doing the Three State Challenge or the Damascus Marathon, I wanted to pick my own. My reasoning was simple: it was a new challenge, and I wanted to know what my limitations were since I've never really pushed myself to my physical limits. Sure, I knew there were risks involved, mentally and physically, but the challenge was birthed in my mind and my mind was already biased and made up. Bear Tracks and I reviewed the maps and found a 26 mile section in Tennessee from Hogback Mountain Shelter into Erwin, Tennessee. We called it the "KrispyKritter Challenge". I left the shelter early in the morning and began the test of my endurance. Bear Tracks was still in his sleeping bag and said he would catch up with me. I made Big Bald at 11:00 and saw beautiful mountain views that inspired me from the get-go. I had lunch at Bald Mountain Shelter: 10 miles down, 16 to go. I took an early afternoon siesta during the hottest part of the day, woke up refreshed 40 minutes later and continued the challenge. I passed Spivey Gap and still no Bear Tracks in sight; I continued. I reached No Business Knob Shelter at 5:30 and met up with Grizzly Dave and Fritz, as well as some other hikers, but still no Bear Tracks. Fritz was getting ready to hike on to Erwin, my last 6 miles and the hostel at Miss Janet's. We waited until 6 for Bear Tracks, who didn't show. I left word with the shelter residents of my intentions. I wrote in the shelter registry "20 down, six to go and I will take, "AT Trivia" for $100, Alex. Wait a minute, too much cowboy TV - reality check, I have a Challenge to finish," so off we went. (Cowboy TV is what hikers call a fire.)

As we descend from the mountains we had gorgeous views of the Nolichucky River. We arrived at the river 1 hour and 57 minutes from the shelter. Fritz and I congratulated each other for doing six miles in less than 2 hours. We caught a shuttle into Miss Janet's and I surprised everybody, yelling "Lucy, I'm home!" Fire Marshal, Kelley and Courtney (by then the duo was renamed Bonnie and Clyde), Mad Scientist, Gaia, Pegasus, Paddler, Beatbox were all there greeting me

Krispykritter on McAfee Knob, Virginia – the most photograph spot on the AT

with hugs and warm welcomes. I was glad to be reunited with my trail family and better yet to have completed the KrispyKritter Challenge - a total of 26.9 miles. I did it.

The next morning my left ankle was swollen and had a dull pain that extended up the shin. "Bear Tracks" came in after spending the night with coyotes under his hammock at Spivey Gap. The comfort of Miss Janet's hostel was tempting to zero and rest, but the woods were calling and I had to make a choice. Stay and nurse my ankle or, leave and continue my quest to find the last northern white blaze. I really considered no option but continuing at this point; I could still walk with a hobble "No Pain, No Maine," as they say. So I packed my backpack and was ready to leave with Bonnie and Bear Tracks after breakfast.

The next several days, the ankle got worse. Finally, at Kincora Hostel there was concern with my hiking family that the swelling was not going down and that I might be doing permanent damage if I continued to hike. I called Lady Kritter and explained what was going on. I was afraid that if I got medical attention it would take me off trail. My spirits were really low - to the point of tears - and I did not want to leave the trail. Lady Kritter convinced me that no matter what, I should seek medical advice and then make a decision after being treated. I just knew in my mind that I had a stress fracture from that stupid "KrispyKritter Challenge" and I was going home.

I left the next morning with the owner of Kincora Hostel, Bob Peoples, who dropped me off at a medical walk-in clinic and said he would pick me up in an hour. I had visions of walking into a room of germ warfare with sniffling babies and coughing adults in a not-so-clean environment. This was not a good omen. I took a deep breath and hobbled in.

I entered an immaculately well organized waiting room. I was immediately impressed with the facility and its personnel. After a brief meeting with the receptionist, I was directed to an examination room. A female doctor walked into the room and asked several questions about my leg. I could smell the sweet fragrance of civilization coming from her as she leaned over to examine my leg. Several times the doctor applied pressure points to different areas and asked if it hurt. The doctor looked up at me and said, "I would like to take an x-ray of your ankle and also have another doctor look at it to confirm my diagnosis." "Sure." I said, sadly thinking this was not a good sign.

The second doctor walked through the door with authority. He was of medium height, barrel chest, short hair with a square jaw, wearing a heavy starched white smock with two emblems on each lapel over street clothes. I was puzzled as the figure walked towards me. I thought it odd this masculine, almost military looking man did not have the appearance of the typical doctor type. He approached the examining table and stated, "I understand you may have a hiking injury." I nodded. The doctor sat on the small stool, wheeled up to my leg and began to apply pressure to the same areas as the female doctor. It was then I noticed the two emblems. The first one was a Winged Staff with Two Snakes Entwined about it. The second emblem contained two arrows crossing one another with a KA-BAR Knife intersecting the arrows pointing up. Under the arrows were the words "DE OPPRESSO LIBER". "Special Forces?" I asked him. Without looking up he said quite simply, "Army, retired." Completing his examination I asked the doctor for his prognosis. But the words that I dreaded hearing did not come out of his mouth. Instead, I heard that he confirmed the female doctor's opinion and told me, "You have soft tissue damage with no broken bones, a shin splint. Normally, I would recommend 3 weeks rest but I don't think you are going to give me that, are you?" "No sir," I said. Then he asked if I could give him a couple of days. He then told me that rest and ice on the swollen area, followed with a couple low mileage days should take care of the injury. And then, as if he was reading my mind, the doctor looked directly into my eyes and stated "I've must have seen thousands of feet like yours, just tissue damage. It will be painful. And, I am going to tell you the same thing I told those soldiers. GO UP THAT MOUNTAIN AND FINISH YOUR HIKE!" I almost stood at attention and saluted as he walked out of the examination room. I sat on the examination table relieved to know I was not going off trail for good. Two days later, I was healthy enough to continue my quest to find the last northern white blaze.

My other low point on the trail actually was spread out over three separate occasions, each involving three separate named hurricanes. While I was on trail fulfilling a lifelong dream, my home state of Florida got battered by 3 hurricanes and 1 tropical storm, causing millions of dollars of damage. Lady Kritter and I live on the periphery of a forest and the trees along with the Kritter Den (our home) were not immune to the damaging winds. It was not an easy time to be away from home.

On August 12th I was having my usual day of sloshing through the Vermont rain and mud when one of the kids I had been hiking with walked up to me and said "Kritter, aren't you from Florida?" "Yes," I replied. Then he said "Did you know Florida is going to get hit by a hurricane?" I quickly told this kid that I didn't think his joke was funny, that hurricanes are serious matters. His lack of smile showed his honesty. "No, seriously," he said. "I just heard two hikers talking about it after one of them heard it on a radio, and thought you should know."

In the fog of endless thoughts, I barely remember telling my fellow hiker "thanks for the trail mail". All sorts of things were going through my mind. I stopped abruptly in the center of the trail, reached down into my backpack, grabbed my radio, inserted the earphones and heard the news. Hurricane Charley was a powerful Category 4 storm from the Gulf of Mexico getting ready to slice Florida in two with estimated wind speeds of 145 mph. My concern for family and friends in Florida was always on my mind, but there was more bad news that needed immediate attention. I was about to have my own set of weather problems from the remnants of Tropical Storm Bonnie (that had already hit Florida) as it traveled up the Appalachian Mountain Range and was set to produce heavy rains for Vermont, New Hampshire and Maine. Murphy's Law was in full-effect and the bad weather news was not done. A cold front had stalled over the area where I was hiking, causing increasingly unsettled weather before the storm arrived. A flood watch had been posted for the whole area until 6:00 am on August 14th. And, for good measure, the weather folks mentioned that they didn't know what Charley would do when it moved north into the New England states. "Damn, too many storms to think about at one time. Let's stick to worrying about one storm at a time and concentrate on what Lady Kritter is about to go through, then the FUBAR (f#%ked up beyond all recognition) I'm about to walk into."

As I was at least a day and a half from a trail town, I did not know where I was going to find a phone to talk with Lady Kritter. And then, even if I found a phone, I was afraid I'd get a busy signal due to the possibility of telephone lines and cell towers being down in Florida. I was not a happy hiker. This was not a good condition to be in; for every footfall can be disastrous when you have a wandering mind. A hard rain fell on the metal roof of the shelter where I'd pulled in for the night, adding restlessness to the misery of the evening.

Quest, CatDog, Hawk and I left the Thistle Hill Shelter in the morning with a light mist and temperatures in the low 50's. Often times, your thoughts turn in mindless rabbit trails after just a few days on the trail, thinking of stupid things just to pass the time away as your rhythmic feet touch the trail. But on that day, my thoughts were focused, honed in on my wife and our home. I started remembering my experiences of riding out the fury of past hurricanes and felt pretty sure Lady Kritter would do everything right. Then I started thinking about what would happen if one of the great oaks surrounding our home crashed into the house. Everybody would likely be safe, but we would need to build a new home. My mind was working overtime and the hiking time was whizzing by. I started drawing architectural plans of our new house. I've never had the luxury of a garage in any of my past houses, so my drawings began with a two car garage. Next, a basement underneath the home. Then for at least another hour, I was rearranged the rooms in the floor plan. I woke up from my architectural fantasy when I realized the quietness of the forest was being replaced by the noises of a residential area. I realized I was not hiking alone as the four of us crossed a bridge over a rain swollen White River and were now in West Hartford, VT. We picked up Hawk's mail drop and ate breakfast at Rick and Tina's Country Store. I entered the store and lo and behold, there was a payphone. I was so relieved to hear Lady Kritter's voice on the phone. She spoke in a calm and in-charge tone, confirming a deadly hurricane was going to hit the lower west coast of Florida and cut across the state at a 45 degree angle east of due north. Quickly, I asked Lady Kritter if everything was okay on the home front and with family members. I was assured everyone was fine and then unconsciously blurted out, "Baby, I am off trail. I'm coming home!" I knew in the back of my mind there was no way I could find a bus to the nearest airport and fly into Orlando in time before it closed. And then, I would have been stranded in the middle of nowhere. I felt helpless, but I had to say it. Lady Kritter assured me all preparations were completed and at this point in time there was nothing I could do. She thought it best, and I agreed, that I would continue my hike to Hanover, New Hampshire where I would stay and try to contact Lady Kritter after the storm passed over. I had to find some type of humor in all this to keep my sanity. I soon found hilarity as we left West Hartford and the country store as I turned down a road named, Podunk. "Well now," I said to myself, "I can now tell everyone I've been to Podunk!" It wasn't much, but it helped me.

As we climbed Griggs Mountain, the light rain that had started to fall quickly turned into a downpour that would've given even the most modest frog an orgasm. Quest and Hawk - who were in Norwich, Vermont - took off into the rain. Quest, who lived in the area of Florida where the predicted landfall was to occur, had similar concerns as me. Attempts to communicate with home failed for Quest. He decided to pick-up his pace, leave the group and push for Hanover, New Hampshire. Hawk went with Quest to keep him company and for safety of not hiking alone and I stayed with CatDog.

CatDog and I crossed the Connecticut River in the pouring down rain and entered into New Hampshire, our thirteenth state. As we entered the center of Hanover we were enveloped by a sea of people and traffic noise. I caught the sight of a familiar hiker, hobbling across the street. I yelled out, "Jack!" A head turned and the hiker figure was confirmed, Baltimore Jack, a friend I'd met on several occasions on my AT journey. He congratulated me for making it to New Hampshire, and we got out of the rain to talk. I told him about my situation at home. I was stunned when Jack offered me a place to stay while I was in Hanover. There I could watch the news and use the phone to call Lady Kritter. We made plans to meet at the famous 5 Olde Bar and Restaurant later that evening.

The first thing I did on Saturday morning August 14th was watch the initial reports of the devastation from Hurricane Charley as I tried to make contact with home. Hourly I called, only to hear the busy signal again and again. I nervously waited, throughout the day, for word. Finally, in the late evening the home phone was ringing and the sultry voice of Lady Kritter was in my ear. Out of breath, Lady Kritter explained they were without electricity. During the daylight hours she was out with the chainsaw helping neighbors cut and move downed trees from the roads. Just a side note, you really don't want to piss off a woman who knows how to operate chain saw. The winds, I was told, were a sustained 80 mph for about an hour with intermediate stronger gusts and tornadoes. Our house and oak trees survived the winds and heavy rain. Lady Kritter did a great job organizing the before and after events on the home front. My only regret was that I was not there to be with her during this ordeal. Lady Kritter also told me all family members throughout the state made it through safely with minor wind and water damage. The positive phone call with Lady Kritter was a huge burden off my shoulders.

Knowing that all was well, I took two days to rest and hopped back on the trail. Hawk and I were climbing out of Hanover when I felt a strange sensation on my forehead. Hawk had a similar experience shortly before mine, sweat. Two days of indoor living, clean clothes, healthy meals and no sweating can erase that animalistic behavior of the forest and make you civilized while in the concrete jungle. The bead of sweat reminded me it was time for work, time to power up that human engine towards Katahdin. And that felt good.

Two and a half weeks later the same kid came up to me and said "Krispy, please tell me you know about the hurricane hitting

Florida." "Not funny," I said. "No, really!" he quickly replied and with his arms reached out in assurance. Déjà' vu hits. There I was, stopped in the middle of the trail reaching into the depths of my backpack for the radio again, and the news was not good. Hurricane Frances was a Category 4 storm approaching Florida from the Bahamas, and I was worried all over again for the survival of Lady Kritter, my family, friends and home. I felt as if I placed undue burden on my wife to handle the home front in my absence, alone. I wanted to be at her side to comfort and support her. I could not do that from the mountains of New Hampshire.

My dream to hike the trail didn't seem so important anymore. What were important were my wife and family. I was so torn inside. Being so close to Katahdin, yet so far away from home, the mental pain and anguish of not being there to help were excruciating. After hearing the broadcast on the radio I began to seriously doubt the future completion of the AT. Dealing with back-to-back hurricanes is an unwanted anxiety, and is mentally exhausting knowing loved ones are in survival mode with you helplessly thousands of miles away. My mind was made-up to go off trail. I created this unusually negative attitude of "what in the hell are you doing out here?" This was truly the first time in my trip where I was completely unhappy. It was raining. My body, like everybody else's was wearing down with aches and pains from the constant pounding, ascents and descents. That night I would be in Gorham, New Hampshire to make plans for my departure. I called Lady Kritter on the telephone and explained how I felt, that I wanted to come home and be there for her, just like she had been there for me. Already preparing for the storm, Lady Kritter said there was really nothing for me to do; though she wanted me home too, the preparations were done, and as I was so close to the end of my journey, I should continue on the trail. Reluctantly, I agreed to continue and would call as soon as I got into Andover, Maine - about two days away. I knew I needed to push myself forward, to get out of town as quickly as possible, before I made a drastic decision to end the mental/emotional torment.

I was still in town on the side of the road hitchhiking when Diesel came up to me saying he and Maya Ques had a ride out to the trailhead and asked if I wanted to go. At 9:45 I was back on the trail and the one thing I did not want to do was to think about what was going on at home.

The rain stopped, and the sun was trying to come out. The trail was wet and muddy from the last two nights of rain - looking more like a stream or brook than a trail. The sun came out and Diesel, Maya Ques and I had lunch at Trident Col campsite. We laid out in the sun and took an afternoon nap, resting our wearied bodies. After we got up, we spent more time walking in water before we finally arrived at Gentian Pond Shelter. The views of purple mountains overlooking the shelter in the late afternoon sun were truly awesome. A pond was located down from the shelter with a brook running down a small rock gorge. To top it off, in the pond I saw my first moose, a female with two calves. The adult moose was standing in the water, sticking her head underwater. When her head came up, water poured off her antlers and cascaded down her facial hair. The calves were hiding in the tree line of the woods until their mother was finished. The last golden rays of daylight were hitting the mountains as I finished my dinner and thought that I just might have salvaged this day from one that was within seconds of riding the swirling, counter clockwise water going down the toilet.

Two days later, I entered the toughest mile on the entire AT, the Mahoosuc Notch. At that moment I WAS NOT HAVING FUN. Not because of the hike or the weather, but because I felt guilty having allowed Lady Kritter to fight another hurricane alone. Yes, she had friends and family to help her, but we are a team and I had felt the need to be there to help and support the home front. It was hard to sit on a mountaintop looking at the beauty surrounding me knowing she was being battered by winds and flooded with rain. The handbook recommends going through the notch with a partner because of the difficulty. I felt, in a small way, if my partner, Lady Kritter, was facing the storm without me, I could do the Mahoosuc Notch alone – without a partner. So, I set off to tackle it myself.

The Mahoosuc Notch is a small, narrow, canyon whose floor is covered with assorted size boulders ranging from massive house-size rocks down to pebbles with no uniformity to their placement. The notch is so narrow that the looming mountain cliffs on either side gave me the sensation of being squeezed. I had to crawl over, slide in between, jump and squirm under boulders in this maze of a trail. In a couple of places, I entered and crawled under huge boulders only to get stuck trying to exit out of a small opening on the opposite side. I had to back out, get un-stuck, take my pack off in closed quarters, exit the opening, then pull the pack through. I was startled at one point when I was about to enter an opening between two boulders and a female day hiker came exploding out. After my heart rate and breathing went to normal levels, I learned the hiker was the caretaker of Speck's Campsite on a day hike. She quickly apologized for scaring the bejesus out of me. My time through the notch was a blur. Most of it was spent thinking of home while I navigated the notch and all its difficulty. It is common for a hiker to donate blood to the Notch and Arm, and I was no exception, falling once and leaving a small amount of skin and blood on the rocks.

Successfully completing the Mahoosuc Notch only meant I was going into the next phase of this arduous section called Mahoosuc Arm. This one-two punch was a grueling climb to a mountain summit. It seemed to take forever, climbing rock face after rock face, grabbing roots and anything else that I could grab or step on to make the 3,701 feet-above-sea-level mountain top. I reached the summit with a long, deep breath and was rewarded with splendid views of the mountain range as I exhaled and strengthened as I gazed out. A few hours later I was enjoying the sun setting over the clear mountain waters of a pond at Speck Pond Shelter. Thru-hiker Christine let me use her cell phone to make contact with Lady Kritter. My wife's voice and positive attitude towards me to finish this hike lifted my spirits.

The next day I found myself spending the night in Andover, Maine with Honey and Bear at their hostel called, *The Cabin*. The first thing I did was watch the news. I was expecting to see the devastation aftermath of the storm. Instead, I watched the track of the storm as it sat just off the coast, stalled between Florida and the Bahamas. It hadn't hit yet.

That put me in a stall. Bear suggested I could slack pack (a day hike without a backpack for a long distance hiker) on the AT as I awaited word from Lady Kritter on how she survived the hurricane. I tried calling before going out, but I couldn't get through. Quest and CatDog were there and decided to go with me, that way we are getting some miles under our feet, taking an easy day, keeping a track on the hurricane and staying in touch with home.

When we returned, I finally made contact with Lady Kritter. Hurricane Frances battered Lady Kritter for thirty hours with hurricane force winds that exceeded 100 M.P.H. She wrote in her journal "We lost power and water for 9 days, not to mention all phones and cell towers, cable and internet. Trees 3, Roof 1. Living in the Twilight Zone." Our house had survived the winds, but sustained minor roof damage when a large limb from one of the oak trees fell and was heavy enough to crush a small portion of the plywood roof on impact. Two other large limbs fell with no damage. All trees accounted for.

Four days after hitting Florida it was now my turn to battle the remnants of Hurricane Frances as she moved up the Appalachian range and into the Northeast. The first wave only lasted for a half hour, but the weather forecast reported a cold front passing through with the remains of Hurricane Frances riding the front. The next three days were going to be wet - and for a change, the weatherman got it right. The third day's morning light revealed dark gray clouds hugging the surrounding mountains, hiding them from view. The ground in town was saturated with water so it didn't take a rocket scientist to know the normal looking footpath was going to be an actual running creek and very muddy. The last 4,000-foot mountain until Katahdin was in the Bigelow Mountains Range. Mount Bigelow was just another peak that I needed to go up and over to reach my goal.

Like the other mountains behind me, I expected the climb to be a thigh burner with rivulets of water cascading down the worn path, and I wasn't wrong. The wind blew harder and was colder as I gained elevation. Windswept clouds blew across the trail in front of me. All the great viewpoints that I heard about were complete whiteouts due to the low ceiling cloud cover. Lunch-thirty was at the historic day-use-only lean-to at Horns Pond (increments of time is really not an issue on the trail. Hikers will designate time using thirty at the end of a word. For example time at night is referred to as night-thirty, time of day as day-thirty, etc.). This was one of the few remaining Civilian Conservation Corps (CCC) built shelters left on the trail and I used it as a refuge to escape the biting cold wind. The climb up the West Peak of Bigelow Mtn. (4,145 ft) was most memorable. Out of the mountain forest, I entered the alpine zone and followed the white blazes marked on the rock face. Stunted plant life was located on either side of the rock face trail. As I neared the 4,000-foot level the majority of the plant life disappeared, exposing the entirety of the rock. A horizontal line of rocks and small boulders helped loosely mark the borders of the trail, and the wind was strong enough to knock you right off your feet, or off the trail if you were not careful. I had to walk leaning into the wind and use my trekking poles as support to keep from being blown completely over. I estimated that the steady wind speed was in excess of 45-50 mph with occasional gusts in the 60 mph range. At one point they were so strong that I had to crawl on my hands and knees. The howl of the wind made it almost impossible to hear the person next to you even if they were shouting.

Visibility was so poor at times from the blankets of fog-like clouds I could only see a few feet ahead of me. Near the summit, I couldn't find the white blaze and got temporarily lost on the trail.

Scarecrow came up behind me and shouted that he thought he found a blaze. We reversed our travel and found the trail going up and over a large elevated rock face. Once we made the summit, the struggle over Bigelow was only half completed. The second half was a descent under the same conditions. The whole process was repeated for my next climb over Avery Peak. I found the whole experience exhilarating - dealing with the severe forces of nature, it was really my adrenaline and amazement that allowed me to push through. It was also then that I realized I was still in my short pants. I normally wear long pants to summit because of the cold temperatures. I apparently didn't feel the cold on my natural high. Little Bigelow Mtn. (3025 ft.) was a milestone event. It meant I had hiked over 2,000 miles on the trail. I was confident, barring serious injury, that I would accomplish my goal of being a thru-hiker on the Appalachian Trail.

But, remarkably, the low that I'd experienced from the Florida storms wasn't over yet. Though the odds of it happening were incredibly low, yet another hurricane threatened Florida - and with it, the possibility that Lady Kritter would not be able to fly out of Orlando to meet me in Maine as I completed the trail. Hurricane Jeanne was the tenth named storm, the seventh hurricane and the fifth major hurricane of the 2004 Atlantic Hurricane Season. It was also the third hurricane and fourth named storm of the season to hit Florida. Lady Kritter, frustrated beyond belief, tired and hurricane shocked, simply said "Just finish the damn trail. I may or may not be able to meet you in Maine". In the end, Lady Kritter was able to take one of the last flights out of Orlando, take a vacation from hurricane alley and join me on Katahdin.

Even though I was the one who did the walking on this adventure, I was only one member of a two person team that helped me towards that dream; Lady Kritter was the other. Her energy supported me both physically and mentally, she held my heart while talking on the phone, and maintained our household through everyday occurrences and natural disasters. She was there on that first day in the drizzling rain saying goodbye, not knowing what the future would hold for either of us. It was only fair, and my desire, to have Lady Kritter hike by my side in those final miles and sharing in the triumph and adulation of completing the Appalachian Trail. The choice, however, was not mine to make. The decision was Lady Kritter's. She was less than 48 hours off the plane from the flatlands of Florida and apprehensive about making the climb without a chance to get her trail legs. I told Lady Kritter it would be an honor for her to be my final hiking partner, and as a team, summit together.

She would've had it no other way.

And so, as our first footsteps fell on Hunt Trail, Lady Kritter and I began following, hand in hand, the morning's assemblage of thru-hikers towards Mt. Baxter. The trail followed a gradual grade along the Katahdin Stream, and after the first mile steepened. The anticipation of the day's hike, and - for me - the climactic excitement of completing the trail, gave us the illusion of time moving slowly and our feet floating over the trail. Quest, CatDog and company waited for us to catch up. I thanked them for their courtesy and asked them to go ahead at their pace. I felt ours would be slow considering Lady Kritter's neophyte trail legs. Steadily, the trail lost its identity as a footpath. We ascended past the tree line and followed the painted white blaze over rock face and a boulder field. Climbing became hand over hand, and at several points, iron bars were embedded into the rock for hand and foot holds. Lady Kritter was feeling the effects and asked me to consider going onward and catching-up with my thru-hiking companions." No!" I said, "We started as a team, we will summit as a team, and we will leave Katahdin as a team."

Katahdin, though, was relentless. We entered a part of the trail some hikers call the "Hunt Spur" or the "Spine" - a very steep and difficult boulder field that you had to strain your neck to look up to the top. Slowly, each individual boulder and rock face was scaled. On either side of our ascent was the open void of space.

Krispykritter, Spiceman, Joker and Lorax towards the end of their journey with Katahdin in the background

Lady Kritter on the Spine of Katahdin

Below, the sun reflected off hundreds of lakes and ponds like pieces of scattered broken mirror. The landscape of mountains and valleys stretched to the horizon. The top of the "Spine" (called the "Gateway"), was a relatively flat, rocky area, (called the "Tableland") approximately a mile in length that led up to Baxter Peak. Just below the summit, I changed into my tuxedo attire that Lady Kritter had brought for the summit photographs. She and I reached the northern terminus of the Appalachian Trail on Sept. 24th at 1:00 pm in the afternoon. I was dressed in a white t-shirt under an Oscar de la Renta tuxedo (with tails), black shorts, hiking boots with short gaiters and - to complete the ensemble - a leather skull cap and sunglasses.

Krispykritter and Lady Kritter at the end of the Appalachian Trail – Katahdin

The champagne cork was popped; the cigar lit and assorted photographs were taken of Lady Kritter and me at the Katahdin sign. I stood on a rock overlooking Chimney Pond during a lull in our celebration. Tears filled my eyes as I was overwhelmed with swells of emotion. People, places and shared moments flashed in my mind. I also realized that I had just joined an international fraternity of less than 10,000 hikers who have completed the Appalachian Trail in one season - a thru-hiker. I was also proud of Lady Kritter's hike to the summit and as we embraced, I told her so. The scenery before us on Baxter Peak was incredible. The clarity of the surrounding mountains and valleys was extraordinary. Ponds and lakes again reflected sunlight like broken pieces of mirror throughout the valley.

After the high of climbing Katahdin, we had the realization of what we endured going up, and that we now faced it as a descent. Knowing what the trail was like helped mentally, but we were getting physically exhausted and knew the hike down would be tough. We ate a quick lunch and, after staying only one hour on the peak, started our return. Four hours into the descent Lady Kritter's knees and thighs were screaming for mercy. The muscles in Lady Kritter's legs were like Jell-O. Each step was painful. The sun was setting and we still had two hours of hiking before returning to the Katahdin Stream Campground. When dark-thirty arrived I gave Lady Kritter my headlamp and I took the lead using a small LED light. I would walk several yards ahead of Lady Kritter, and then return to her to help her along. The next two hours were very long, helping talk Lady Kritter down the mountain. Finally at 9:45 pm we reached our vehicle in the parking lot. The next morning all the thru-hikers were meeting at the AYCE breakfast in the hotel's lobby. When Lady Kritter came hobbling down, everyone commented on how she had the hiker hobble.

And so, Lady Kritter became an honorary member of a group of thru-hikers who climbed Katahdin on September 24, 2004.

One of the hardest things for me to do after completing the trail was the thought of leaving the mountains and returning home to Florida, 27 feet above sea level. It definitely was an adjustment for me. I always wanted to live for extended periods of time in the mountains - waking up and falling asleep day in and day out.

I knew why I had been there - to live in the beauty and wonderment of Mother Nature's bosom - the mountains. Yet, my Appalachian Trail journey was over that September day when Lady Kritter and I climbed Katahdin. Many thru-hikers couldn't wait to get back home and leave the misery and hardship of the AT behind them. Now that Lady Kritter was here with me, my misery and pain were over. We were a team no longer separated by thousands of miles.

We spent the next 2 1/2 weeks traveling in the state of Maine on what I jokingly called the "KrispyKritter's Getting Re-acquainted with Lady Kritter Tour". We stayed in Maine for two reasons. One, to let Lady Kritter wind down from the pressures of enduring the natural disasters, and two, I did not want to leave the mountains. I did not want to leave the trail.

Our first stop was a peaceful four days at Whitehouse Landing Wilderness Camp, located in the Hundred Mile Wilderness on the AT. I rented a cabin at White House Landing for the solitude of Lake Pemadumcook and to hear the periodic blast of the air horn announcing the arrival of hikers. I was hoping to see, one last time, familiar faces of my nomadic thru-hiking family. I was not disappointed. Pegasus, Boo-Boo, Papillion, Gaia, K-Less, Bramble, Rael and several new faces came through on their final days towards Katahdin. Lady Kritter and I spent wonderful times together hiking and canoeing on the lake, getting to know each other again. We said good-bye to Bill and Linda, the owners of White House Landing, and traveled to Greenville to see Paddler and spent two days with him. Once on the road again, we stopped just outside Caratunk and spent the night at Northern Outdoor Center. We had a splendid display of the fall colors as we traveled through the Rangeley Lakes Region with our final day's destination at Bear and Honey's "The Cabin". We spent 5 days there, met the Garland Family and spent our days hiking and rock hounding.

During our travels, I had to change my mindset from the slow pace of the trail to the fast pace of the automobile. I had to leave town because of what I perceived as crowds in the small town of Norway, population 1,500. Our travels intersected portions of the trail that I had crossed as a thru-hiker. I remember my reaction during those times as I stood on the roadside and felt the wind from speeding cars and wondered why everyone was moving so fast? Once I was safely across, I was happy to re-enter the forest and escape the noise of modern man. But I found myself riding in one of those modern chariots, taking my Lady Kritter distances that took me days to cover on foot in a matter of minutes.

Time was, and still is, a hard adjustment for me.

We spent the last two days in Freeport, Maine walking through streets of outlet stores (L.L. Bean, North Face and Patagonia, to be precise). People...so many people. It reminded me of a colony of ants, an endless stream of moving bodies along established trails, ducking in and out of holes and continually bobbing and weaving in search of something. Lady Kritter and I had dinner with Pipesmoke and his wife Jeannie who dropped us off at the airport in Manchester,

New Hampshire for our flight home. Our late flight landed at Orlando International Airport, the gateway to a fantasy paradise of Mickey Mouse, Sea World and Universal Studios. Friends from another lifetime (John, Mary, Neil and Rhonda) picked us up and we rode the busy highways of Orlando to a restaurant for a short visit. I was not accustomed to the loud noises of the big city. I was not prepared for Modern Man's furiously fast transportation, whisking me away from the stillness of the mountains and depositing me in a sea of complexities.

I learned to live the simple life on the trail. Everything I needed was on my back. I wanted to continue this simple philosophy at home. And so, I began, on my first full day at home, getting rid of personal belongings. Over the years I have been known to be a packrat, accumulating so much stuff. Stuff no longer needed, memories no longer wanted and stuff no longer useful or duplicated and triplicated in unknown piles of other stuff. Slowly, these items began entering a new phase of existence for somebody else. I find it hard at times to organize rooms containing possessions, especially since all I had to organize for those six glorious months on the trail was my backpack. I find myself outdoors more than I was before I left. I often build a small fire in our backyard fire pit and listen to the sounds of the nightlife, unfortunately most of it is human. After two weeks home I was already longing to see a green tunnel of a trail wandering through a forest. I heard Mother Nature calling and one week later, for three days, we saw each other again for an extended period of time on the Florida Trail.

Since I have been home, one of the questions most asked is "Do I miss the trail?"

I miss what was on the trail...

I miss the challenges of daily life on the trail: 'What new adventure awaited me?' 'What's in store for me today?' 'Where will I get my water?' 'What to eat?' 'What animals will I see?' 'Where will I rest my head at the end of the day?' 'Will my body hold up?'

I miss the dark night sky lit up with huge twinkling diamond-like stars with the faintest creamy color of the Milky Way splashed across the sky.

I miss seeing the small towns of America, meeting faces of people I never knew, who shared their kindness, their homes, and their zest for life.

I miss the acts of trail angels I never met, who made my journey an easier walk in the woods.

I miss the cry of the coyote and the song of the loon.

I miss the sounds of running water cascading down mountain streams and the wind blowing through the trees.

I miss the colors that radiate in the forests, the alpine meadows and bogs bringing a beauty to my eyes and the earthy smells to my nose.

And most of all, I miss the men and women of my nomadic family who shared a common bond of living together, surviving snow storms, high humidity, heat, rain, bugs, hard climbs and steep descents. We shared a camaraderie that most people cannot fathom. I will always remember their words of encouragement, smiling faces and the look of astonishment on those faces at our successful achievements throughout our journey on the Appalachian Trail.

KrispyKritter's final moments on the AT

CHAPTER 3
Hiking... I Mean, Walking The Pennine Way

She called again, Mother Nature, with more lessons to learn - to teach more about harmony between man and nature. And so began my next long distance adventure.

There is a small ribbon of rock, dirt and peat that travels through the bogs and high moorlands of England - some even call it "the backbone of England". The Pennine Way is regarded as the most challenging and toughest long distance walk in Great Britain. Influenced by Benton MacKaye's 1927 Journal of American Institute of Architects article that had given birth to the Appalachian Trail, journalist Tom Stephenson in the 1930's wrote several articles suggesting a similar pathway in England. In 1965, Tom Stephenson saw his dream become reality as the Pennine Way (PW too many) became the first National Long Distance Trail in England. I find it fitting that my second long distance hike was inspired by the Appalachian Trail.

The Pennine Way travels up the middle of England with the southern terminus located east of the city of Manchester, in a small village named Edale. 270 miles later the northern terminus is located in another small village named Kirk Yetholm in Scotland. The first and last day are considered by many to be the toughest and most hazardous. Inclement weather on the Pennine Way is said to be a true test of navigational skills as a hiker. A thru-hiker on the PW negotiates 287 gates that separate pastures, 249 timber stiles built over stone walls that separate pastures, 183 stone stiles (steps built into the stone wall to go up and over), 204 bridges, 319 km of public footpaths, 112 km on public bridleways, 32 km on public highway and thousands upon thousands of sheep. You walk to the highest waterfall in England (Highforce in Teesdale), the highest road (on Great Dun Fell), the highest Inn (Tan Inn), the highest market town (Alston) and to the longest canal (the Leeds and Liverpool Canal). A hiker on the PW will step on stone roads laid by the Romans, walk alongside a portion of Hadrian's Wall, built from sea to sea during the Roman conquest to keep out barbaric tribes from the north, walk through areas steeped in British history, view the surroundings landscapes that inspired literary works, visit geographic wonders and cross the vastness of the Cheviot Hills that lead into Scotland.

At first, the plan was to hike the Pennine Way alone. Then I talked about the hike to my friend Brian (trail name Greyhound) and saw the same enthusiasm on his face that I felt in my heart. The more I talked about my upcoming hike, the more he engaged and his interest awakened. It was only natural then to invite him along, which he gladly accepted.

The hike was simple. We had no definite plan, but were governed by two dates: August 6th was our beginning and August 29th the end. Life on the trail between those two dates would be dictated by weather, topography, mental - as well as - physical well being, and where we'd find pints of ale from the local British pubs.

And so the adventure planning began!

Compared to the preparing for my AT hike, I felt a greater level of intensity in the preparation of the Pennine Way. On the Appalachian Trail, I had a good idea what to expect because of my many section hikes. I believe the excitement in planning this adventure was magnified for several reasons. First, and foremost, traveling in a different country, separated from home by thousands of miles of water. Going home was not an easy logistical matter if something went wrong. I couldn't just get in a car, drive down the interstate and be home, or jump on an airplane and be at my doorstep within two or three hours. Next, I knew from reading books and the journals of past hikers on the Pennine Way, that I would be living in and discovering yet another side of Mother Nature's topography and weather. I was going to see landscapes unique in natural features. And then, I would be meeting people rich in a culture that I'd never experienced on the AT. I would be visiting places in England where history and doctrine played a big part in the people who sailed west across the Atlantic Ocean and shaped new countries on the North American continent.

I knew from traveling to England in the past, that the British use different words than Americans do to describe certain things. I needed to start understanding their lingo if I was to communicate with other hikers. Plus, I did not want to stand out as another arrogant American not willing to adjust to local customs. I found in my research of the Pennine Way that my backpack and the equipment that it carries are called a kit. Deciding what to take and what to leave behind in this kit took some thought because I'd never hiked in this climate – for this duration. Deliberating for days on what to bring and leave at home, I decided in the end, to choose my gear using the basic instinct of preparing for the worst and surviving through adopting, overcoming and improvising. I was mentally and physically ready for the challenge and to be once again on the bosom of Mother Nature.

The day of departure arrived; I kissed Lady Kritter good-bye and boarded a plane for a day of planes, trains and custom agents. I left the Sanford International Airport and - after a quick layover in Reykjavik, Iceland – landed in London. And that is where the fun began. I went through British customs and a female customs agent was having a problem understanding what exactly it was I'd be doing in country. Passengers on the flight from Reykjavik were given a form to fill out. I filled in all the sections except for the one asking "What address are you staying at during your stay in England." I left it blank. The custom agent wanted to know why the address section was not filled out. I tried to explain to her that because I was going to be backpacking and would have a new and different address every day. After several attempts to convince her of my intentions, I thought we are making progress, because we moved to the next question. I was thinking, "OK, over the first hurdle." The custom agent then wanted to know how long I would be in the UK. "2 months," I said. Then she asked how much money I had with me. "400 pounds," (USD 800) I said. "Oh my God!" she said, as she went into a tirade that 400 pounds is not enough money for 2 months, her face was contorted and I think she believed she had apprehended a bearded, national threat. Hearing the commotion, her supervisor arrived and stood next to her. I started from the beginning, and basically gave them a course in Backpacking 101. Satisfied that I was not a threat, the UK National security settled back to DEFCON 5 and I was off to meet Greyhound in another part of the airport.

We finally found each other, which was a feat in itself in a sea of people, and boarded our flight to Manchester. Upon arrival, we took the train to Edale and by 9:00 pm Greyhound and I were having a pint at the Old Nags Head to celebrate our arrival at the Pennine Way's southern terminus. We set up our tents in the dark and drizzle of the night at Cooper's Field Campground. Sleep came suddenly as the sheep baaed in the background.

A blistering, chilly wind greeted me when I woke up, but that soon died down to a strong breeze. Edale is a very small village with old stone buildings, and has a reputation in the UK for being one of the premier centers for outdoor activities. Greyhound and I went back to the Old Nags Head Pub; not to drink pints, but to take the ceremonial pictures at the plaque designating the beginning of the Pennine Way and to sign the official logbook. Greyhound wrote by his name, "unleashing the hounds." After a brief visit to the post office/general store, we were off and walking through Edale Valley.

Our first climb, a short gain in elevation, was to a place called Jacob's Ladder. In one direction, I could see the expanse of Edale Valley in different hues of green with flecks of white (sheep) scattered about. In the other direction I could see the rolling hills of the moorlands, a barren land with low vegetation and miles and miles of peat bogs (a type of wetland that for centuries accumulated the remains of dead plants in layers several feet thick). A gray path parted the moorlands and diminished as it went up and over the hill. We soon learned that the gray path contained large slabs of stone that had been taken from dismantled cotton mills and placed into the bogs as stepping stones. The hiker, prior to the stepping stones being laid, had to wade through that mess. They stood on their back legs, with the bog up to their thighs and slowly moved their back leg up and out of the decaying muck - accompanied with a wet popping sound. The peat then moved quickly (like wet concrete) and filled the void previously occupied by their leg. Once free and balancing on the hind leg, they placed their leg forward and let it sink down into the gooey mess. Only to be repeated over and over again. Slowly, this would go on for hours and hours.

The beginning of the Pennine Way starts at a pub – where do you think it ends?

I know because Greyhound and I tried it with the gray path next to us. The endeavor of past hikers to slosh through the bogs was quite an extraordinary enterprise. Within minutes, I was dirty and fatigued. I had the deepest respect for the accomplishments endured by the peat bog hikers of the past.

The path, immediately after crossing Kinder Low, followed on top of a steep cliff looking down into the valley. Greyhound and I found a rock similar to McAfee's Knob (on the AT in Virginia) that looked like a human nose so we called it Kinder's Nose. We each had a picture taken of us standing on the rock overlooking the valley below.

The early afternoon was spent walking through the bogs over Mill Hill, through a track in the bottom of a deeply sunken gully with peat all around known as the Devil's Dike, then up to a mountain of peat named Bleaklow. As far as the eye could see, the landscape contained pockets and small channels of black-peat. It made me feel like I was a visitor on another planet.

North of Bleaklow, I found a small canyon where a stream cascaded to the bottom. I thought this location would be a good place for a break and reflect on how I could find the beauty of

Krispykritter on Kinder's Nose

Mother Nature in all types of different locations in the world). The walk down Clough Edge brought us to Torside Reservoir where we walked through a forest of pine trees. We spent the night at a campground in a place called Crowden and got intimate with pesky, biting insects called midges. In between the swatting and swearing we talked with hikers on the trail. As we prepared for bed the sun went down around 10:00 pm and so did I for a restful night on the Pennine Way.

The next day began with an early sunrise at around 4:30 AM. Back on the PW, Greyhound and I started off with a great walk through the Crowden Valley up to a large rocky cliff called Laddow Rocks. I felt like I was in a shooting gallery as we walked along the edge of Laddow Rocks. Everywhere I looked, up close or far away, the landscape suddenly changed as sheep's heads were always popping up above the heather, or disappearing behind hidden crags - all the time they were chewing. Other times we heard a sheep's baa up close, then far away, but couldn't see them, a 360 degree surround sound of "BAAA". I later learned that, though sheep were frequently kept in pens, they were found everywhere; in the pastures, on the roads, in the villages. And so was their poop. My boots will forever have a fine coating of the pungent goo. All day long as we walked through that section of the PW was the sound of the sheep.

Continuing along the trail, we started seeing grouses (the next target in the shooting gallery). They regularly startled me as they abruptly took off in flight from a hidden spots near me. It was almost as if I heard, only slightly, the word "PULL!" just before they took off. The last animal of the shooting gallery was the rabbit. The small furry animal kept jumping out of 'nowhere' and hopping quickly to another hidden spot. (Note: no animals were harmed in the making of this hike.)

A moderate mist overtook us as we walked up the stone slabs of Black Hill. The hill had an eerie, surreal feel to it, and with the mist, created a dream-like landscape. Much of the day was spent on the stone slabs walking over more bogs in the moorlands. Similar to road walking the hard slabs were brutal on my feet.

The grey path of stepping stones going up Black Hill

Greyhound and I, towards late afternoon, came upon the Great Western Inn located in Standedge. The owners (Rachel and Alex) have a delicious food menu, great selection of beer and an offering of good friendship, so we decided to spend the night. I noticed in the guide book that one could stay at the Inn or camp, so true to our noble, backpacking way of life, I asked Rachel, "Where can we camp for the night." "Go around behind the Inn, on the grass, in the area surrounded by a fence." Rachel stated.. Her word choice contained two clues to what type of camping it would be - "grass" and "fence". The word grass brought to mind the plush softness for a bed. The word fence brought to mind an area without sheep and a good night sleep. I was soon to learn that my expectations were not to be met - at least, not exactly. Greyhound and I, pleasantly full from our evening meal, picked up our kits and walked to the back of the inn. The fenced-in grassy area spread out before us, ready for our tents. But the area also contained a small herd of sheep, and *everywhere* on the grass we looked were sheep nuggets. We had to take the time to brush clear a site of nuggets before setting up and nestling into our tents.

All night long the woolly creatures created a restless night with their incessantly baa. I no longer had to close my eyes and count sheep to go to sleep. They were always outside my tent. I tolerated the baas of the sheep, but I was not about to trade in my trekking poles for a shepherd's staff.

I woke up the next morning, unzipped my tent fly and was face to face with a chewing sheep who was staring directly in at me. In the twilight of morning, in that state of not being fully awake, I think I heard the sheep either greet me with "Good Morning", or maybe he just baa'ed at me. But either way, it meant "Welcome to England."

The third day on the Pennine Way we were in more peat bogs of the moorlands. They were everywhere, and we were already getting our fill of them. Greyhound and I came to a sign stating that, at one time, the landscape of the present moorlands was covered in forests. Britain's early inhabitants, long before the invading armies of the Romans, cut the trees down for farming, fuel and building. Over the centuries, the vegetation re-growth became low lying peat bogs that dominated much of the landscape.

We came to a highway rest area (called a layby in England) on A672 and found a snack caravan cooking up breakfast sandwiches, tea and coffee. The line was full of businessmen and police officers getting their breakfast. I had the best bacon, sausage and egg sandwich that I could remember and coffee, my luxury item to have when in civilization. Talking with some of the chaps; I mentioned how the area once had trees. One of the lads replied, "We know, there is a sign that says you are entering the Black Forest. When you look away from the sign you see 6 trees." Everyone laughed.

It is amazing to me when I look out and see Mother Nature's artwork, how certain areas you see remind you of other areas you have visited in the past. This was the case at a rocky area called Blackstone Edge. Boulders of all shapes - as big as a house, and as small as a basketball - littered the rocky hillside, reminding me of parts of Maine. Coming off the Edge we walked on our first Roman road! The stones were nicely laid so that wagon wheels could easily ride over them, even still. In the middle was a culvert system to drain the water down the hill into a reservoir.

The terrain leveled off for several miles as we walked alongside several reservoirs in brisk wind. Throughout the morning the wind steadily increased. We were walking the reservoirs with a head wind of 20-25 mph winds. By noon, winds of 30-35 mph with gust of over 40 mph were hitting us, as we approached Stoodley Pike Monument, elevation 1310 ft.

The wind was so strong that I could see Greyhound walking in front of me getting thrown off balance by the blast. The gusts would suddenly quit and the force he was using to counter the wind threw him the opposite way.

Stoodley Pike is a needle-shaped monument, 120 feet tall overlooking the Calderdale Valley and is a landmark that can be seen from miles around. The monument was erected in 1814 to celebrate the defeat of Napoleon, and was completed in 1815. Stoodley Pike, because of the soft peat, has fallen and been rebuilt several times. The monument is roughly 40 miles from Edale, and those who pass it experience a change in landscape; leaving the moorlands behind and entering into a countryside of farmlands and small villages.

Greyhound and I found one of the best re-supply places we had ever encountered at Highgate Farms in Colden. Directly across the farmhouse, a small one room, general store was built into the carriage house and old barn called, Aladdin's Cave. The small store sells a little bit of everything and had a steady stream of customers from the local farming community. Not a space on the wall, countertops, or shelves was wasted. That store put American convenience stores to shame. The deli and bakery were so good; a steak and onion pie with a pint of ale immediately brought a smile to my face and more-than-satisfied my hiker hunger. The proprietor of the store was a spry, aristocratic elderly lady. By the name of May. She was delighted to show Greyhound and I the invitation to and pictures of the Queen's garden tea party she recently attended in London. We had such a great time foraging in the store and restocking our food supplies. May told us we could camp on a grassy knoll behind the store, and we saw a double rainbow over the farm as we stepped outside to look at the knoll. Good food, resupply, good company and a sign of good karma; it was a no brainer; we were staying here for the night. Once again the ground was covered in sheep nuggets.

May at her counter at the general store called Aladdin's Cave

I have found throughout my time here on earth that there always seems to be a balance in the differences of scenery and in the life of the land - the ying and the yang. Greyhound and I have discovered this balance, too, hiking in England. We traveled through patches of pasture land after leaving Highgate Farms and realized how much we missed the moor highlands. We walked our way through decrepit cabins used for hunting and sloshed through a cattle farm ankle deep in cow poop. Suddenly, sheep poop didn't seem all that bad. This was not one of our favorite mornings for hiking. But, the yang came through when the Pennine Way took us through the beautiful villages of Ponden, Ickornshaw and Lothersdale. Each village seemed prettier than the last.

I had learned to admire and appreciate the moors. They are one of Mother Nature's ways of rebuilding what man has destroyed. The moors are left alone by most, drained and sold as fertilizer by some, and protected by few that hope to retain their beauty in the landscape. The moors to me are similar to the Florida Everglades. Some people see the everglades as swampland and miles of nothing but sawgrass. But, to those of us in balance with nature, we see the vastness of the everglades as mini ecosystems of beauty. At first, as I began hiking in England, all I saw was the vast rolling hills of purple heather, a low lying, purple blossomed shrubs and the bogs. The longer I stayed in the moors, my senses began to develop a respect for England's natural beauty. The heather would explode from the flight of the red grouse, or the running hop of the rabbit. Britain's smallest falcon, the Merlin, can be seen flying overhead. I watched, as far as the eye could see, fields of swaying heather, waving as the wind caresses them. At times, small flowers peek out between the rocks and caught my eyes. As we were walking, Greyhound asked me if I liked the moors. I told him it was funny that he should ask me that question, because I was just thinking how much I did. We had developed a kindred spirit in that.

At the conclusion of the first week of hiking the Pennine Way, I'd already had some wonderful memories. The most vivid of those from the bloody (not the body kind) sheep and the bloody wind. I was truly excited for what the second week held.

The beginning of the second week on the Pennine Way found Greyhound and I walking into the Village of Gargrave. The noise, traffic and many brick buildings gave the village the hustle and bustle of a small town. Greyhound and I did not waste any time saving our trail food and eating lunch at a local pub that overlooked the main intersection of the village.

Full, we waddled over to the local grocery store and re-supplied. On our way out of the village we found one of the famous red British telephone booths along a path on the banks of River Aire. Greyhound and I hadn't talked with our wives since we began our walk; so, with a glance, we agreed to stop and give our wives a bell (British for a telephone call). It was *so* good to hear Lady Kritter's voice. I caught up on news on the home front and learned about the terrorist plot at the airports in England and the United States! I immediately understood why I'd had a bout with the custom agent upon my arrival to England; she was doing her job and doing it well. The town noises of Gargrave got to Greyhound and I, and less than three hours later, we were above Gargrave walking amidst quiet pastures. I was surprised to say it, but we welcomed the baa's of the sheep.

I was reading the British Walking Guide Series, *Pennine Way* by Edward De La Billiere and Keith Carter, and really liked what I had read about the Village of Malham. When Greyhound and I arrived there, we were not disappointed. We crossed Malham Beck (a large creek) and entered a village made of stone buildings. In the center of the village was the Malham Youth Hostel. I had never stayed at a Youth Hostel before and I was curious as I read what it was like: cozy bed, warm shower, machine to launder clothes *and* pub food. It didn't take but a nano second to decide that we were staying there. When the doors opened to the hostel, Greyhound and I were the first registered guests. A chap by the name of Dave was on leave from the British Navy and was assigned to our bunk room. He, too, was hiking the Pennine Way. The three of us had dinner at a local pub where Dave introduced us to a local ale called "Old Peculier", an enjoyably flavored, intoxicating ale. Our faces were hurting so much from the laughter as we talked about the trail, and compared countries and women. Waking up in the comfort of a bed and enjoying the morning hospitality of the hostel introduced a new way for me to spend nights while traveling in the civilized world. To top it off, I realized the best part of sleeping in the hostel - not one baa.

As Greyhound and I continued to hike north on the Pennine Way, more and more of Mother Nature's wonderment began to appear. Leaving the Village of Malham, the Pennine Way traveled through an area called Malham Cove in the Yorkshire Dales National Park. Malham Cove is a curved crag (cliff) of limestone, approximately 240 feet high and 900 feet wide. Melt water from the last Ice Age created Malham Tarn (a lake) and a stream that once ran over the crag in an imposing waterfall that gave the cove its curved shape. We climbed steep steps embedded in the side of the crag and emerged on top of the cove. Its surface contained a magnificent pavement of limestone with deep fissures and channels. The resulting limestone pavement is known as 'clints' and 'grykes', whereby the naked limestone lumps are the clints and the fissures in between are the grykes. The grykes are home to many rare, shade-loving plants: harts-tongue fern, wood-sorrel, wood-garlic, geranium, anemone, rue, and enchanter's nightshade. Greyhound and I were blasted by high winds and rain as we carefully hop scotched across the clints. It did not help matters that we climbed up a narrow valley with high cliffs on either side, which created a natural wind tunnel that funneled powerful wind and rain into our faces. We emerged from the canyon-like valley and found ourselves back in the moors with a grand view of the wind whipped waves of Malham Tarn. We could see in the distance, through the gray mist and rain a small grove of trees standing in the middle of nowhere.

Greyhound and I looked at each other, pointed towards the trees and in the scream of the wind rushing by our ears; we barely heard each other yell, "Shelter!" We found that sweet spot in the trees that sheltered us from the beating fury that was hitting us and ate a soggy lunch. Rested, with stomachs full, we secured our weather gear around us and with our heads down, stepped back onto the trail. We crossed Fountain's Fell, a mountain that once housed a thriving coal mining community that was potted with deep holes left by the miners. It was imperative to stay on the trail in this area or risk falling into one of numerous vertical abandoned mine shafts, lost forever.

The weather would often change at the blink of an eye. As we left Fountain's Fell the sun broke through the clouds; burning off the gray mass to reveal blue skies - and just in time, Pen-y-ghent, the highest mountain in England, stood in front of us.

The Pennine Way climbs up Pen-y-ghent as a steep ascent with a series of vertical rocky steps that leads to a plateau like summit. The mountain towers over the landscape at an elevation of 2,278 feet, with splendid views. Sometimes called, "The Hill Of The Winds" Pen-y-ghent lived up to its nickname as everyone visiting the summit was seeking shelter behind stone walls to escape the cold winds. Truly, the backbone of England, rainfall on Pen-y-ghent either flows west towards the Irish Sea, or east towards the North Sea.

A slow descent off Pen-y-ghent brought Greyhound and I to the Village of Horton In Ribblesdale.

Krispykritter overlooking Pen-y-ghent

The guide book referred to camping at Holmes Farm where we found the owner riding a lawn mower in a pasture. He was cutting the grass in straight lines, crossing over those in another series of straight lines, creating checkerboard squares. The well-manicured field contained an assortment of tents and caravans (travel trailers). The machine-riding architect turned down the rpm's on the mower as Greyhound and I approached with our backpacks on. "Three pounds ($6.00) each and pick any open square for tent camping. Showers are located in the building next to the barn," he stated. I looked up and realized each tent was located in a square. I picked a nice soft cushion of grass, set up my tent and took a shower. "*Wow!*" I thought. I was going to own a piece of English real estate for the evening and the farmer had found a unique way of making money by grazing humans. *What a concept!*

It was early afternoon and Greyhound and I were hungry for some pub food. I surveyed several campers and was told the Pen-y-ghent Cafe, just down the road from the farm, was the most popular choice. We could hear guitars, violins and other stringed instruments playing music as we approached the cafe. There we were on the backbone of England, getting ready to eat pub food, drink pints and listen to authentic English music; I was excited. However, I forgot Murphy's Law. The music stopped as Greyhound and I entered the cafe. The circle of musicians changed seats and passed back and forth stringed instruments. Greyhound and I ordered our food during this lull and found an empty table in the crowded room to eat at and be serenaded. And then, it happened. A banjo twanged out the first notes of the music from the movie Deliverance. Immediately following was the guitar, playing the same notes. The music was repeated over, again and again, each time the tempo going a little faster. The crowd erupted into whoops and applause, Hee Haw style, as the song Dueling Banjos reverberated off the walls. The players were good, but this was not the English folk music I was hoping for. The next song wasn't either; it was a fast Country Bluegrass number, followed by another. I don't know if it was because Greyhound and I ordered the traditional American hamburger and chips (French fries) but the rest of afternoon was filled with American Country music. Thanks Murph!

The next morning the clouds were gray and covered the top of Pen-y-ghent in mist. Without the sun shining and the moisture heavy in the air it looked like we were in for a cold hike. Greyhound and I left Horton-in-Ribblesdale and hiked back into the moors. We stumbled upon, Ling Hill, a very pleasant ravine designated as a Nature Reserve. The chasm was cut by a stream, carving a deep gash into the limestone; and though it was not very long in length, it was a unique, fenced-off environment of wildflowers, trees and wildlife. Greyhound and I thought this would be a great place to explore, letting the world above us go by.

Instead, we respected the 'No Trespassing' notices and continued on our way. The historic Ling Gill Bridge crossed the stream north of Ling Gill. It started raining. This time Greyhound and I took refuge sitting behind the bridge's ancient parapet (when you are outside in the elements of nature it is amazing the different styles of shelter one can find from the weather). We settled down for a snack break so that the wall blocked the wind and rain from our bodies. We could see on one of the parapet walls a barely readable inscription referring, I thought, to the bridge being rebuilt with the worn numbers 1765. I could only imagine the history that passed over this bridge.

Greyhound and I observed several large tree farms below us as we followed the trail along the crest of the moorlands. We both wondered why the trail didn't go through the forest and felt walking among the trees would have been a good change of scenery. Seeing the hillsides covered in trees from above did give us a brief glimpse as to what the landscape looked like in ancient times. Walking in the moors, we followed a stony-walled Roman path called, Cam High Road that led into West Cam Road and then into the village of Hawes. These two roads have been used for centuries. It was hard to believe that my footsteps were hitting on the same roads as did those of legions of Roman soldiers.

Hawes was nestled into a delightful valley called Wensleydale. Bigger in size than Malham, both villages bristled with tourist and caravans (travel trailers) passing through. I imagined Hawes being the equivalent to Gatlinburg, near Great Smoky Mountain National Park. Our timing for arrival in Hawes was perfect: a weather front was moving in and the rain had been steady since we arrived. Located in the village was the Hawes Youth Hostel - a perfect place to escape the well-known cold and wet English weather. Dave and Alster, a chap from New Zealand, arrived later and told us how they were fogged in on their way down into the village. Our room's window looked out in the direction from which we had come into the valley, and we saw the fog slowly envelop the hilltops.

Greyhound and I decided to schedule a zero day (rest day in trail lingo) in Hawes. After our decision, the weather took a turn for the worse. The cold rain continued throughout the night and into the morning as we nestled in our hostel beds. Dave shoved off after breakfast to stay on his schedule. Greyhound and I did the usual things a thru-hiker does in a trail town; laundry, re-supply food, go to the post office, and find an internet cafe.

Once finished with town chores, the rest of the day was spent exploring the village. The highlight of our village visit was visiting a rope-maker shop and the Wensleydale Creamery - maker of fine cheeses. The rope maker was cool, but the cheese shop was the best part. Sampling free food is a thru hiker's dream, and the fresh cheeses were delicious. And after eating such a large amount of it, I felt like a local connoisseur of cheese.

The village had two outdoor centers and Greyhound and I went in to see the similarities and differences with Travel Country

Outdoors - where we've both worked for years. We walked in and the first thing we noticed was that - ironically - the owner was walking around greeting customers, while the help sat behind the counter. There wasn't a great selection of clothing and gear, just mostly items used by day hikers. The majority of outdoor activity in the National Parks, from what I can see in England, is walking. People walk greater distances than in America and it shows in their physical appearance. One does not see very many obese individuals, including children.

The villages we were passing through differed greatly from American small towns. We didn't see gas stations on every street corner, fast food restaurants, drug stores, shopping centers or stripped malls. The overall presence of police vehicles and officers wearing weapons was limited. The villages for the most part are clean and have walking footpaths everywhere.

The afternoon, unlike the morning, turned into a wonderful, sunny day. We took advantage of the weather and had a great lunch on a hill overlooking the village and Wensleydale Valley. Lunch consisted of cheese, wine and loaves of baguette bread.

I spent the rest of my zero day recuperating sore muscles. By the way, we did pass a petrol stop (gas station) and saw the price of petrol. The liquid gold was no longer sold by the imperial gallon. Instead, the price at the time of our hike was one pound per liter. In Florida that would equal about eight dollars per gallon (2008 prices). I'd found the answer to America's obesity - keep raising the gas prices.

The highest inn in England is called the Tan Hill Inn. Walking north of Keld in the rolling purple colored moors called Stonesdale Moor, we steadily climbed until a completely isolated, and two story building came into view as a speck on the horizon. It took a while, but we finally reached the inn. Outside, by the front door, was a plaque that read:

TAN HILL INN
Great Britians highest Inn at 1732 ft A.S.L.
En-Suite Accommodation-morning coffee and meals
Rustic Barn, Wedding Licence
Tel:01833 628246 – www.tannhillinn.com

Tan Hill – the highest inn in England

We dropped our packs outside the door and entered. The atmosphere was extraordinary: low ceilinged pub, lots of wood and old furnishings, a coal fire was burning in the fireplace, a dog was sleeping on a chair next to the fire, a pet sheep was running throughout the interior and then jumped through the open window, people were taking pictures of the sheep, others were eating and drinking - simply happy to be there. Greyhound and I had a pint or two and toasted each other, and the Inn for its achievements of standing through time for the wayfarer of the moors.

We set-up our tents in the back yard and were greeted by a menagerie of animals: four inquisitive chickens, numerous sheep checking out our tents, rabbits bouncing back and forth outside our tent screen and birds landing and taking off in the grass adjacent to our tents like an aircraft carrier.

Afterwards, Greyhound and I had supper with two other Pennine Way thru-hikers. One was a middle-aged man claiming to be on his third thru-hike. I forgot his real name, but we ended up giving him the trail name "Duckman" because he walked with a plastic yellow duck on his shoulder, saying it was a way to meet women.

Wild camping at Tan Hill

Trust me, ladies of England, run if you see this combination of man and plastic duck.

The other hiker was an 18 year old lad by the name of Chris. Chris represents the new generation of England, and Duckman, well he still thinks England is sending their Red Coat Army to fight the colonies in America. He even asked me, "How are the colonies doing?" I am not kidding.

It was interesting to hear their interpretations of the hike. The folks in England walk the Pennine Way with hardly any food or portable shelter (tent, bivy or tarp) to protect themselves from the elements, or sleeping bags. They check in at Bed and Breakfast establishments, inns, youth hostels, or the home of a friend, get a nice warm shower, sit down to an evening meal prepared for them at an extra charge, or go to the local village pub for supper. The night is spent in a warm comfortable bed. They wake up for a cooked breakfast (extra) and, as they walk out the door, are handed a brown paper bag containing a sandwich and snacks for their day's walk.

Throughout our hikes, Greyhound and I would have discussions on nature, life, backpacking, work, and so on. One such discussion occurred as Greyhound and I were lying in our sleeping bags next to the inn listening to the baa of the sheep. Greyhound called over to me and asked if I caught the conversation on how the British considered hiking the Pennine Way. We started asking each other questions as to why we called it a hike and the English called it a walk. According to the Webster's Dictionary, a hike is "to go on an extended walk". A walk is "to go or cause to go on foot or a slow gait". Hiking to Greyhound and I is the unassisted living and sleeping in nature, with whatever is in your kit. You become a part of Mother Nature, instead of just being a visitor. England does not have any wild lands like we know as being wild in the United States. That was taken care of centuries ago when the land was raped by the cutting down of the forests and the many of the wild beasts hunted and killed to extinction. The hikers of England, who hike long distances, in essence, separate their journey into an accumulation of several day hikes. They walk each day, stop at night for food and lodging in the villages, and then start over again the next day. They do this not only on the Pennine Way, but on all the trails in the United Kingdom. And when they camp in a tent, it is called wild camping. Greyhound and I still had all our gear, but decided to adopt the phrase; "When in Rome, do as the Romans," and apply it to our hike in England by going for a walk - staying in the hostels and eating in cities most nights.

Rain pelted our tent walls on and off during the night. The early morning sun was a big orange ball breaking through two horizontal sections of blue gray clouds. Nature has a way of balancing the growth and development of her surroundings. Watching the rising sun was a positive sign for a fantastic day to come. The morning hike was through some beautiful heather fields that had a sweet floral aroma. Alongside the trail was a small creek called Frumming Beck that ran through the peat bogs. I noticed a brown bird that runs like a roadrunner, only flying as a last resort. We passed more farmland and then walked through the tiny village of Baldersdale; the halfway point on the Pennine Way. In the early afternoon Greyhound and I came to the village Middleton-in-Teesdale. We started to re-supply when all the stores began closing for the day. I asked a passing woman what was going on, and she said it was half-day Wednesday. "What is that?" I asked. "Oh!" she replied, "that is when the stores close early for mid-week, so we can do our weekly chores." I was enamored at the concept of planning time in the middle of the week to do personal business!

Once again, in true English fashion, a weather front was moving in. Greyhound and I left the Dufton Hostel exceptionally early to beat the fast moving front. We were probably the only people that day to see a clear view of the village below from Knock Fell (2,604 ft). As we looked up, the outline of the mountain - Great Dun Fell - was shrouded in mist. The higher we climbed, the harder the wind blew and the more the temperature dropped. Every now and then the opaque mist would swirl away, giving us a clear view of the alpine-like terrain of Cross Fell (2,930 ft). The mist turned into a heavy fog and navigation was strictly by compass and map leaping from cairn to cairn. Five minutes before reaching Greg's Hut, a bothy (shelter) used as a refuge for bad weather, a heavy rain began. We stayed in the rock shelter as the initial rain storm dropped its deluge. With no end in sight of the rain, we left the bothy, descended off Cross Fell and settled in for a mundane, wet walk. To compound matters, the footing was especially precarious; it was one of the rockiest roads I ever hiked. Greyhound and I spent hours on that difficult-to-manage road, wrapped up in our hard shell rain gear, our exposed bodies being pelted by the relentless rain. Chris, who we met at Tanner Inn and spent the night with us at the Dufton Hostel, caught up with Greyhound and I somewhere in the rain and the three of us entered the village of Garrigill. Dripping wet, we entered the village pub, warmed up next to the coal fire, and drank pub refreshments. It was really hard for the three of us, after a brief rest and being almost dry, to leave the comforts of the pub's interior and resume our walk in the wet environment to Alston.

Chris, Greyhound and I stayed at the Alston Youth Hostel that night. Several hours later Dave, another Pennine Way hiker we had been running into off and on since Malham Youth Hostel, showed up - his gear, kit and clothing completely wet, inside and out. Dave couldn't understand why his North Face Gore-Tex jacket didn't keep him dry. I asked, "Where did you get the jacket." He replied that while on deployment with the Navy, he bought the jacket at the market in Asia for a good price. Greyhound and I immediately said, "A knock off"(a fake). Chris, Greyhound and I started laughing. The only thing Gore-Tex on that jacket was the wording on the label. Dave also told us he was the last one to cross the high fell. He said several walkers turned back because of the visibility. I went to bed early in a warm and dry bed. My last thought before slumber was "I think I like this walking stuff."

The four of us stayed in town most of the morning and walked around, exploring. We visited the bakery, a small outfitter, and the co-op food store. I liked the atmosphere of the quaint town that claims to be the highest market town in England. The narrow main street of Alston was located on a steep hill with old, brick, two and three story buildings on either side. The first floor contained compact storefronts with the upper floors occupied mostly as residences. The invention of electricity and the development of plumbing with metal pipes occurred long after the buildings were constructed, so their distribution equipment could be seen attached to the exterior walls. Almost all the buildings are older than the United States, as are many buildings in England.

One proprietor that Greyhound and I spoke with in Hawes told us his basement used to be a pub 250 years ago! He then added that people generally have no interest in history unless a building is over 300 years old. As in most villages and towns, the centre opens up and contains either a small square with a significant monument to local history or, a small area dedicated to the parking of the most recent invention, the automobile.

Greyhound, Chris, Dave and I, left Alston and headed for Knarsdale. When we left the village, we immediately found ourselves back in the farmlands. Greyhound and I initially thought, during the first days of our hike, that the moorlands on the Pennine Way were used as connectors between the villages. We decided after nearly two weeks on the Pennine Way that the farmlands, the beautiful hamlets, villages and scenic features made by man were - instead - the connectors between the green and purple hues of the Mother Nature's moorlands.

Farmland walking meant walking through numerous pastures that were set apart from others by stone walls to keep livestock in. We'd have to go up and over the walls on stiles, a passage through or over a fence or boundary via steps, ladders or narrow gaps A wooden stile would fill the narrow gap with a gate. Most of stiles contained wooden or stone steps built into the stone wall on both sides. The footing on these steps was slippery from sheep dung and/or moisture from dew or rain. Climbing the stiles, opening and closing the gate, squeezing through the narrow opening and watching-your-step all took time and broke the rhythm of the hike. There were, however, some people who had constructed a newer way to go through the pastures. It is similar to a small swing gate; you walk part way into the enclosure, close the gate behind you and walk through the other side of the enclosure, and through the wall. That was more time consuming but saved the knees from climbing and the possibility of falling from slippery steps.

We ate lunch at a pub outside Knarsdale as the afternoon rains began. Once again the afternoon walk was a soggy one through the high marsh grass of the moors. Crossing more bogs, pastures and a golf course we finally arrived at the Greenhead Youth Hostel tired and wet.

What a difference a little rest made. After the previous day's walk in wet boots, my feet hurt and looked like white prunes. Greyhound and I had done laundry the night before and placed our clothes in the drying room. Hostels on the Pennine Way do not have dryers. Instead, they have what is called a drying room that is heated by a radiator. Wet clothing and gear are placed on racks and hooks surrounding the room to dry. I decided to wash both my clothes and my boots and asked that the heat be kept on all night. With all the mud and animal dung caking my boots, part of my foot problem was that they couldn't breathe through the boots.

When I woke up the next morning and went to the drying room, I was shocked to find the room stone cold and all the boots, clothing, and gear still wet. I was not a happy camper. And, I was not the only one. Dave and several others had wet items in the room to dry. After speaking with a hostel worker, the heat was turned up, the clothes were dried and the boots got partly dried.

I was excited to be on the next segment where the Pennine Way parallels the historic Hadrian's Wall. Before we saw it, though - Brian, Chris and I came to the ruins of Thirlwall Castle that had been built from stones taken from the Roman Wall. At the Walltown Quarry and Walltown Crags, we finally came face to face with the wall. And, it was spectacular. The wall was built by the Roman Emperor Hadrian as a defense against the Picts (tribes from Northern Britain, now Scotland). Constructed along a fault line, the wall sits on top of many hills and crags, protecting the northern frontier with approximately 73 miles of fortifications. Included in that were turrets

KrispyKritter on Hadrian's Wall

or milecastles every Roman mile (approximately 4,851 ft.) and larger forts at predetermined intervals along its length.

There we were, Brian, Chris and I walking alongside the wall built 2000 years ago by thousands of Roman soldiers. To touch a rock laid by someone from that era was quite a feeling, a physical connection to history from times long past. I think all of us, privately in our own ways, walked a part of the wall pretending to be a Roman Centurion on duty overlooking the landscape for invading bands. For me, my imagination took root when we were at a place called Milecastle 41. This area was a guarded gateway into the frontier of the barbarian tribes. Beyond it was the last frontier, where no Roman had gone before, to explore new worlds, seeking out new life and civilization...wait, whoops, while all that is basically true - I'm thinking of the wrong dimension (insert appreciative smiles from the Star Trek fans).

Looking to the northwest the dark skies meant only one thing, rain. One of the big reasons those drying rooms were so valuable. Greyhound and I made a dash to our next destination, the youth hostel in Once Brewed. It was full because it was still raining, so we spent the afternoon at the dry (and less crowded) Once Brewed

Tourist Information Centre. We watched a movie about the Romans and the history of why and how they built the wall. The rain continued to come down so we spent more time looking in the gift shop. It was here that we met up with Poor Dave and caught a glimpse of some trail magic.

A couple who stayed with us at the Greenhead Hostel had a room with 4 extra beds. Dave, who was soaking wet and limping around on blistered feet, met up with the couple. I guess they felt sorry for him and appreciated us taking Dave under our wings, because they offered their room for the three of us Trail magic when you least expect it - even across the big pond. It reminded me of a phrase I liked: "Gratia gratiam parit" (kindness produces kindness).

We woke up in the morning to a light drizzle. Thankfully, this time the drying room did its job so all equipment and clothing was dry. The morning walk continued along several more miles of Hadrian's Wall causing many more vivid mental images of life at the wall.

The trail parted ways with the old structure and soon we were hiking in Wark Forest. Majestic pine trees lined the trail through tall wet grass. I had to stop and take it in. It was so beautiful. I sat down and let the sights, smells and sounds of the forest take over my environment. I was no longer on a walk; I was sitting on a carpet of pine needles on a journey with Mother Nature. I could hear the faint cry of an owl in the distance or, the beating of small wings flying overhead in-between the long trunks of pines, chirping a song. Waves of the earthly musk from the forest floor floated into my nostrils. Looking beyond the first line of trees and into the darkness of shadows, I found the camouflaged remains of an old stone building. I got up and went to the ruin and discovered that the building was rather large, containing many stone walls inside it that created rooms with pine trees growing inside. Touching the four foot high stone wall, I closed my eyes and envisioned a family from a time past living in this structure that was both residence and barn.

Today, the only residents were the pine trees and creatures of the forest. Greyhound stopped to sit at the site and felt the spirit of those giants that surrounded us. We, once again without talking, found a deep connection to Mother Nature in England. Towards the end of this sensuous forest experience, Chris arrived and took in the energy flow of the forest as well.

The middle of the afternoon found us walking in pastures, through more sheep and cow poop. Even the footbridges across the Houxty Burn had a coating of the number two. I don't know if this was done intentionally, but the name of this area was Shitlington.

When we arrived into the old market town of Bellingham, I had enough layers of the brown stuff on my boots that I couldn't read the label on them any longer. We dropped our packs in Bellingham and walked into the butcher shop and bought hot meat and potato pies with drinks.

There was nothing like a fresh English meat pie after a day of hiking. So satisfying. We spent the rest of the afternoon in town, and, in the rain went on to the Bellingham Youth Hostel. During the evening, the hostel warden (that is the actual title of the person in charge of the hostel) told us that the Bellingham and Byrness Youth Hostel, as well as several others hostels in England, were being phased out at the end of the season. Greyhound and I looked at each other and had the same thought: Future thru-walkers would have to carry a tent or tarp since there would be no facilities to stay at, thus making them thru-hikers, American style.

Chris, Greyhound and I sat down in the hostel to go over the final push to Kirk Yetholm, the northern terminus of the Pennine Way. Dave stayed behind nursing some terrible blisters from the constant wetness. I, too, had blisters: one on my little left toe, one small one on the right heel and one big one on the left heel. I tried everything to protect the hot spots: duct tape, gorilla tape, changing socks and all the new fancy pads from the British outfitters. Nothing worked, and probably because of the large amounts of water inside my boots - the boots were supposed to be waterproof and had somehow failed. There were times that I would walk through grass saturated with morning dew and my socks were soaking wet. It even stumped Greyhound as to the cause, maybe they were also knock-offs - the only thing Gore-Tex being the label.

The final two days were supposed to be the most demanding and challenging on the Pennine Way. This was due, in part, to a 27 mile section of nothing but high barren moorlands stretched across an area called the Cheviot that straddle the England – Scotland border. The biggest concern in this section was the weather. The alpine environment combined with the constantly changing northern

England climate of being wet, windy and foggy was a recipe for a possible treacherous crossing.

Alertness was a vital key to survival. Many hikers challenge their endurance and attempted to complete the section in one day. Looking over the maps and guide book, we felt that we could accomplish walking from Bellingham to Kirk Yetholm, a greater distance (42 miles), in a two day period creating less punishment for our bodies.

The next morning Greyhound and I were out the door and waving good-bye to Bellingham, the last big settlement before entering the frontier. Chris was not far behind. Within a few hours, my feet were again soaking wet from the waterlogged peat moors and wet grass. We walked along the edge of Clydesdale Forest and were finally on a track (forest road) walking through a beautiful forest. Large sections of valleys and distant low, round mountains covered in conifer trees reminded me of northern New Hampshire and Maine. Heading for a small community called Byrness, we walked alongside the River Reed that entered a beautiful natural woodland that reminded Greyhound of sections in the High Sierra. If we would have previously known of the gentle ease in elevation, the road walk to this spot and the grassy sites along the river with picnic tables, surrounded by majestic trees, we would have pressed on from Bellingham to wild camp at this tranquil location. We entered the hamlet of Byrness and found a great surprise; the First and Last Cafe, a small store/restaurant and gas station on a road going into Scotland. There, I cooked the last of the dehydrated spaghetti sauce and pasta that Lady Kritter had prepared for me. We bought dessert in the shop, loaded up with enough water for the next day and a half. We left the café and followed The West Highland Way up a sharp climb to enter the high moorlands.

We walked the next 8 miles over stone slabs, wooden duckboards (boardwalks) and through very wet bogs. Near Ravens Know (1,729 ft) we had to engage a very wet bog. Chris went one way and ended up waist deep in bog. I decided to stay closer to the fence line and was stepping rather quickly in front of Greyhound. One minute I was on solid ground, the next step I was knee deep in a bog. As fast as a bolt of lightning I was out and walking on water. Greyhound stopped when I fell in and found dry land on the other side of the fence. Chris, Greyhound and I finally got together and broke out in laughter at the sight of Chris and me covered in muck from the chest down. In the late afternoon we found ourselves walking past the mounds of Chew Green, the site of a Roman Camp, and then walked on Dee Street, a Roman road that linked York with Scotland. We ended the day's hike at the first Mountain Refuge Hut, 23 miles from our day's beginning in Bellingham.

The first thing we had to do before entering the hut was to shoo away the guard sheep lying and standing on the wooden planked porch. The front door had slats of wood going across the bottom third of the entrance to keep out the sheep. The wooden building had one solid window located in the front. We entered the hut and found a small area with a bench running along three walls. It was a little over shoulder width and with more than enough length for the three of us to lie down. There were instructions on the wall stating that if we heard loud explosions to cup our ears and hit the floor for protection. We also saw signs as we came in that informed us we were next to a military zone. The shelter register had some entries from folks that had experienced the military ordinance, noting that they'd had to deal with heavy gunfire or artillery. We settled in and slept peacefully throughout the night. Waking up and still in our sleeping bags, we discussed how surprised we were that all day, and through the night, there was no rain, only mild wind and beautiful scenic views.

I woke up early that morning probably because of the anxiety of it being the last day. I got out of the sleeping bag and looked out the window. All I saw in front of me was a sheet of white fog. After breakfast I, taped my blisters as best I could (which ended up lasting 30 minutes), geared up and then did one final chore: putting on my wet boots. Sliding the boots over blistered feet was more like a tug of war. I could hear them screaming as I pressed down. "No! No! Not again, we can't take much more." The screams were turned into simply muffled bitching as the foot was encased inside their saturated habitat. The fog lifted as we left the hut, but we were immediately greeted by a heavy drizzle. Most of the morning, we slogged through wet bogs in between the stone slabs and wooden duckboards and once again was in a heavy fog. Chris' initial intention was to climb the rocky Cheviot and take pictures of the views. He decided against

Our last night on the Pennine Way a bothy (shelter) on the Cheviot massif with Chris and Greyhound

it because of the whiteout conditions and said he could take the same white picture from the duckboards as he would from the Cheviot. As we descended from the Schiller (1,985 ft) we came out of the fog and into the farmlands and sunshine.

The final few miles were a walk on an asphalt road that dropped us into Kirk Yetholm. How fitting it was that we entered the Border Hotel for our free half pint of ale, for being a length man, in the rain. We took the congratulatory photographs, and signed the register inside the inn's pub.

We then went outside to touch the sign, officially ending our journey on the Pennine Way. But, we couldn't find it. We asked someone where it was located and they told us it was destroyed during a recent fire at the inn and not yet replaced. The ending was anti-climatic, nothing like the completion of the Appalachian Trail, where everyone was emotional. We walked for a few minutes in our own foggy thoughts. For me, I was glad to be here, at the finish, healthy and most of all, free from the farmlands and sheep landmines of poop.

Three new members of being "length men" with their free pint

Chris, Greyhound and I hopped a bus to Kelsey, took a taxi to Berwick-upon-Tweed, and finally took a train to Newcastle. As the train slowed down for Newcastle, Brain and I said goodbye to our new mate, Chris. We hopped off the train, entered the world of civilization, and found a place to spend the night called the Backpacker Inn. What was the first thing I did in town? You guessed it. I took off those shit dipped boots and gave them away to a thrift shop.

I always have mixed emotions about leaving a trail. I miss being with Lady Kritter and I want my five senses to take in her essences, to be physically one again, yet, I know I will miss being on trail, enjoying the ribbon of dirt winding through nature's beauty. The Pennine Way was no different. I learned to hike (I mean walk) the trail of another country, in the style that was customary for that country. It did not matter if I liked it, or not (although I did); what mattered was that I saw that great land firsthand, as its countrymen do. I saw their beautiful wild lands called the moors. I saw forces of energy in High and Low Force, High Cup Nick, and in the pure air of the high moorlands called the Cheviot. I witnessed the cordial and generous people of country towns and villages, and most of all, I got to touch and see history pass by everyday as I walked. If given the opportunity I don't think I would thru-hike the Pennine Way again. Instead, I would go back to my favorite places to day hike and explore. Most of all, I am proud to be called a length man of the Pennine Way.

Krispykritter with a street statue in Newcastle

CHAPTER 4
Scotland and the West Highland Way

Greyhound and I, during our preparation of the Pennine Way, started talking about taking advantage of being in Europe and hiking other trails. It was only fitting then to consider one of the top ten hiking trails in the world, The West Highland Way in Scotland. We decided that while Lady Kritter was finishing her visit with relatives in Southern England, Greyhound and I would take a few days off after completing the Pennine Way. Then, she was to meet us in Scotland to hike that country's famous long distance trail - The West Highland Way. Well, that was the plan.
Murphy's Law interjected and threw Plan A for a loop.
The curveball came when Greyhound and I finished the Pennine Way six days ahead of schedule. We walked throughout the city of Newcastle and talked about what we would do with almost two weeks of free time. We discussed doing another short hike for about five days (Plan B), or, him going to the mainland to hike in the Alps, as I went to southern England to meet Lady Kritter and relatives (Plan C). The problem was that I gave my bloody boots away. That did away with me hiking again until I could get my other boots that Lady Kritter was bringing with her. And, Greyhound couldn't stay idle for two weeks. In the end, we each did what was needed to be done. At 1:15 in the morning I initiated Plan C and left Greyhound in Newcastle as I boarded a bus for London. I then took a train from London to Southampton, and finally the arms of Lady Kritter. Greyhound ended up doing the West Highland Way ahead of us, jumped over to Ireland to walk the Wicklow Way, and then flew home. Greyhound left having completed three major European trails.

Meanwhile, I had some down time to heal my feet and explore southern England before the wedding. A couple days later Lady Kritter and I said goodbye to family, shouldered our luggage of 2 camping backpacks, one massive duffle bag, and a luggage bag on wheels and flew to Glasgow, Scotland.

Without the help of family to carry our luggage, Lady Kritter and I shouldered and wheeled our baggage the best we could from the baggage claim, through the airport terminal to the bus station outside. The crowd parted as we struggled with our luggage and I felt Scottish eyes gazing at us. I thought they might be silently saying to themselves, "Must be Americans!"

We caught the bus at the airport and rode to the center of Glasgow, where we were dropped off at Queen Street Station. Here we were in the center of a concrete jungle, two little fish in the sea of a Scottish metropolis, trying to orient ourselves to the city map. The best thing to do when you are lost, I mean misplaced, is to sit down and evaluate your situation. So we found a pub. As we walked up to the counter the barkeep said, in a Scottish accent, "From the US?" "How could you tell?" I replied sarcastically. Lady Kritter ordered her drink of choice (coffee) and I ordered mine (a pint of ale). We were relaxed, but I was already tired of breathing the "fresh" city air, so we went over the map, got our bearings and came up with a plan. Because the city had excellent public transportation, we decided on using the subway. It had a station close to the Glasgow Youth Hostel, where we'd be staying. The ride, however, was a bit hectic in the five o'clock crowd.

We exited the subway tunnel and kept pace with the flow of people. Once again we found ourselves dazed and confused as we tried to orient ourselves to street intersections and the map. I guess my map and compass training from Search and Rescue days paid off because, finally there we were, standing at the front steps of the Glasgow Youth Hostel. We entered the lobby and I handed our reservations to the hostel representative behind the desk. And that was the point when you might have pictured Ed McMahon from the Tonight Show, saying "AND HEREEEEEEE'S MURPHY." (Another guest appearance of Murphy's Law.)

. The clerk told us that I had made reservations for two separate beds, one in the male dormitory, and one in the female dormitory. Because the hostel was full, they did not have a private room available (like the one I thought I reserved). I turned to talk to Lady Kritter and the small slits hiding her beautiful eyes said it all. Saying she was not very happy about spending the night in a dorm with strange women was an understatement. I wasn't a bundle of joy either, knowing I was going to be sleeping in a room with a bunch of guys instead of my wife.

A basic philosophy that I like to use to help prepare me for the arrival of Murphy's Law is this: Take a negative, turn it around, and, make something positive out of it. SO the positive would be I would be meeting and sleeping with people from around the world. My perspective started to slowly change a bit, but I didn't think Lady Kritter was convinced. I don't know which room Murphy's Law was in at the hostel, but apparently we were accompanied by him from that point on.

Lady Kritter and I woke up refreshed and ready to take on Glasgow, aided by another saying, "Everyday is a new day!" which I repeated to myself every morning. We met at the predetermined time in the dining room for breakfast and exchanged small talk about our sleep mates before quickly shifting into the discussion of what to do in Glasgow. As we looked outside the hostel's window and watched heavy rain hit the glass, we agreed that whatever we did it would be inside.

Going over the city map, we saw that the hostel was within walking distance from the Kelvingrove Park and the Kelvingrove Art Gallery and Museum. We learned that this museum was considered one of Glasgow's and Scotland's premier museums and art galleries, and offered one of Europe's great civic art collections.

And so, Lady Kritter and I walked in the rain, happy at least to be alone with each other. After thirty minutes at a fun-loving pace, we were standing in front of a huge, red sandstone historic structure with unique architectural features. We entered the building to the sound of a soft female Scottish voice explaining that the museum was free. For the rest of the day Lady Kritter and I roamed the art galleries and museum looking at paintings by Botticelli, Rembrandt, Millet, Monet, Van Gogh, Derain and Picasso. We walked through halls of archaeology, natural history and Scottish history (including European armour, prehistoric relics and military weapons). I cannot tell you how many times I stopped in bewilderment at the different exhibits and could not believe what I was looking at...and that it was free. At the end of our visit, I left a donation in gratitude and appreciation for their excellent exhibitions.

On the walk back to the hostel, Lady Kritter and I talked about the next day's start of our West Highland Way adventure. Exhausted and hungry, we arrived for a quiet evening at the hostel, or so we'd thought. During our museum visit, fifty noisy German students arrived at the hostel, having just been released from being cooped up in a bus. Murphy's Law.

The West Highland Way was designated as the first official long distance path in Scotland and was brought about by the development of the Pennine Way in England. The first half of the path begins at Milngavie (pronounced "mullguy"), just north of Glasgow and travels over tracks, drover's paths and old military roads through valleys and along Britain's largest body of inland water, Loch (Lake) Lomond. The second half crosses the Scottish Highlands, winds around the base of the highest natural point in the United Kingdom, Ben Nevis, and terminates at Fort William 95 miles later. All along The West Highland Way were the ruins from Scotland's earlier inhabitants and the continual reminders of its current populace.

Lady Kritter and I left the hostel in the morning rain, entered Queen Street Station and boarded a train for Milngavie. Within 30 minutes after leaving Glasgow, we were stepping out of Milngavie's train station and walking the streets of the beautiful village. The sun broke out, the air was crisp, and friendly villagers greeted us as we walked through a weekend market. Things were looking much better for us than when we first arrived in Scotland.

We found the pointed granite obelisk sticking out of the pavement that announced the southern terminus of The West Highland Way. Across from the obelisk was an indoor/outdoor cafe. I walked over to one of the outdoor tables, sat down and ordered two mugs of coffee. I was hoping this gesture would be a good way to begin our adventure (Lady Kritter loves drinking coffee throughout the day) and I didn't know when coffee would pass her lips again.

We sat there in silence, nervously looking at the obelisk - knowing that the two of us had a history of backpacking trips that didn't work out too well. But I could not contain the uncontrollable build up of excitement within me. I thought, "I'm feeling what a horse feels like in the starting gate just before bells go off and the gates open." I got up and walked around to release some of my pent-up energy. I found a park bench next to a stairway with the words "West Highland Way" etched into the metal seat back. Not far away I found the West Highland Way Information Centre selling WHW mementos and last minute hiking gear. I went back to Lady Kritter, picked up my backpack, took a deep breath and said, "It's time." Lady Kritter downed her last sip of coffee, picked up her backpack and slung it over her shoulder as we walked over to the obelisk. We posed for photographs with the monument as a local villager came over to take our pictures. In the early afternoon, I touched the first marker designating the West Highland Way, a White Thistle within a hexagon. We began our journey north.

Krispykritter and Lady Kritter at the beginning of the West Highland Way

The first six miles was a gentle walk out of the village. We meandered on a footpath along the Allander Water and then through the Mugdock Woods. The path continued northward as we passed the first loch (lake) called Craigallian Loch. The path then rambled along rolling farmlands that had a sentry of an ancient mountain top called Dumgoyach. The views were fantastic.

Just off The West Highland Way we played tourist and stopped for a tour at Glengoyne Distillery. The tour concluded with a nice pick me up from a dram of single malt whiskey. Oh so very smooth. We stopped to talk with a couple who were day hiking. They told us of a great place to have lunch called Beech Tree Inn. They were not wrong. Lady Kritter had Haggis (a savory pudding containing sheep's pluck (heart, liver and lungs) and she loved it! I simply thought there was something wrong with that woman's taste buds.

For the next four miles we followed alongside a main road on a path converted from an old railroad bed. The road noise was irritating, but we found a blackberry bush that held the largest blackberries I've ever seen and the juiciest I have ever tasted.

Lady Kritter and I won a race with an afternoon shower just south of Drymen (pronounced "drimmen"). We could see the rain falling in the distant valley as we were approaching Easter Drumquhassle Farm, our first night's destination. The farm was an actual working farm directly on The West Highland Way and the owners supplemented their income by renting wigwams and campsites to the walkers At the farm, we met Galvin and made a quick exchange of money for keys and entered the wigwam as the raindrops fell.

A wigwam is a clever, solid built shelter based on the Native American teepee. The internal frame is wood and the exterior is clapboard. They're supposed to sleep up to six people yet, by the size of the wigwam, I'd say these six would have to be very close friends. The rain lasted only 15 minutes, then the sun came out and we sat on the little porch of the wigwam to watch the Scottish sunset. What we'd hear them say about the weather there was true: if you wait 15 minutes, the weather will change. The Scottish folks also say that in one day you can have all four seasons, and I was not looking forward to that happening. Lady Kritter and I had the wigwam to ourselves for a very cozy night. The chill winds blew outside and, from the

Lady Kritter on the porch of our wigwam

small window, the illumination from the full moon created a soft glow on the wigwam's interior.

Lady Kritter and I left the comfortable wigwam in the morning and headed for the village of Drymen. The local village store was open early so we bought instant coffee and powdered cream to treat ourselves at the end of the day with our new delights. We walked past the Clachan Inn, the oldest pub in Scotland (1734) and thought for a moment what the interior walls - if they could talk - would say about its history. I treated Lady Kritter to breakfast at the Winnock Hotel in the village. If you asked Lady Kritter, she would come right out and tell you she is not a hiker, so I thought I would reward her for a great day yesterday. Her great spirits, finishing the day with a smile on her face, and sitting by her side as we overlooked the Scottish sunset was indeed something I will always cherish.

We left Drymen and entered Scotland's first National Park, The Loch Lomond & Trossachs National Park. Within this park lies the Queen Elizabeth Forest Park. The majestic pine trees there were simply stunning. The high canopy blocked out the sun, creating a dark and mysterious forest of tree trunks. I can now understand how past generations of English folklore conjured up stories of monsters, dragons, and magical myths lurking in the forest. The air was crisp with the fresh fragrance of pine combined with the opulent earth aromas of the forest's carpet-like floor of moss. A steady climb up the forest track brought us to our first glimpse of the beautiful Loch Lomond.

The first real test of the hike was a moderate climb and descent of Conic Hill. We came to a trail junction where one can either take the low route around or the high strenuous route to the top. , I would have thought Lady Kritter would take the low route. Before I had a chance to ask her, Lady Kritter turn towards me and said she wanted to do the high route. I was stunned. She continued saying she knew I'd want to and wanted to share the views from the top with me. Just before reaching the base of the hill, we hiked up and over two ravines with cascading streams running through them. We decided to stop at the second stream to cool our feet, have a snack and rest up for the climb. Well, that was the intent, until the Midges (a biting black fly), found us for a meal and shortened our stay.

The arduous walk up Conic Hill took some time, but Lady Kritter made it. The views overlooking Loch Lomond in the bright sunshine were spectacular, a panoramic picture unveiled below us. Starting from the left and running right as far as the eye could see, laid a large expanse of water. Assorted shaped islands of green looked as if they were floating on the water below. According to the guide book, the islands are on a fault line called the Highland Boundary Fault. Surrounding the loch, mountains rose up 2,000 ft high from the shoreline. We rested there for lunch on a grassy knoll, amidst the beauty of that panoramic scenery.

On the way down misfortune struck. Lady Kritter stepped on a rock that shifted as soon as she put her weight on it. She lost her balance and fell, painfully twisting her knee in the process. We limped off the hill and gave the knee a rest at a cafe in a village called Balmaha. Over a cup of coffee, we contemplated our next decision, either to stay in Balmaha, or continue. Our reception as West Highland Way hikers in Balmaha was not the most hospitable we had encountered thus far. We decided not to spend any more money in a place where we were not wanted. *Plus*, Lady Kritter, who did not want to be defeated by a rock, had hopes that the pain would eventually subside. Two miles into the hike and with several ups and downs straining the knee, the smile disappeared from my Lady's face.

Lady Kritter going down Conic Hill moments before her fall

We were running out of daylight and against Lady Kritter's wishes I made a command decision. I loaded her backpack against my chest and held it in place with my pack across my back. I had hoped this would take the weight off her knee and help us along. Exhausted, we entered the youth hostel in Rowardennan as the final light of the day faded and four and a half miles were under the Vibram soles of our boots.

That night, I was privileged to one of the most incredible night scenes that I had ever witnessed. I got up to go to the bathroom and walked past the window, when I was hit by a ray of pearl glow. Without thinking, my sleepy eyes gravitated to the explosion of light from the full moon and the vibrant reflection of moon light emitting off the loch's water. I closed my eyes, and then opened them again, and the full picture came into focus. The Harvest Moon was unbelievably grandiose and floating above the silhouetted mountains across the loch. The same equivalent of moon and mountains, only upside down, bounced in reflections off the still waters. I stood for an indeterminable amount of time, mesmerized by the stunning panorama before me, then went back to sleep.

The beautiful youth hostel in Rowardennan

The next morning, I woke up wondering if that picture in the window was real, or just a dream - it was so far out of normal reality.

I walked briskly to the window and looked out to see the same shaped mountains bathed in daylight, and knew my window pane of light energy was just as real as the reason why I got up to go to the bathroom in the first place.

Lady Kritter got up and her knee was not better. I decided it was best not to push and scheduled a zero day. I planned two zero days for the hike, so I was not worried about the time table. Throughout the morning and early afternoon, Lady Kritter tested the knee on short walks around the hostel and along the loch's beach. Another crucial decision was beginning to formulate in the back of my mind, and I knew I might eventually have to make it.

I came up with different plans on what to do. Ultimately I decided to leave Lady Kritter at the hostel so she could rest up I had met the folks running the hostel at Rowardennan and felt confident Lady Kritter would be safe. Doing this would give her several more days of rest so we could continue our planned adventure through Scotland after the West Highland Way. I worked out a schedule for Lady Kritter on the third day to take the ferry from Rowardennan and cross the loch to a bus stop in Inverbeg. At the stop she would catch the northbound bus traveling to Tarbet. Lady Kritter would get off the bus at the train station in Tarbet and then catch one of several trains going to Ft. William. During those three days I would continue on the West Highland Way to Ft. William, the northern terminus of The West Highland Way and meet my Lady Kritter. I felt the plan was solid and was confident with it, as long as Murphy's Law didn't interfere.

I am very proud of Lady Kritter's hike. It was her longest two day total of continuous trail, and we both had smiles on our faces for most of our journey. We both have a love for Mother Nature as well, and it was a joy to spend together that time walking in it. We spent the rest of our last day exploring pebble beaches along the loch and Lady Kritter was blessed by finding a perfect heart-shaped rock at the water's edge. Lady Kritter turned to me with a tear running down her face and handed me the rock. I now carried both of her hearts.

Morning came swiftly. In a matter of minutes I was out of bed, had my kit on my back and once again I was heading north on The West Highland Way. Lady Kritter wanted to walk down the trail with me as a final gesture of being on the trail together. Near the entrance to Ptarmigan Lodge we said our goodbyes. I was sad and lonely as I took my first step north without my Lady.

There are two routes you can choose north of Rowardennan. I picked the normal route along a track, rather than lower, difficult route along the loch shore. I needed to take the easiest route to stay within my time limit of three days. Also, the guide book stated the higher route had more waterfalls and I am a sucker for waterfalls. I was not disappointed. Throughout the morning hike, the sights and sounds of falling water were incredible in the forest. Each step unveiled a new sound. One moment the sound of trickling water dropping from exposed roots could be heard. The next moment a concerto of water was cascading down rock faces on one side of the trail. The creek passed underneath the trail and faded away as the water leaped frogged over rocks towards the loch. I was greeted a short time later by the grand finale of that water world. As I continued along the dirt path I became aware of a faint sound of falling water. The consistent sound grew louder as I walked, until I saw a magnificent waterfall with thunderous water falling into a pool. The hamlet was called Inversnaid.

The waterfall at Inversnaid

North of Inversnaid in a rocky crag near the loch's shore, there is a cave called Rob Roy's Cave. Folklore in this area claimed the cave was used as a hideout by Rob Roy MacGregor from the British. Better known as Rob Roy, he was a famous Scottish folk hero and outlaw of the early 18th century and is sometimes referred to as the Scottish "Robin Hood". Above one cave opening, painted in big white letters, was the word CAVE. How curious! Some of the locals say it was the result of graffiti. Sitting on a rock below the opening, I pondered why someone would do such a thing. It didn't take long for the answer to arrive. I could hear a man's voice echoing off the water over a loudspeaker, telling a brief history of Rob Roy and his cave. I looked up and saw, approaching on the waters of the loch from the south, a boat loaded with tourists. I realized the graffiti would let the boat passengers know the location of the cave's opening. This particular group got an added bonus. There he was, Rob Roy himself, in plain view. From a distance they saw a Sean Connery-look-alike with a white beard, sitting at the cave entrance, waving to the people. I had myself a chuckle wondering how many of their photo albums I would be in.

The sights and sounds of water that surrounded me got even better as I continued north towards Inverarnan. I heard the symphonic sounds increase in intensity in the diverse aquatic sounds; from falling waters to the small waves of the loch lapping the beach. The further north I walked, the more the clarity of the water improved. Sparkling, crystal clear, spring mountain water freely flowed in creeks and streams seeking the waters of the loch. The views of the mountains rising from the shoreline, some extending over 3,000 feet were wonderful to behold. And with it, the aromatic floral smells of the forest. The type of smell companies try to reproduce, but fail to acquire. I will always remember how acute my sense of sight, hearing and smell became on my journey on the northern end of Loch Lomond.

My original plan was to spend the night camping at Beinglas campsite just north of Inverarnan. I was arrived there at 1:30 pm,. the sun was shining, I was feeling good and I had 8 hours of daylight left. I opted for Plan B, to have lunch and continue north. The next 6 1/2 miles of trail followed the River Falloch through Glen Falloch. I passed scenic rapids, walked over the top of a small but impressive gorge and then walked several miles on a rocky road that once was an 18th century military road. The views had been breathtaking since Milngavie, however each mile north brought even more worthy, pleasing, magnificent mountain views. I tried to take pictures of what was before me and realized that the depth and beauty could not be captured. Instead, I put away my digital camera, stared at the world in front of my eyes, and clicked countless mental picture to be stored onto my hard drive of memories.

North of Crianlarich, I entered a conifer forest that was rolling up and down the mountains. The sights of rolling mountains covered with evergreen trees and the sound of the wind blowing through them re-confirmed my enthusiasm for, and commitment to protect, Mother Earth. I was truly walking in a wonderland. I have earth-touched the carpet of many forest floors, and this forest north of Crianlarich will always be held close to my heart for its beauty. The forest gave way to farmlands and it didn't take long after exiting before I missed the biodiversity of the forest.

I came to the ruins of St. Fillan's Priory late in the afternoon. In the eighth century, St. Fillan (a monk) came to Scotland from Ireland. He built the priory (a monastery of men or women under religious vows, headed by a prior or prioress) on the property at what is now Kirkton's Farm in Auchtertyre, near the village of Tyndrum. One of the more famous folk tales concerning St. Fillan involved a wolf that attacked and killed one of St. Fillan's oxen that was being used to help move materials to construct the priory. It is said that the wolf then offered his services to replace the oxen when he realized that St. Fillan was doing holy work. The word Fillan is believed to come from the old word "faol", meaning "little wolf".

My camp for the night was at Strathfillan Wigwam & Camping on Auchtertyre Farms. I did not want to be indoors so I chose to set up my tent in their campground. Like many other campgrounds I visited in the United Kingdom, I had a choice of which part of the pasture I liked, which, of course, was the area with the least amount of farm animal dung. After a brief battle between me and the infamous midges, I set up my tent. Eventually, I won the fight because the no-see'em netting of my tent kept the thirsty midges buzzing around outside and off of me. Pleasantly exhausted, I had completed another fantastic day on the West Highland Way.

Camp at Strathfillan Wigwam & Camping on Auchtertyre Farms

I woke up during the night to go to the bathroom. I unzipped the tent door and was greeted by a sheet of white fog. Visibility was less than 25 feet. Since I was in soft grass, I figured I would walk barefooted. I took about 50 steps in one direction, then looked back into a white void where my tent should have been standing. I knew there was a full moon somewhere above me, but I couldn't find it. I did my thing, then followed my footsteps in the wet grass leading back to the tent. The first thought that came to mind: "Hiking is going to be interesting in the morning."

I slept in to give the fog time to burn off. As I was breaking camp and putting on my socks and boots, I felt a small bump on the top of my ankle. Looking back, I remember nonchalantly squeezing the bump and thinking it was a large blackhead or pimple. I never really gave it a good look.

I left Auchtertyre Farms the next morning with a very soggy tent and walked in and out of heavy blankets of fog. After leaving the River Fillan, the topography changed into an eerie landscape of mounds everywhere, with ponds of various sizes in between the mounds. The fog added to the supernatural scenes. I knew from looking in the guide book that I was in a particular area of prior glacier activity. The land rose into mounds creating fuzzy outlines, or hillocks called kames that were formed from deposits of gravel left over from the glacier. The depressions in between the kames were nicknamed "kettle holes" filled with water and were called lochans. As I followed the path, I had an eerie sixth sense that something, or someone, was watching me. Onward I went, with all systems on alert mode. The mystical fog swirled at this one particular pond, so I stopped to watch the beauty of the spinning cotton candy-like clouds ride the air currents. I looked down and, by my feet, was a large King Arthur looking sword etched into a concrete placard. I had no idea why there was a placard there, but it was wonderful. I felt like something magical was happening. That I was somehow a part of history. And I was ready for whatever came next, even if I didn't know what it was. I found another placard nearby stating that I was on hallowed ground that honors the memory of those killed in a clan war called The Battle of Dalrigh in 1306. During the battle, it is believed that one of the clan leader's sword was thrown into a nearby lochan to keep it from enemy hands. I felt the wind pick up just a notch and watched a particular patch of gyrating fog advance in my direction. Through the fog I thought I saw a faint apparition of several silhouettes emerging in the form of highlander warriors wearing kilts and battle gear. It looked real, but I knew it was my imagination creating the warriors, guardians of the sword. Or was it? I now knew why I felt the way I did entering the region - in addition to the fact that the sixties were good to me.

An hour later I was in a small village called Tyndrum. Walking in Tyndrum there was a sign that revealed how the villagers felt about their environment. It stated:

"We are not just planting a woodland, we are watching an idea grow..."
Tyndrum Community Woodland

If more communities throughout the world, like Tyndrum, were conscience of their footprint left on Mother Earth, I truly believe future generations would have a greener and healthier life.

I had been leapfrogging four other guys that were traveling as a group. Three of them were friends from Southampton and the fourth from Glasgow who was picked up as a hiking mate on the first day. We finally met and introduced ourselves at a food store in Tyndrum and had a good chat over snacks. They were trying to finish the Est Highland Way in the next 3 days, then - weather permitting - summit Ben Nevis near the northern terminus of Ft. William. It seemed all five of us had the same schedule in mind, so we became a small hiking family of five.

Outside of Tyndrum, the fog lifted and again before us were great views of mountains and valleys. The West Highland Way traveled an old, rocky military road north of the Village of Tyndrum. The roads were built to move British troops quickly through the mountains during the 17th and 18th centuries. The afternoon turned into a beautiful, sunny day. I stopped at the Bridge of Orchy Hotel for coffee, lunch and to talk with other hikers. Soon after leaving Bridge of Orchy, I had great views of the twin mountains Beinn Dorain and Beinn an Dorthaidh.

I caught up with the four guys and we decided to stop at the Inveroran Hotel, built in 1708, for a pint. I particularly wanted to stop here because the guide book stated the hotel built a pub just for hikers (I mean walkers) called The Walker's Bar. After we each had two pints of good pain management, we left the hotel and continued our walk on another military road through the largest uninhabited wilderness in Britain called Rannoch Moor.

The moorlands and mountains of Rannoch Moor were indeed desolate and had a wild, unspoiled, undulating beauty I had rarely seen. If it were not for the military road, the going would have been excruciatingly slow through the bogs. I was particularly impressed with the exceptional beauty of the River Ba that flowed through a small ravine at Ba Bridge. I stopped at the river for a break and to drink the crystal clear water of the river. I sat back and took in the scenery of an amplitude of mountains, blue skies dotted with floating cotton ball clouds and a green valley below that was spread out incredibly before me. Most of all, one particularly alluring mountain looked like it was a giant amphitheater behind a lake, facing the west. This cirque, called Coire Ba, is the largest in Scotland.

Looking north from Ba Bridge, the military road rises until it looks like it disappeared into the ridge and sky. I finally reached that point and slowly descended until, in the far off distance, I could see a white speck in a sea of green. The guide book said that white speck was Kings House Hotel, my resting spot for the night. Straight ahead, a massive pyramid shaped mountain called Buachaille Etive Mor, "The Great Herdsman of Etive", stood in front of me. The mountain shape has made Buachaille Etive Mor one of the most recognizable and photographed mountains in Scotland.

Twenty minutes later, I was at the whitewashed two-story Kings House Hotel next to the River Etive. Just behind the hotel was a free camping area along the river. I discovered why it was free. I was violently attacked by squadrons of midges as I was setting up my tent. If you could stand the blankets of midges, you deserved the right to camp for nothing. After setting up my tent in record time, I ran into the hotel and opted for a pub meal instead of midge pie. The boys showed up and they too had fought a losing battle with the vicious flying insects. Soon they were in the hotel's pub with me enjoying the insect-free environment. It was mid-afternoon and a hiker's bond developed as we got to know each other better. Carlos, Bjorn and Richard had been friends for several years but Jason and I were fitting in right nicely. Carlos was nursing a sore knee from a night hike on the first day. The fourth lad, Jason, decided not to stay and wait for the trio; and headed for the Devil's Staircase and the rocky

Buchaille Etive Mor, "The Great Herdsman of Etive"

path down to Kinlochleven. Even though I felt I could do the next 8.5 miles that day, I was happy with the day's total of 23 miles. I did not want to push my luck on tired feet. At the end of the night we ran to our tents through more blankets of midges. After a quick zip-in, I was safe from the most annoying insect Mother Nature has produced. I vowed to never say a bad word again about the Florida mosquito.

The next morning I woke up, ate breakfast and packed my kit inside my tent. I unzipped the screen door of the tent and immediately was swarmed in blankets of midges. Word must have spread throughout the highlands last night that fresh meat was available at River Etive. There was no escape for me. I put on my rain pants, rain jacket, worn gloves and a hat. I even wore a mosquito head net with limited success. The little bastards dive bombed through the holes and continued their relentless pursuit of any exposed skin or orifice. It made me glad that I didn't live here in the days of old, with naught but a kilt to keep the midges from attacking more tender spots.

The lads got up and more waves of the little demons attacked. This was a hostility conflict: war. Weapons of mass destruction came out to counter attack. I applied Skin-So-Soft to my skin from a spray bottle. Some satisfaction was achieved when we saw the little blood sucking creatures stick to the liquid. Within minutes exposed skin was black with suffocating insects. The liquid would soon evaporate and be absorbed into the skin, exposing skin to new waves of the tiny flying insects with teeth. The swarms continued to increase with the early morning light. I was packed and waiting on the lads. I was done being midge bait. and told them I would meet them up on the trail. I had to do bodily functions and there was absolutely no way I was pulling my pants down for this herd of meat eaters. I had visions of the midges flying towards my creamy white bulls-eye with the USDA stamp of approval on it. I made my way through the midge swarm and to the trail.

On that morning, I surely learned the meaning of the British phrase, "Bloody Hell". I left the lads, turned and looked back at them one last time. I chuckled to myself as I saw human forms flinging arms and legs in no particular pattern; swatting the air, jumping up and down and - in between all these gyrations - trying to complete their morning chores to get out of camp.

Walking at a quick pace created a slight breeze that left my attackers behind and I was once again enjoying my walk along the valley. I noticed that the morning clouds were filled with moisture and Buachaille Etive Mor was shrouded in the clouds. In fact, I was fortunate to have that type of weather. I don't like sunlight beating down on me when I'm strenuously climbing in elevation.

I climbed to the top of Devil's Staircase and was at the highest point on the West Highland Way (1,797 feet). Looking back into the valley, the sun burned away the morning clouds revealing splendid mountain views. I thought the climb up the switched back trail was not as bad as everyone was making it out to be. A chilled wind blew from the north at the top. I gazed at the immense views of the Scottish highlands opposite Buachaille Etive Mor. I looked north and saw the West Highland Way diminish over a rocky hilltop only to be seen again further down the valley.

The path changed back and forth into a rocky road creating a slower-than-normal descent into a beautiful valley. It seemed to never end. Suddenly, the air was shattered by a loud, thunderous roar and directly above me was a low-flying military jet from the Royal Air Force. The aircraft was flying below the mountain tops and deep into the valley. The sound of the jet's engine was drowned out by a second jet at a lower altitude. The military jets were a formidable sight indeed.

The walk was now on a continuous rocky road suited for only four wheel vehicles, twisting and turning until finally I arrived into the village of Kinlochleven - once a thriving community based on the mining and smelting of aluminum. Recently, the village has been cleaning up its image of being a mining town in an attempt to become a solid outdoor recreation center. I stopped at an outdoor complex that was built inside one of the aluminum factories. It contained a store, cafe, lounge and three climbing walls. Two of the walls had different degrees of difficulty and the third wall was inside a refrigerated room for ice climbing. I sat, relaxed, ordered breakfast and watched the climbers exert themselves...as I did not.

The day turned into a nice sunny one and I decided to continue on to Fort William. As I was leaving the village I ran into Carlos, Bjorn and Richard eating at the Tailrace Inn. They were getting ready to leave and also push for the end. Since we had basically been together the last three days, it was only fitting that we spend the last 14 miles together.

Experienced hikers know that any trail that goes down to enter a trail town/gap/valley will usually have a strenuous climb up the other side. The walk out of Kinlochleven was no exception. The trail out of Kinlochleven went up a mountainside at a steep angle until it reached another military road. The next several miles the three boys and I walked through a valley with magnificent panoramic views of mountains and a river flowing below in a valley to our left. Carlos' knee was giving him a fit, so we decided to rest at the ruins of a farmhouse. Carlos asked if I wanted a "cup-ah". "A what?" I said. "A cup-ah". The look on my face told Carlos I did not have a clue what he was talking about. "A cup of tea", he said. I should have known from my AT hike with Cuppa Joe. The four of us spread out on a grassy area behind the stone walls of the old farmhouse, boiled water and lightened our food bags for the final push into Ft. William.

The final miles of The West Highland Way entered into beautiful forests and we got our first glimpse of the highest mountain in the United Kingdom; Ben Nevis. Bjorn and Richard, in excitement, went

Rest stop from the wind and a cuppa tea

ahead. I stayed with Carlos who was really nursing his knee. I was glad to stay behind with Carlos since the slow walk gave me more time to appreciate the beauty of the forest. Sadly, we rounded a bend on the forest road and saw Ft. William below. We caught up with the other two and together Carlos, Bjorn, Richard and I, entered Ft. William and touched the West Highland Way obelisk, thus ending another fantastic hike. Carlos, Bjorn, Richard and I found, after several attempts, the last available room in Fort William. We showered and the boys wanted to celebrate our accomplishment with a round of pints and a steak dinner, which I was glad to oblige. The next morning the boys left for home and I waited for the arrival of Lady Kritter. I was soooo excited to see her step off the train and to share our stories together. The next morning Lady Kritter and I would be on another adventure in Scotland, but together.

The West Highland Way, for a trail of only 95 miles long, is (mile for mile) one of the most intense trails I've ever seen - containing non-stop splendid views, mountains landscapes that were typically of epic grandeur and worlds full of water that saturated my synapses.

Yes, I did have 5 of the most wonderful days of Scotland weather; however, I feel that (even in a drizzly light rain) the views of Mother Nature would make the trip a worthwhile adventure for anyone. It is a world class trail that should be added to anyone's top ten list of trails to walk. The only question I had upon my completion of the West Highland Way was this: "In days of olde, without the convenience of modern technology, how did the Scotsman who were wearing kilts, keep the midges away from their family jewels?"

Kri

spykritter, Richard, Bjorn and Carlos in Ft. William

CHAPTER 5
The West Highland Aftermath

F t. William is a beautiful city to walk around, so I took the opportunity to join Carlos, Bjorn and Richard on their walk to the train station for their departure home. The weather was quickly changing to a dreary overcast day with a light sprinkle. I spent the rest of the morning ducking in and out of the street shops, keeping a mental note on which ones Lady Kritter might like to visit. I was enjoying this time as it gave me the opportunity to decompress from being on trail; and to reflect back and reminisce about the sights and sounds of the Scottish Highlands. When I thought it was about time for the first train to arrive from Tarbet, I went to the train station and watched passengers unload. The last passenger walked passed me – no Lady Kritter. I went back in the late morning for the next arriving train with the same results. I found myself in the afternoon hanging around the train station more and more hoping to see my red-headed lady limping down the platform. I walked to the train station and watched the passengers unload from the rail cars only to find myself lonely, and concerned, without Lady Kritter. I looked at the train schedule and realized there were only a few more trains left for the day. I was getting a "wee bit" worried. Finally, on the last train of the day, I observed a familiar backpack and Lady Kritter hobbling on a sore knee and blistered little toe along the pavement. Relieved, I held Lady Kritter in my arms once again.

We found our way to the Glen Nevis Hostel, nestled at the foot of Britain's highest mountain, Ben Nevis. Once we were settled in, I caught up on Lady Kritter's adventure of catching the ferry, having one bus pass her bus stop (with the driver smiling and waving as he went by), catching another and hopping on the last train to Ft. William.

The weather remained soggy and cold with low clouds shrouding the summit of Ben Nevis. Our initial plan was to climb Nevis, and then leave the next day by train and travel north to Culrain. There we'd stay at a castle that was converted into a hostel, named Carbisdale Castle. However, the weather forecast was not looking good. In fact, Mountain Rescue was activated to aid several walkers caught in the weather system on the mountain. Lady Kritter excitedly wanted to know if we could alter plans and visit a circle of stones she had heard about while staying at the Rowardennan Hostel. I liked the great back up plan and it was perfect timing for research on a crappy day smothered in rain clouds.

The next day we went into Ft. William, found a computer and began our research to formulate Plan B. What we planned, I found out later, was better than anything I could have ever imagined. The Callanish Stones were located in a group of islands off the Scottish coast called the Outer Hebrides. The stones were located on the western side of the Isle of Lewis, near the village of Calanais. The website reported the circle of stones to be one of the most remote and ancient monuments in Europe. I was captivated by the description. After hours of online study, we had bus routes to ferries, bus routes in the Hebrides and places to stay with the Scottish Youth Hostel Association once we got there.

The next morning Lady Kritter and I boarded a coach bus in Ft. William to continue our Scotland adventure...on Plan B. We rode westward, stopping in small villages and towns separated by the moorlands, letting passengers on and off. Five hours later, the driver stopped the bus on the Isle of Skye on top of a hill at the intersection of the main road and a smaller one. The driver turned to Lady Kritter and I and stated, Uig (pronounced "Oo-ig") Hostel. We exited the bus and watched it disappear down the hill, leaving us standing on the side of the road, precisely at In-The-Middle-Of-Nowhere, Scotland.

Across the main road, and below us, laid a large bay. A small village of buildings, barely visible, could be seen sitting on its shore. Behind us was a steep grassy hill separated by a dirt road. Lady Kritter and I looked at each other, then back up the hill, then back at each other. Together we shrugged our shoulders and with facial expressions that said "What the f#&@." We swung our backpacks over our shoulders and started walking up the dirt road. Within minutes we were standing at the front door of Uig Hostel.

The hostel sat high above the cliffs and overlooked the bay and Uig Village below, known as "The Gateway to the Outer Hebridean Islands". We could see just below the horizon, the wake of the ferry approaching the docks of the village. The same ferry that would take us to the Hebrides tomorrow.

The hostel's interior was small with quaint, cozy and a warm atmosphere. Since we arrived in the middle of the afternoon, we asked the hostel keeper if there was any good hiking in the area. The keeper made it a point to make eye contact with both Lady Kritter and I, and then, in a gentle Scottish brogue, asked, "Do you believe in fairies?"

Instantly we both said, "Yes."

"Then", he said, "I will draw you a map to Faerie Glen".

"Faerie Glen?" we asked. "Faerie Glen", he repeated and said, "Follow the map and if you believe, then you will find Faerie Glen."

There we were in an enchanted land, charmed in mystical lore and then we were being directed to a local, magical place. It was perfect!

After looking at the map, it seemed to be too far for Lady Kritter to hobble there and back. Hearing our discussion, the keeper, offered us a ride to the point where a path leaves the road. However, he could not pick us up and we would have to hike back to the hostel following the map's directions. Lady Kritter and I accepted the offer. In the car, the keeper emphasized again how Faerie Glen was a very special place, and could not explain why he offered us the ride. According to him this was the first time the offer was made to guests.

Once again, being strangers in a strange land, we were dropped off In-The-Middle-Of-Nowhere, Scotland. I oriented us to the map and found the landmarks that led us cross country from the road. The rolling farmland of green grass reminded me of sections of the Pennine Way, with black faced sheep and their nuggets scattered about. We came upon a foundation of old stone blocks tumbled in disarray in the formation of a long rectangle. There was no doubt, we were looking at the ruins of an ancient home/barn. We took turns speculating how the building was utilized and who were the people who built them. Lady Kritter and I could feel an excitement in the air as we left the ruins and continued on our journey. I followed a slightly worn path as it went high and Lady Kritter followed another path as it descended into the glen. I crested a hill and before me, many strangely Tolkien-like cone-shaped hills covered in tufts of green grass that resembled lacework cut by the wind, laid before me. Spellbound, Lady Kritter and I met near a Rowan tree, itself a mythical and magical tree of the ancient lore.

I turned around to see a dirt trail leading up a rugged rock formation, easily the highest point in the glen. Of course, I had to climb it. I followed the trail as my imagination ran wild with unicorns, dragons and fairies dancing in my head. I came to a small plateau at the top through a small cut in the rock. I looked below and saw Lady Kritter standing in the green grass. Not far from where she was standing I could see a stone spiral circle, a heart and other figures protruding from the grass. I pointed towards the circle and yelled at Lady Kritter in excitement. She couldn't hear a word I was saying because of the gusting wind, but began to move in the direction I was pointing. I could see from a distance her face suddenly light up with amazement as she found and entered the circle. I looked across the valley and in the distance saw large waterfalls cascading into the glen. This magical and mysterious spot can only be described as otherworldly and peaceful. We left Faerie Glen in epic grandeur with the sun setting in orange, yellow and purple hues. Once on the road heading back to the hostel, I asked Lady Kritter if she saw any fairies. She said no, and she asked if I did as well. I also said no, but that I'd certainly felt their presence. I pictured them hiding from view behind rocks, giggling to each other, as they watched Lady Kritter and I amusing ourselves on their playground. I also asked Lady Kritter how her knee was doing. She told me in all the excitement she had forgotten her pain. A great ending to a beautiful day in Scotland.

Lady Kritter and I were back at the hostel preparing our dinner in the kitchen, when three young men entered into the dining/living area talking with a Spanish-sounding accent. I started talking to one of them in English and asked the usual hostel questions when you first meet someone: about name, where you're from, where you've been, where you are going. The guys were from Brazil and had rented a car to travel throughout Scotland.

Sometime during the early evening, I did not feel like myself. I felt like maybe I was coming down with the flu or some sickness. I lost my appetite and didn't finish my dinner. I told Lady Kritter that I was tired, excused myself and went to bed. I had no idea life changing events were taking place inside my body.

We left the hostel the next morning and just missed the bus that would take us to the docks. Time became critical for us. We needed to catch the only ferry for the day to the Outer Hebrides. Lady Kritter and I started hitch hiking, hoping to catch a ride on the sparsely traveled road to the village. It looked like we would be spending another day in Uig. Just then, a vehicle passed by stopping ahead of us. It was the guys from Brazil. We found enough space for our backpacks, loaded the small vehicle with all five of us with sardine-in-a-can-like precision. Lady Kritter and I made it to the docks just in time to catch the ferry.

Coming over me again was that eerie, sick in the stomach feeling. I knew I was coming down with something when an ordinary cup of coffee I had on the ferry made me nauseated. I held back telling Lady Kritter how I felt, thinking it was only temporary and it would pass.

The ferry docked at East Tarbert on the Isle of Harris and once again we loaded up on a coach bus, this time heading for the city of Stornoway on the Isle of Lewis. We changed buses in Stornoway for another bus that took us to an even smaller bus, and then finally to our destination for the night at a primitive hostel called Gearrannan Blackhouse Hostel in a small village called Garenin. The hostel was located in a traditional Scottish house called a blackhouse and was constructed of stone walls and thatched roof. The scenery was extraordinary. Our blackhouse sat on top of a cliff along with several other blackhouses and overlooked a secluded bay on the western Atlantic coast of the Isle of Lewis.

By the time Lady Kritter and I arrived I was running a fever and the only thing I wanted to do was collapse in bed. I figured I had caught a 24-hour bug and would be up in the morning to resume our adventure. I lay in bed with all my clothes on, layers of blankets on top of me, shivering and sweating up a storm. Every joint in my body ached. Lady Kritter helplessly checked in on me from time to time as she walked the village of blackhouses, the high cliffs above the bay and the stone beach down below.

I was delirious throughout the afternoon and night, and still have a fuzzy memory as to where I was and who was, in the hostel.

Gearrannan Blackhouse Hostel, on Garenin, the Isle of Lewis

I awoke very weak the next morning without a fever. Lady Kritter told me at breakfast she knew I was really sick because I was the only male in a hostel of women, and so stayed in bed.

Feeling better, Lady Kritter and I decided to continue our journey to our primary destination, the Callanish Stones.

We took a small bus to the outskirts of the village of Calanais and were dropped off at the visitor centre managed by the Urras nan Tursachan (Gaelic for The Standing Stones Trust). During the bus ride my left leg developed, what I thought, was a heat rash - I assumed it was caused by the wool socks during the feverish sweats the night before. Again, I didn't mention it to Lady Kritter and we continued on our adventure.

We arrived early to the standing stones and the museum doors were not yet opened. Unlike Stonehenge, fencing did not circle the stones. Lady Kritter and I took advantage of the time and the opportunity, to walk by ourselves before the rush of people.

Entering the site was an extraordinary feeling - knowing that in the same spot, it was over 5,000 years ago that a group of people were constructing that circle of stones. In fact, the Callanish Stones were erected in the late-Neolithic period and some have said that they are older than the stones of Stonehenge.

The spot was magnificent, 50 monolithic stones of Lewisian Gneiss rock were set in the ground on a ridge of land overlooking Loch Roag. A bird's eye view of the stones shows how the builders arranged the stones into the appearance of a Celtic cross. A large ring of monolithic stones circled a huge monolith located in the center. Within this ring, a stone chambered cairn was found containing human bones. An avenue-like entrance into the circle was created by two parallel lines of standing stone that were 270 feet from the center of the circle, through the wall due north. Three other lines of stone also radiate out from the circle with the last stone of each line facing towards the cardinal directions. The story was told to me that a farmer discovered the stones while digging for peat in 1857. When I visited the site at Stonehenge, it was awe inspiring (due to its size), but, I had to stay on the marked path quite a distance from the stones. We were not allowed to walk in between or around the stones. At Calanais, we walked freely and touched the stones. The incredible energy that Lady Kritter and I felt radiating from this site will forever stay with us. We only hoped that these stones wouldn't also have barriers placed around them in the future.

The Calanais Stones

Our next step in our journey was to return by bus to Stornoway, spend the night at a hostel, and on the following day, board another ferry to Ullapool. We would continue our exploration on the mainland of Scotland until our departure from the Glasgow Airport for Iceland. There we would spend our final week of vacation in Iceland, traveling its perimeter coastal highway and staying in hostels.

Stornoway harbor

The bus ride into Stornoway was uneventful. Lady Kritter and I found Stornoway to be a quaint little town surrounding the harbor; which was busy with freight, ferry and its fishing fleet. A major port town for the Outer Hebrides and the largest settlement on the islands, Stornoway is known as "the heartland of Gaelic culture". Lady Kritter and I located the Stornoway Backpackers Hostel on Keith Street, found a bunk room to ourselves and unpacked. Once settled in, we wanted to explore this hiker-friendly town. Lady Kritter and I found the Nan Eilean Museum on Francis Street, not far from the hostel. The small two-story building contained archeology, and the social, domestic and economic history of the islands. While Lady Kritter was walking around the museum, I decided to take a closer look at my leg, which was beginning to itch and starting to hurt.

What I saw next took me by complete surprise. My lower leg was swollen from the knee down and everything swollen was covered in red rash. What scared me the most was that the red rash was under my skin and not a typical, on the surface heat rash. I called Lady Kritter over, placed my foot on a chair and as I raised my pant leg, told her, "I think I need to see a doctor". Lady Kritter's eyes became as big as silver dollars as she, "Oh my God!"

Events happened rather quickly from that point. We asked a young lady at the museum desk where we could go for medical attention. She made a phone call to her doctor down the street. The doctor's office said it was ok for us to come in immediately and they would see me at the end of the scheduled appointments (an advantage of being in a small community). Mind you, it was after 4:00 in the afternoon and businesses were closing for the day. I am sure if this had occurred in many places in the United States, I would be told I could not come in without appointment or, first check to see which type of health insurance I carried.

Lady Kritter walked, as I hobbled, the short distance to the doctor's office. Within minutes, I was in the examination room showing my leg to the doctor. Even I was shocked at the full view of my leg with my pants off. The leg was badly swollen from the ankle up to the knee. The rash circled my leg and ran from the ankle up to beyond my knee. Where the rash stopped on my inner thigh, two red lines streaked up into my groin. It looked like something right out of a science fiction movie. An animal or, alien entity had overtaken my body and was on the move. Things were not looking real good for the Kritter. The doctor completed her examination, walked over to her desk and began to write.. I asked the doctor if she was writing a prescription. Her answer shocked me.

"No" she said. "I m writing your admittance into the A&E".

"What is an A&E?" I said.

The doctor replied, "the Accident and Emergency of the hospital."

"WHAT?" Lady Kritter and I looked at each other as we watched each other's jaws drop to the floor. Stumbling for words, either Lady Kritter, or I, said, "But, but we have another 10 days left of our vacation and in three days fly to Reykjavik, Iceland".

The doctor replied, "You are a very sick man with an infection called cellulitis and could be in the hospital up to 7 to 10 days.".

I looked at her with a puzzled look on my face and said, "Cellulite-what, you mean the cheesy looking fat on the thighs of fat people?"

"No" the doctor said. "Cellulitis," the doctor continued, "is a very serious bacterial skin infection and you have a high fever that requires hospital treatment. We need to treat the infection with massive doses of antibiotics in an IV'".

The doctor called us a taxi and before I knew it, I was laying on a gurney being wheeled into different hospital rooms for testing. One of the nurses drew an outline of the rash with a black magic marker. Lady Kritter thought I was being used as a new board game in Scotland, but the nurse explained the outline was to show how quickly the infection was spreading. Another nurse came in, examined my leg, and - with her Scottish accent - exclaimed, "You have a Nasty-Wee-Beastie bite!"

"A WHAT", I replied.

"A Nasty-Wee-Beastie" the nurse said again, as she points to a dot on my skin at the curve where the ankle meets my lower leg.

"WHAT THE HELL IS A NASTY-WEE-BEASTIE", I said, thinking I just heard my death sentence. Searching for the right American phrase to say, the nurse replied, "I guess in the United States you would call it a tick bite. The bite caused the infection and rash on your leg."

I asked, "You have seen this before?"

"Oh yes", the nurse said, "at least two or three times a year."

I was at least relieved the medical team was dealing with something they knew about. I laid my head back down on the pillow and started thinking, "A tick bite? Where in the hell did I get a tick bite?" I start replaying the West Highland Way hike in my head. Suddenly, I remembered my tent stay at Strathfillan Wigwams & Camping on the pastures of Auchtertyre Farms. I left my tent barefooted during the night and walked in the pasture grass to go to the bathroom. I woke up in the morning, and as I was putting on my socks, felt a small bump (the same exact spot the nurse pointed out a week later). Not having my glasses on, I assumed it was a pimple and squeezed with my two thumbnails. Successfully popped, I put on my dirty socks and continued my journey. I never once took into consideration ticks in Scotland. I had been wrong.

The first two days, I was in and out of consciousness with a fever. My memory of those days were like looking through a kaleidoscope. Except, for me the changing glass was in the form of indiscriminate events appearing and disappearing like scattered dreams. Scenes of the West Highland Way, Uig, Blackhouses, Lady Kritter, an environment of white, surrounded by tubes sticking out of

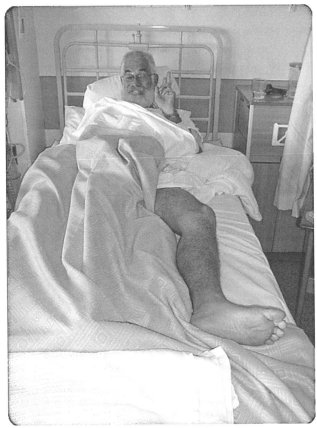

The day after my fever broke

my arm and in my nose, delirious with Nasty-Wee-Beasties dancing in my head and people speaking English with a different accent, asking, "What is your name?" "Do you know where you are?" On the third day my fever broke. The doctor came in and had a heart to heart talk with me.

First, he let it be known how fortunate I was to be in Stornoway where the only hospital in the islands was located. The next nearest hospital was over two hundred miles away in Glasgow. Second, he informed me of how dire my condition was, as my body was deteriorating through septic shock. Another 24 to 48 hours and the infection would have gone systemic, meaning organ failure. Hopefully, he said, massive doses of antibodies given through an IV and taken orally would attack the infection and stop it from spreading through my body. Third, there was a chance that I may have permanent damage to my leg. And fourth, the remainder of our vacation was canceled. I would be in the hospital for at least another week with a long recovery period ahead of me after that. Damn Nasty-Wee-Beastie.

I was reassigned to a male ward containing six beds once my fever broke. I will always remember three of my ward mates: MacLeod, Gregor and Ronnie. MacLeod was a large man with an infectious smile, who occupied a bed by the window with a gangrenous leg. In a baritone Scottish voice that would rival Sean Connery's, Mr. MacLeod came over to my bed in a wheelchair, introduced himself and asked if I was the American with the Nasty-Wee-Beastie bite?" "Aye", I replied.

"Tis a fine way to visit Scotland', he sarcastically said.

"I have a fondness for nurses with a Scottish accent," I told him.

"Aye, me too", he said, and we both laughed.

MacLeod was the self designated "Welcome Wagon" for the ward, telling me all about the other patients. Every time a new patient would come in during my stay he would wheel over to the bed, welcome the newcomer, and then look over in my direction and tell them, "We even have a Yank across the way." You couldn't help but love the spirit of this man. MacLeod and I developed a kinship in no time. We spent countless hours together during the hospital's designated quiet times, looking out the window and talking. He proudly told me about the Macleod clan and its role in the history of Scotland, especially on the Isle of Lewis. I, in turn, would tell him about the United States and how my ancestors helped shape the thirteen colonies into a nation.

Gregor was an up and coming local artist who was stricken by a diabolical nervous system disease that paralyzed him from the neck down. Gregor's mother and brother were devoted daily visitors spending every possible moment to make Gregor comfortable. Lady Kritter became friends with his mother and brother and told them she would look after Gregor. I watched Gregor's eyes light up with a smile whenever Lady Kritter would go to his bedside and bend over to hear his soft whispering voice. Gregor would do the same thing with the female nurses. You could tell he so loved women. Lady Kritter is a healer with her energy and spirit. I could feel the energy vibrate in the room as she went to visit each patient in the ward, especially with Gregor.

And then, there was Ronnie, a magnificent young man who had a developmental disability characterized by significantly impaired cognitive function. He was in the hospital with a severe respiratory infection. Most of the day he would sit in front of the ward's TV and watch cartoons until Lady Kritter arrived.

The day my fever broke Nurse Donnaq arrived fresh from her two days off. Dressed in her white uniform, she was a natural beauty with a soft creamy color complexion, medium height, a slender body, hair touched by the sun and the face of an angel, walking through the ward's door. What attracted me towards her was her voice. A velvety tone that mesmerized me with the enchanting sing-song of the Scottish accent. The female version of the Sean Connery voice that you could listen too, all day long. My first impression was that I was still under the spell of the fever and hallucinating.

She walked up to my bed and said, "Madainn mhath!"

I looked up at her with a wrinkled forehead and said, "WHAT?

My response and accent cause her cherub face to look momentarily puzzled, then, regaining her smile, she spoke in English and asked if I was the American patient in the hospital. I nodded.

I then had this great idea. I could learn Gaelic during my stay by having the hospital staff teach me the language. It worked pretty well! By the time I left the hospital, I had regularly had this conversation in Gaelic with Nurse Donnaq. Mind you, my r's didn't roll smoothly and my guttural sound resembled the harshness of phlegm creeping up my throat.

Donnaq: "Madainn mhath!" (Good Morning!)

Krispykritter: "Mandainn mhath, Donnaq!" (Good morning, Donnaq.)

Donnaq: "Ciamar a tha thu?" (How are you?)

Krispykritter: "Tha gu math, tapadh leat". (Well, thanks.)

As Donnag placed my breakfast tray in front of me I would say. "Moran taing". (Many thanks.)

About a half hour later Donnaq would return and ask. "Deiseil?" (Finished?)

KrispyKritter: "Tha" (Yes)

Donnaq: As she left the room. "Chi mi rithist thu". (I'll see you later.)

KrispyKritter: "Mar sin leat". (Good Bye.)

I also used this phrase a lot. "Chan veil mi a' sinning". (I don't understand.)

The daily routine quickly became mundane. The morning consisted of breakfast, taking meds, cleaning up the room and patients, doctor visits, then some personal time. Lunch was served around noon followed by a unique period called "quite time". During this period the wards lights were turned down and the patients had to lie down and either take a nap or be still and quiet. Actually, I thought it was more of a quite time for the hospital staff to collect their wits before the rush of visiting hours. Quite time was over when the lights were turned back on and a tray of tea and biscuits were brought to each patient. Two o'clock began visiting hours and was always a treat because that was when I could see Lady Kritter until nine o'clock in the evening.

The first couple of days of Lady Kritter's visits were dream-like and I would remember hearing only parts of her adventures and exploits around town. It was hard for her to be alone in a foreign country with her husband lying in a hospital bed - lifeline attached to his arm - whilst herself staying in the hostel. It was strange to hear that she spent the night with different men who spoke different languages in a bunk room of a hostel each night. When Lady Kritter was not spending time with me she was exploring. She visited Lews Castle, the harbor and the shops around Stornoway. And as the days went by she was becoming a celebrity of sorts in Stornoway - the southern accented wife of a hospitalized American.

As a side note: in all my wanderings prior to this European trip, I'd never taken out trip insurance. But for our Great Britain and Ireland extravaganza, Lady Kritter and I became members of the International Youth Hostels, which included optional trip insurance in that membership. I had decided that it would be a good investment to take out the insurance just in case anything should happened to us during our two months in Europe; stitches, broken bones, etc. But I was certainly glad that it covered "Nasty-Wee-Beastie" bites.

Seven days after checking in, I was released from the hospital. Unlike the hospitals in the United States, I was not hassled to pay my bill before leaving the property. They had my insurance papers and were content with that. Their main concern was that my condition continued to improve. (And by way, it took the hospital almost a year to get their money. My primary insurance company, well known in the industry, wouldn't pay because I was out of the country. The company defaulted on the basis that I did not inform them I was leaving. How lame. The trip insurance covered - without question - the almost $20,000 dollars of medical and travel bills that we incurred during that week in Stornoway. Thank you Travel Guard International.

The day after my release, Lady Kritter and I met up with one of the friends she had made while I was in the hospital. Analyse, a shop owner from town, wanted to take Lady Kritter and me on a picnic to Bosta Beach on the Island of Great Bernera. Analyse claimed we needed to purge the hospital air from our bodies and infuse some fresh ocean air. We rode about an hour and a half through the bogs and small villages of the northern Hebrides. The road ended on Bosta Beach, an incredibly beautiful sheltered bay on the Atlantic Ocean. The water was crystal clear blue and gently caressed a sandy white beach. Rugged islets poked through the water off shore, creating a surreal landscape.

Nestled in this wild flower glenn on the shores of the beach were the remains of a 6th century Iron Age village. The village had been discovered in the mid 1990's during a strong Hebridean storm that pushed back the sands to reveal the historical treasure. Archaeologists had then recreated one of the houses (called a 'jelly bean house' because of its shape).

I was in heaven. I left the girls alone and set off on my own exploration of the wee glenn. I climbed/limped up the steep hill - picturing myself back in the 6th century overlooking my village. I was amazed how well the village was concealed from the ocean - surely a survival technique to hide the village from the Nordic warriors that used to plunder the coastal waters. On top of the hill, I had beautiful, scenic view of land and ocean - mountains rising up out of the crystal clear water. I found it hard to believe I was still in Scotland. From up here, I saw the girls below, though they looked like small dots from the height I was at.

I climbed back down to the girls pleasantly exhausted from my jaunt. In front of the girls was a picnic feast fit for a king: wine, salads, crab legs and Scottish delicacies. It was completely perfect...except for one thing. The *bloody* MIDGES. They were on us in no time, finding exposed skin - almost forcing the three of us to leave. Instead, we enjoyed our meal overlooking the ocean - though we were swatting the whole time.

It was so good to be roaming outdoors again, breathing fresh air and enjoying the raw beauty of Mother Nature. The three of us wanted to stay longer, but in the end, time - and the relentless midges - won.

The next afternoon, a huge dinner was held in honor of Lady Kritter and me - given by Chris, (another friend Lady Kritter met in Stornoway) and Chris' landlord. After dinner we were entertained by the talented guitar playing landlord, who played and sang Scottish folksongs, as we sipped very smooth single malt scotch whiskey. I will be forever grateful to the people of Stornoway and the West Isle hospital for taking care of Lady Kritter and me during our unexpected stay.

In order to get back home, Lady Kritter and I had to make the trip in three legs. The first began as we said our emotional goodbyes to our new friends at the Stornoway Airport and boarded a flight for Glasgow. Landing once again at Glasgow International, it was hard to believe it was only two long weeks ago we started this adventure from here. And, to think what we had been through in those two weeks. It seemed a lifetime ago. We picked up our remaining luggage at the youth hostel, and began the second leg of our trip, a flight to Reykjavík, Iceland. Little did we know our misadventures were to continue.

Due to my weakened condition, the doctor had given me written orders to give to the airlines stating that I needed medical assistance. It read, "At present he has difficulty walking and needs assistance. He is not fit enough to carry heavy weight and will need assistance from his wife to carry his luggage." In essence, I needed a wheelchair for transportation at each of the airports. Everything went fine from Stornoway to Glasgow, but then in Glasgow, Murphy's Law was waiting to rear its ugly head.

We arrived at the airport on the day of departure and checked in with the airline company. The ticket agent said we were not registered in the computer for the flight. I showed the agent our paperwork and the search was on. Finally, after several minutes the ticket agent confirmed that we were on the flight, but said there was one small problem. "It seems the two of you are separated, she said." I had been placed in first class and Lady Kritter was to ride in coach. Not horrible, but I was not happy. Additionally, I asked the ticket agent if I could have a wheelchair waiting for me in Reykjavík. "No problem" she replied.

The flight to Reykjavík was uneventful but, our short stay in Reykjavik was a wholly negative experience. We de-boarded the plane and entered a terminal that was devoid of airline personnel, and the promised wheelchair nowhere to be found. Even the information booth was empty. After minutes of looking, we finally found a person in an airline uniform. She informed us that she was unable to help , as she was on her break. Customer service?

It took Lady Kritter and I over an hour and a half to finally talk to someone who would listen to our plight. Her name was Rachel and she was fantastic. She listened to us patiently and when we finished telling our story of woe, she took it upon herself to make Lady Kritter and me as comfortable as possible. During this time Lady Kritter and I missed a bus excursion to Blue Lagoon, a famous hot spring spa. To help us out, Rachel clocked out of work and drove us in her own vehicle to the lagoon - and then made arrangements for the bus to take us back to the airport. Rachel dropped us at the front door of the spa and we found the bus that was to take us back to the airport. The bus driver told us the bus was leaving in 30 minutes and boarding would begin in 15 minutes. So...our visit to Blue Lagoon was quick, but it was worth it. Lady Kritter walked and I hobbled to the blue water pool with steam coming off the surface. We stuck our toes in the water to make sure it was warm – and, yep, it was. Then we returned to the bus, by-passing the souvenir shop. We stayed at the spa for the full 15 minutes and were one of the first ones to board the bus. We wanted to see and feel the spa in fast forward not wanting to miss the bus and get stuck there.,

The third leg of the trip home was from Reykjavik back to Orlando, Florida. Rachel must have sent word to the crew of the plane of our plight. An airline attendant moved Lady Kritter after takeoff directly behind me, though still in coach. We were able to converse on the long trip across the Atlantic Ocean and I was able to share my first class meal and snacks with her, passing them under a divider curtain.

The wheels touched down at Orlando International Airport and we were safely home. A few days later I wrote an e-mail to the airline company, to the Iceland tourist department, and the City of

Reykjavík. The only reply I got was from the airline company that simply stated, 'sorry about your bad luck'. At least their customer service was consistent, top to bottom.

All in all, pretty much everything that happened after the West Highland Way wasn't expected, but it was actually a great experience. Even in the midst of dragging our luggage across the country and being hospitalized with a life-threatening injury, the beauty of the Scottish country and people made the trip worthwhile for us.

But next time, they can keep their Nasty-Wee-Beasties to themselves.

CHAPTER 6
Getting Muired! Part I
Tahoe Rim Trail

In 2007, Greyhound and I were planning to hike three of the long distance hiking jewels of the West, The Wonderland Trail (WT), Tahoe Rim Trail (TRT) and the John Muir Trail (JMT). However, anyone that knows me also knows that Murphy's Law has a habit of messing with me. 2007 was no exception. The original plan was to begin in Washington State and circumnavigate Mt. Rainier on the Wonderland Trail. Then we would travel south to Tahoe City, California and circumnavigate Lake Tahoe on the Tahoe Rim Trail. Our final destination would be in the famous Yosemite National Park where we would start at the northern trailhead of the John Muir Trail and finish on top of Mt. Whitney. This is where Murphy's Law came in. A reminder that even the best plans can be flushed down the toilet.

Heavy seasonal rains during the late fall washed out several sections of the Wonderland Trail closing it down for a thru-hike. No problem, we would just scratched off the Wonderland Trail for another time and began on The Tahoe Rim Trail. But then, the Tahoe Rim Trail was involved in wildland fires west of South Tahoe City closing the trail. Then family matters were creeping in on several fronts for me and Greyhound was still somewhere in Wyoming on the Continental Divide Trail (CDT) finishing up his Triple Crown. I didn't have to be continually hit over the head with a 2 x 4 to realize the vortex of the summer trip of 2007 was swirling in a clockwise direction down the toilet. It was obvious that the universe was dropping hints that I should postpone the trip. So, when Greyhound called from the CDT, we discussed our options. In the end we both felt this was not the time for this trip to happen. So, he stayed on the CDT to complete his epic journey. And together we decided to wait until the next summer for our California hiking together.

Since I knew that I would eventually be hiking in the High Sierras, I talked and asked questions of customers who came into Travel Country Outdoors who said they had hiked out west. Their faces would light up with excitement as they struggled finding adjectives to describe the beauty they saw in the High Sierras. "Breathtaking", "Majestic", "Magnificent panoramic mountain scenery", "Turquoise colored alpine lakes", were all great descriptors, but according to them, "You have to be there to appreciate the beauty surrounding you." In 1912, John Muir wrote:

"Then it seemed to me the Sierra should not be called the Nevada, or Snowy Range, but the Range of Light. And after ten years spent in the heart of it, rejoicing and wondering, bathing in its glorious floods of light, seeing the sunbursts of morning among the icy peaks, the noonday radiance on the trees and rocks and snow, the flush of the alpenglow, and a thousand dashing waterfalls with their marvelous abundance of irised spray, it still seems to be above all others the Range of Light, the most divinely beautiful of all the mountain chains I have ever seen."

There is a small group of us who, like John Muir, are naturalists and concerned about the well-being of Mother Earth. When we see something of exceptional beauty we simply call it "getting Muired" in honor of John Muir. So I was going out west to get "Muired."

A year later, Greyhound and I were planning another long distance hike. At first, we were going to again try to and begin on the

Wonderland Trail. However, another fall storm caused further damage, washing out new sections of trail. I believe circumstances beyond our control happen for a reason. We objectively discarded the Wonderland Trail segment and re-evaluated our options. Going over maps and guide books, we realized the Tahoe Rim Trail (TRT) and the John Muir Trail were connected by the Pacific Crest Trail (PCT). The Tahoe Rim Trail (TRT), is one of the few long distance loop hiking trails in the country. Loop trails are great because you can start at any of the trailheads and finish where you began, a plus for logistical purposes. For us it also meant we didn't have to find transportation to three different trailheads. Since the TRT was a loop trail, Greyhound and I saw this as an opportunity to start in the south near the PCT, at Big Meadow, hike around the lake in a clockwise direction, re-supply, return to the start, then hike south on the PCT (Pacific Crest Trail) using it as a connector trail to Yosemite National Park, where the John Muir Trail begins (or ends), in Happy Isles. Another benefit of starting with the Tahoe Rim Trail and hiking southward was the gradual acclimation to the altitude. The elevation gains slowly increased from our starting point at Big Meadow (7,500 feet) staying on a ridge line between 8,000 to 9,000 feet to the highest point at 10,000 feet which would be about a week into the hike. Towards the end of the John Muir Trail we would have our trail legs and hopefully our lungs for the 12,000 and 13,000 feet mountain passes and the highest point in the lower 48 states, Mt. Whitney, at 14,494 feet. Based on the mileage, the planned hike would take approximately 6 weeks; combining three long distance trails through the High Sierra Mountains of California, to create one long distance hike. And so, Greyhound and I came up with an awesome 500+ mile, long distance hike that we called our *Summer Hike in the High Sierras*.

With less than a week to go, Greyhound and I were waiting in anticipation like race horses waiting for the starting gate to open. Our airline tickets had been bought, our food sent to drop off locations, backpacks packed (and re-packed) and ready for deployment. The wild land fires in California were again being a nuisance, but so far not threatening our area.

Our plan was to fly into Reno, hop a shuttle to Tahoe City, then a bus to South Lake Tahoe. Arriving by noon, Lake Tahoe time; we would be looking at the mountains that carried a ribbon of dirt on its ridge line around the lake called the Tahoe Rim Trail.

It was hard to believe, but Greyhound and I were sitting on a plane, wheels up and heading west for the Sierra Nevada Mountain Range on a summer day. My first hint that things would certainly be different out west happened as we headed down the walkway towards the baggage claim area at the Reno - Tahoe International Airport. The lights and sounds of slot machines flashing and ringing focused my attention on the frantic pace of people hoping to score that one last "JACKPOT!" before boarding their planes for home. Walking out of the gated area and past the TSA security checkpoint, I noticed the metal detectors were not going off as frequently as they did in Orlando. I thought to myself, "Why was that?." Then it hit me and I had a good laugh. I pictured some of the people leaving their gold and silver jewelry at pawn shops for the green currency in the last attempt to hit the jackpot. Another thought occurred to me, and I quickly looked around to see if anyone lost their shirt, too.

The rest of that day and the following day, Greyhound and I spent our time around South Lake Tahoe getting acclimated to the high altitude. I couldn't handle the city any longer. The frantic pace and noise of it were getting to me, and all I could see surrounding me were beautiful mountains. I did not go there to be a tourist. I went to be cleansed by the sights and sounds of Mother Nature. I needed to be up among the mountain streams and lakes, away from the civilized world going crazy for money around me.

I figured if the altitude was going to give me a headache, I might as well have that headache in the upper reaches of Mother Nature's beauty and not the noise from all that nonsense. I knew there would be no argument from Greyhound. All of this reminded me of another quote from John Muir, "The gross heathenism of civilization has generally destroyed nature, and poetry, and all that is spiritual."

Greyhound and I woke up early the next day and decided to have a quick breakfast before hitchhiking out to the trailhead. As we were eating breakfast in a local restaurant, a hiker walked in with his backpack. As he was passing, I asked him if he was hiking the Tahoe Rim Trail - in the hopes of getting information on trail conditions. "Yes", he replied. I then asked his name. "Sauerkraut" was his response. "SAUERKRAUT! Did you hike the AT in '04?" He looked at me with a 'how did he know that' expression and said, "Yes." I stood up, knowing there could probably be only one Sauerkraut and told him my name was KrispyKritter. "Oh my God," he replied in his thick German accent. He and I had hiked together for a short time on the AT and he was back in the states hiking the PCT with his girlfriend. We talked at length about the hikers we knew and what we had done since the AT. The hiking community is such a select group of individuals that Greyhound was not excluded from the conversation, because he knew some of the same people too. After this energetic conversation, Sauerkraut gave us some great information on trail conditions.

Greyhound and I left town and found a ride to Myers, then another one to the trailhead, all within an hour. Stepping onto the dirt trail that wound up through the Ponderosa Pines was exhilarating. I was in sensory overload within 30 minutes. On a bright sunny day with blue skies above me, I was standing in the middle of a mountain meadow encircled by a floor of green vegetation sprinkled with flowers in hues of purple, orange, white, blue and red. As I turned and looked above the meadow, I had a 360-degree panorama view of mountain formations. The air was fresh with the fragrances of pine and flowers dancing on the wind.

The trail threaded through a grove of tall pine trees and opened up to my first small California mountain lake called, Round Lake. I stopped in amazement. I just had to sit and let my five senses take over. I found a massive fallen down tree trunk jetting into the lake's water and did so.

An Osprey took off from a pine tree, rode the thermal winds with sharp eyes searching the water for dinner. Twice, he pulled back his wings and dove into the water with a splash, flying out empty handed. The backdrop during all the aerial acrobatics were the white granite mountains dotted with trees, making it hard to concentrate on the osprey. My nostrils were filled with the fragrance of Mother Earth's musk smell mixed in with the scent of pine riding the mountain breeze and the odor of fresh water. The auditory sensations of the mountain air whispered through the trees, the chirps of the osprey and the water lapping the shoreline occupied my ears. Touch? I had the lake wind on my face, the tree bark on my ass (via my pants) and the coarse sand in between my toes. At one point during this sensory overload, Greyhound came up to the trunk and sat down. When he finally got my attention I turned to him as he said, "Was I lying?! Didn't I tell you! Wait until the John Muir Trail!"

Five miles from the trailhead, Greyhound and I came to Meiss Meadow and saw the cowboy cabins that signify the joining of the Tahoe Rim Trail and the PCT. I was officially walking on the PCT and I was *stoked*. The remainder of the day continued with more meadows, more lakes and of course, more mountains, along with Greyhound saying "Was I lying? Didn't I tell you... Wait until the John Muir Trail!" And to think this was just our first day.

The second day, though I wouldn't have previously thought it possible, was even better. Greyhound and I hiked alongside the blue waters of Lower and Upper Echo Lakes, surrounded by white granite mountains and granite islands floating in aqua blue waters of the upper lake. We entered the Desolation Wilderness Area to find an array of pristine mountain lakes. That is when we came across one of the most beautiful lakes I had ever seen, Aloha Lake. The lake was surrounded by the Crystal Range with its granite slopes coming right up to the water's edge. Speckled throughout the clear water were various size islands of granite, some with boulders sitting on top, left

Aloha Lak

there thousands of years ago when the glaciers melted away. Trees sporadically dotted the barren landscape bringing a unique and beautiful loneliness to the high country.

Once the Tahoe Rim Trail left the PCT (near Twin Peaks) we had to share the trail with mountain bikers. It was easy seeing one coming at you, but a different matter from behind. Sometimes you would hear a bicycle bell going off behind you or, more likely, be startled by a rider yelling "BIKER, ON LEFT." We'd look back and see a fast moving object barreling towards us down a steep rock and boulder trail. There was no way the rider could completely stop his or her momentum. We had just enough time to step to the right and let them pass without incident. God forbid we'd stepped to the left for a nasty collision between hiker and biker. The rider would sometimes yell during the brief encounter to tell us how many riders were behind them. As they sped away, I would yell "One hiker in front!" I was amazed how fast these riders would travel over boulders, rock ledges and deep rutted trails. They were polite; but I just could not get use to the feeling of potentially being run down at any moment. In the end we made it safely into Tahoe City with no tire tracks on our backs.

Five days into the hike, Greyhound and I woke up near Watson Lake to the odor of burning wood. I immediately looked outside my tent and could see a pale sheet of white whisking through the pine trees. I had a foreboding feeling the spectacular views of Lake Tahoe described in the trail books would be hidden by the smoke. Trail maintenance crews working on the trail told us about a large fire located almost two hundred miles to the south, just outside Yosemite National Park. Greyhound and I looked at each other, thinking that a portion of the hike might have to be re-routed. We both agreed we had immediate needs to overcome, like hydration, high mountain passes to cross and over 165 miles of trail to safely navigate before entering Yosemite and dealing with fire. So, we put off worrying about the fires unless we had to think about them.

Another major and immediate problem we had to face was the scarcity of water on the northern and eastern sides of the lake. We had to carefully plan where our water sources were located and what our intake for the day was going to be. We heard through trail mail that water was available a mile from Watson Lake, flowing across the trail in a small creek. Just to be sure we both loaded 2 full liters of lake water. Sure enough, when we got to the creek, crystal clear water was flowing. We topped off our liters then cameled up (a term used to drink a lot of water) since this was to be our only water source for the next 17 miles.

The morning's hike stayed in the forest and as the day progressed so did the smoke. Visibility was a mile to a mile-and-a-half. Just before coming to Brockway Summit we hiked through a forest charred by last year's fire. The charred remains were not a pretty sight and part of the reason we did not hike the previous year. The hike from Brockway Summit actually started the climb to the highest point on the Tahoe Rim Trail, Relay Peak at 10,338 feet. The awesome views of the lake were hidden from us by the smoke.

Somewhere near the Nevada/California state line the smoke started to diminish. The trail traveled between the 8,000 to 9,000 foot elevations as we hiked on the sides of Mount Baldy, Rifle Peak and Rose Knob in direct sunlight. The mountainside was mainly covered in yellow flowers and dotted with a pine tree here and there. Near Mud Lake we found a spring with the coldest, sweetest water yet to have traveled across my taste buds. Greyhound took a big gulp and immediately yelled out that he had brain freeze. Rejuvenated we pushed on to Relay Peak.

The air cleared and we found some awesome volcanic rock formations along the way. One particular formation on Slab Cliffs looked like gigantic french fries sticking out of the ground. A steep, rugged mountain resembling National Geographic pictures of the Alps loomed over us on the backside of the french fry formation. We hiked over a small rocky saddle before reaching the summit of Relay Peak. Greyhound and I took pictures of each other to commemorate our achievement of climbing our first 10,000 foot peak.

What a difference a day made. Greyhound and I spent the night at the base of Relay Peak. During the night the mountain winds changed direction and began blowing fairly steadily. The faded outline of the mountains rising above the opposite shore came into view through the smoky air because of the sudden change of wind. Not crystal clear, but clear enough to see. Greyhound and I broke camp and headed for Tahoe Meadows in the early morning light. Along the way we spotted several bucks crossing the trail and heading up the mountain. It reminded me of a group of men returning home from an all-nighter with the boys, who hoped to make it into the house before the women folk woke up.

Greyhound and I were now on the east side of the lake - according to the guide books, in the driest section of the trail. Henceforth, we had to be particularly frugal with our water. There were only two options in this section, cache water, or carry it. Since we did not have a vehicle to leave a cache at a trailhead, we had no choice but to carry our water. The only source for water in this section was at Ophir Creek with the next available source 23 miles away at Spooner Lake.

The hike beyond Tahoe Meadows went through a dry and dusty landscape covered in a light brown, almost white, coarse sand. Speckling the rugged terrain, white boulders of granite laid in the sand, sometimes individually, sometimes in groups. Usually the groups were higher up and great for taking a break from hiking to scramble on. Pine trees punctuated the landscape and since there was barely any underbrush, it gave a vast, open feeling. Greyhound said it best when he turned to me, pointer fingers on outstretched arms scanning the horizon and stating, "This is what the moon would look like if it had trees."

As we climbed, we could see the air losing the smoky opaque appearance. I could actually see mountains on the other side of the lake now and looking down at the lake, I could see golden brown beaches with specks of people probably getting sunburned. The water's colors contained so many shades of blue, from the turquoise color near the beach, to the deeper shades of blues marking the various depths of the water. White horizontal lines zinged across the water like the contrails in the blue sky of high altitude jets, denoting another gas guzzling water craft entertaining its occupants. It was hard to believe yesterday was the worst day for viewing scenery, because today was almost picture perfect.

We were high above another lake alongside Lake Tahoe called Marlette Lake, now on the Nevada side of the lake and the trail. The wind above Marlette Lake was blowing at a steady 35 to 40 mph. Sometimes a gust would push me down the trail and I prayed my feet landed in the right spot. Several sections of the mountainside were covered in a sea of purple flowers as far as the eye could see. Their purple heads swayed to and fro as the gusts of wind brushed them. A sweet aroma filled the air as I walked down the trail. The slope of the terrain got steeper and the landscape now offered some of the finest natural rock gardens. Flowers in shades of white, red, yellow and purple surrounded rocks and boulders of so many sizes. The green seed spikes of Sage would wave in the wind above the flowers. Man's attempts to recreate such rock gardens are feeble compared to the work of Mother Nature.

Speaking of man's work, there was a group of Native Americans called the Washoe who lived in this area for 10,000 years. They were hunters and gatherers who lived in harmony with nature. Their beliefs were simple: if you net five fish keep two and send three back into the water. If you pick fruits or berries pick one and leave two. That way Mother Nature will always supply. The first American to allegedly see this land was John Charles Fremont in 1844. It took less than 70 years from that date for the white man to cause the native fish of Lake Tahoe to become extinct. That was accomplished through overfishing and the introduction of aggressive non-native fish to replace those that had been fished out. The land was raped and left naked by the glutton timber companies who were supplying wood for the greed of the mining industries and the towns that grew up around them. When the mining declined, most of the land was abandoned and left in ruins. So, I ask you, Who are the civilized ones?

Twenty-three miles later, when Greyhound and I had barely a sip of water left in our water bottles, we arrived at Spooner Lake. It was a no-brainer that we would spend the night and enjoy the precious water which we shared with a coyote that greeted us at our arrival. The next morning we replenished our two liters of water for the 13 mile stretch hiking up to Spooner Summit without a water source.

The early morning sun was just waking up the mountain side. White, puffy clouds for the first time hugged high above the mountains and Lake Tahoe, giving us views that were even better than the previous few days. We could clearly see up and down the lake as well as across. At South Camp Peak, we sat and watched the morning demarcation line of sunlight march across the water and up South Tahoe City to the surrounding mountains on the western shore. Greyhound and I pointed to the mountains across the lake that we crossed the following week and talked about the places where we had been. A cold wind came in from the lake and gave both of us a chill. The best way to warm up is to hike, so we said good-bye to the lake and our recent memories and continued on our footpath of rock and dirt.

We arrived at the Kingsbury North trailhead and began our 3 mile road walk through residential neighborhoods. The trail passed through Heavenly, a ski resort which is overflowing with skiers during the winter. The lifts were now silent above the green vegetation of summer. The trail passed right by The Fox and Hound Bar and Grill in Heavenly. Like any good long distance hiker should do, we had to check out the hamburgers and grab some french fries and of course copious amounts of coke. The stop was also an added bonus after walking on the hot asphalt roads in the noonday sun.

Well rested and with bellies filled, Greyhound and I waddled back out to the trail and followed the blue and white triangle shaped Tahoe Rim Trail marker out of Heavenly. Not long after leaving the ski resort we were on a high and narrow trail through Mott Canyon and Monument Pass. The cliff edged trail leading up to Monument Pass at 8,820 ft in elevation afforded us a different perspective of mountain scenery. We were on the southeast side of the lake and high on the eastern slopes of the mountains. The views contained several breathtaking overlooks with eastern views into the Carson Valley. This section of trail also contained massive western white pine trees, with thick trunks and full, green tree tops that looked like overgrown broccoli. One particular huge tree was positioned on the turn of a switchback. I referred to him as "King" and called him "His Majesty." The other trees were sentinels protecting the kingdom. Greyhound and I each, in our own way, paid our respects and entered the kingdom of ancient trees. Towards the end of daylight we arrived at Star Lake. Greyhound scouted the lake and found us a camp site with spectacular views of Freel Peak and Jobs Sister reflecting in the cool waters of the lake. Star Lake is the largest mountain lake on the eastern side of the loop trail and was a great water source as well as excellent camping spot.

After leaving camp at Star Lake we entered a wide open area of high country. The trees in this area were stunted, bent, gnarled and twisted by the harsh conditions of the high mountain weather. They stood alone or in small groups among the boulders. Both Greyhound and I were amazed by the beauty of these ancient trees. I knew the only reason these trees were probably still alive was because they were too few with little monetary value and were too far away to be axed or chain sawed. It was a pleasure to look at them and not see graffiti hearts and "so and so" loves "so and so" etched and scratched in the tree's bark. John Muir has a quote that says "God has cared for these trees, saved them from drought, disease, avalanches, and a thousand tempests and floods. But he cannot save them from fools."

We walked on the white sand in another moon-like landscape surrounded by large slabs of white granite rocks and boulders that fell from the sides of the mountain. The rocks piled up on top of one another creating an smorgasbord of caves. We explored some of those close to the trail and wondered how many ancient people used these caves for shelter. For me it was sort of like watching an computer re-enactment from Discovery Channel episode playing in my mind.

Greyhound and I looked across at the caves that were too far away to explore and tried to catch a glimpse of the stealthy movement of a mountain lion. This was their habitat and you could just feel those laser eyes piercing you while you're hoping that sleek, powerful muscular cat machine doesn't have an empty stomach. We failed to catch a glimpse of the elusive cat. We crossed over Armstrong Pass, had one more climb in elevation and then enjoyed a pleasant walk on a high plateau with more rocks and boulders.

I had to be careful not to dehydrate or lose electrolytes at high altitude. I sweat so much that there would be a streak of dried salt running down both sides of my shirt where it came in contact with the Granite Gear Vapor Trail backpack. The front of the shirt looked like a psychedelic white design from the 60's. I drank plenty of water, when we could find it, and ate salt products like Pringles and Fritos to replenish my sodium chloride. I tried to get 10-12 miles of hiking in by mid-day before the sun started to warm up the tan/white sand and reflect the heat back off the white sand and granite boulders.

I would get tired between 12 and 3 in the afternoon, my feet hurting and became a little cranky. Greyhound called it my "Mid-day Meltdown". It has now become a standard phrase incorporated into our hiking vocabulary. I slowed down during this period and took more rest breaks. I started taking breaks near fantastic vistas that would take all my negativity away. Greyhound knew this was the best time to leave me alone. By 3-3:30 I was back in rhythm and clicking off the mileage, again feeling like a champ.

I knew we were coming close to a water source when I could see white and brown earth surrounding a ribbon of lush dark green vegetation with flowers poking out everywhere and a cool mountain stream running through it. This was one of my favorite types of locations to relieve my "Mid-day Meltdown"s.

Nine days after setting foot on Big Meadow, Greyhound and I passed through some small meadows, descended into a thick forest and was back at Big Meadow, completing our thru hike of the TRT. We hitched a ride into town, found our hotel, got some town food into our bellies, and cleaned off, or should I say, scrubbed off 165 miles of dust and dirt. Greyhound called his wife and I called home to let Lady Kritter and family know I was still alive, not eaten by mountain lion or bear. I was bombarded by questions from both Lady Kritter and family on whether or not I had felt the earthquake that had rocked Los Angeles, California. "No", I said. "It must have happened when I did one of my famous 'stumble, catch and balance act.'"

I have a habit of dragging my feet instead of lifting them up, due to medical reasons. It could be the smoothest dirt trail for miles around, and if I was not paying attention, or in a daymare (I will explain in another chapter), I would drag my foot, find anything sticking up, and trip. However, I also used this to my advantage. When I stumbled, trip, or kick up a pile of dirt and dust several times in a row, I know it is time for a rest break. Sometimes while hiking, I played mind games to occupy my mind. One such game involved stumbles and slides going downhill. I would measure the length of the slide or stumble in my mind until it totaled roughly 3 ½ feet. This would be the equivalent of one length of my stride I did not have to take.

Anyways, I was disappointed I did not get to experience the earthquake and felt even better there was little damage or injury to the civilized world. I'll just have to rely on my only other earthquake experience - the day I met Lady Kritter.

The Tahoe Rim Trail was a beautiful 165 mile trail that circumnavigated one of the most beautiful and largest alpine lakes in North America. The lake, 22 miles long and 12 miles wide was surrounded by the mountains and flowered meadows of the High Sierras. Greyhound and I hiked through two states (California and Nevada), three National Forest Wilderness Areas (Mount Rose Wilderness, Desolation Wilderness and Granite Chief Wilderness), the California and Nevada National Forest lands and the Lake Tahoe Nevada State Park. In addition, the Tahoe Rim Trail is one of the youngest long distance trails in the United States being completed in 2001.

I recommend this trail for any long distance hiker's wish list of trails to hike in the world.

CHAPTER 7
Getting Muired! Part II
The Pacific Crest Trail

Greyhound and I were anxious to get back into the mountains after a day of re-supplying and eating town food. We got on the road in front of the hotel trying to hitch a ride back to Big Meadows in the early morning light. The highway was very busy and both Greyhound and I were amazed at how long it took for us to catch a ride. Someone finally stopped (an artist who carved pieces of log with a chainsaw and was from Florida. That wait of one and a half hours, broke the longest time period for each of us in our long distance hiking career to catch a ride – hitchhiking (the record still stands today). By noon we were finally on the PCT heading south for Yosemite.

The Pacific Crest Trail (PCT) crossed a main highway at Carson Pass, named after Kit Carson. He was a scout and hunter for the Fremont expedition in the mid 1800's. The pass became famous when a Mormon battalion was returning home from the Mexican War and found this pass as an easier way to get back home to Salt Lake City. Word spread quickly from the soldiers and the pass became the route to travel if you wanted to go to California overland.

The hike on the PCT lived up to its reputation as a trail running along the slopes of massive mountains, beneath towering jagged granite rock walls - waiting to tumble down at any minute. I could look up from the trail and see hundreds of loose boulders and rock fields that had fallen already. Crystal clear, cold water run-off from

Greyhound on the Pacific Crest Trail north of Sonora Pass

the snowfields ran down the slopes by way of creeks and streams into lakes and ponds. Deep green vegetation, sprinkled with the colors of summer flowers, dominated either side of the water runs - giving life to an arid landscape of grays, whites and volcanic reds.

Greyhound and I were walking high along the side of a mountain top called the Nipple. (By the way, it does actually look like a nipple on top of a breast. Men have died trying to find the other one). We were up high looking down at a lake when Greyhound spotted movement of something brown in the grass between us and the lake. It was a huge mule deer standing on the mountain slope. Suddenly, the mule deer laid down in the grass. I was so excited. This was the first time I witnessed a deer bedding down. I watched closely and noticed there was a second deer in the same bed of grass. Here were two of Mother Nature's critters sharing a bed together. It reminded me of two other Kritters. I looked at my watch and realized a dear was bedding down back in Florida, so I sent a good night to Lady Kritter from across the country.

Greyhound and I entered the Mokelumne Wilderness and began climbing out of the trees. We were treated to some magnificent views every time we climbed over a saddle (a low point of a ridge connecting two peaks). The vegetation and terrain would have a particular look as we climbed up to the saddle, and then completely change on the other side. We crossed over several saddles and on the trail down into the valley found ourselves hiking beneath massive jagged volcanic rock formations that towered over us. I felt so small walking next to the cliffs. The brownish red walls were pocketed with cave openings and crevices. The previous day we saw the same type of formations, except the rock was granite. The land took on a magical wonderland-type appearance. The rocks and soil were colored in bands of grays, deep brown reds, indigo, dirty yellows, oranges and light olive green, depending what their chemical makeup. There were times I would walk along the trail and the color bands would change every 20 ft or so. I called this an Earth Rainbow.

Another thing I noticed was the harshness of the environment. The high country during the summer is extremely dry. Yet, you can see evidence everywhere of water erosion and the force from the waters of the spring snow melt as it became a powerful earth mover to the movement of rocks and boulders. We came upon water falling down the mountainside in a creek, our oasis in the Mokelumne Wilderness. Cold water was dancing down the rocks from the higher elevations with flowers and trees bordering the stream. Greyhound and I sat motionless and listened to the water rushing down the mountain and watched as different aquatic life came out of hiding. I was truly in a garden paradise.

Greyhound saw a bear and her three cubs playing in a field north of Asa Lake. He hid behind a tree and peeked around the trunk every so often to get a view of the frolicking cubs. Mama bear could smell Greyhound, but she couldn't see him and was getting anxious of the new animal smell. I was 10 minutes behind Greyhound, sitting on a boulder eating my Pop-Tarts and dreaming of coffee, as I looked out onto a pretty meadow hoping to see a bear. I didn't see a bear and I missed all the action by the time I got to Greyhound. However, on my way I had my own encounter with some other animals. I observed two mule deer, a buck and a doe each by themselves. The doe was so funny. I was walking up the trail and turned a corner to see her standing to my right, staring at me, right there on the trail. I wanted to grab my camera and take a picture, but was afraid the movement would spook her. I stood motionless and stared back. So there we were in a Mexican standoff, me frozen on the trail and the doe looking at me, saying, "Don't you want a picture of me?" I slowly removed my camera from its shoulder case, readied it and put it up to my eye for the shot. I looked at the deer once more and she was still looking at me, posing. I took the picture and it was as if I could hear the deer say "Finally", as she ran into the forest.

Doe posing for the camera

One day during the hike, I thought I started to hear the faint sounds of bells clanging as I was hiking up the slope of a valley near Murray Canyon. Then, I thought I was hearing the musical sounds of wind chimes hanging in the trees. "What's next, dragons and fairies?"

A short time later the mystery was solved. I recognized cow patties laying on the trail and then finally came upon a herd of cattle that were grazing in the valley, across the trail and under the shade of the trees. As I walked up to the cows, I saw that each cow had a bell around its neck. The closest one started walking away from me, bell clanging, then ran into a second cow, then a third, and so on. Soon, the whole herd was in motion – which is where the wind chime affect came from.

Greyhound and I started spending our nights camping in the cooler, higher elevations. We settled in for the night higher than a majority folks going to bed in the lower 48. One particular night above Wolf Creek Lake (elevation 10,250 feet) the wind interrupted my peaceful sleep. Throughout the night, the cold wind howled outside our tents causing anything loose to flap, especially when hit with gusts. A particularly strong gust came through camp and pulled one of my tent stakes up. I had to get out of my warm sleeping bag, go outside in the chilly wind and fix my tent. When I did, I was almost blown away by the intensity of the wind. Undaunted, I found a large rock to anchor down the tent corner. I crawled back into my still semi-warm sleeping bag and within minutes was snugly warm and comfortably falling back to sleep. Greyhound said he slept through the night listening to the rhythm of his tarp flapping in the wind.

The next morning, I woke up with the sun shining and chilly wind still blowing. We broke camp early because we knew we were going into civilization to re-supply, shower and eat town food. In the early morning light, we made it to a two-lane lonely mountain road at Sonora Pass. Seeing the desolated road and the time of day, I thought there was a good chance we would break our time record of not getting a ride Like the one we'd just established outside the city of South Lake Tahoe. There were plenty of rocks laying around, so Greyhound and I played a game of Target while waiting for a vehicle to pass. Target is throwing rocks at an object with each hit being a point. The one with the most points – wins. Surprisingly, within an hour of waiting for a hitch, we caught a ride into the PCT trail town of Bridgeport, 30 miles from the trailhead. It was just in time too, because Greyhound was catching up to me in points.

We arrived in town via Route 395 running down main street. The town was a quarter of a mile from end to the end, which meant everything we needed was within walking distance. We stayed at a motel well known to PCT hikers and the first thing I did was take a shower. I cannot express how good that shower felt - after walking for days in an arid land where every foot fall would create a puffy cloud of dirt and dust. There was a coating of dirt on every piece of clothing and equipment that I carried, as well as most body parts. The cleaning of clothing, equipment and bodies was sheer delight and good for the soul.

The following day, we made last minute phone calls to our wives, said goodbye to our comfortable beds and in the early morning light, with full stomachs and clean clothes, we were on the edge of town hitchhiking back to Sonora Pass. The first ride was a rather large boned man (in other words heavy set) going to his doctor's appointment. He was eating glazed donuts while driving; he turned to me and said, "I guess this isn't good for the doctor visit," then looked back at the road and took another big bite. He dropped us off at the intersection of Route 108, a 13 mile winding mountain road that goes up to Sonora Pass and Route 395. We were only part-way back to the trailhead. I wished our driver good luck on his doctors visit.

Within minutes of standing on the side of the road for our next ride, a deputy sheriff pulled up in a marked 4-wheel drive unit. The deputy opened his door, stood with one elbow on the top of the door, the other elbow on top of the roof with a microphone in his hand talking to dispatch. The deputy then put the mic down, looked at Greyhound and I and asked if we were hikers, and where were we going? We answered that, "Yes. And we are going up to Sonora Pass to get back on the PCT." The deputy then asked if we wanted a ride or if we wanted to wait for another - as it started to sprinkle.

Greyhound and I looked at each other for confirmation and we both said "Yes." Then, I asked, just to be positive, that his ride was to Sonora Pass and not back to Bridgeport as a guest of the county. He confirmed Sonora Pass, and not the county jail, was where he wanted to take us - with the only stipulation that we show photo ID. The deputy said, "It could be embarrassing if I gave you a ride, then found out you were wanted for murder or some other serious crime." We all laughed. Greyhound pulled out his driver's license as I was still looking for mine and he was cleared by dispatch. The deputy said, "It's OK, just give me your name and date of birth." Waiting for a response back from dispatch, we climbed into the caged back seat and started heading for the pass. The radio speaker crackled with the dispatch voice saying, "No record of subject found." OOOPS. I *had* to find my ID. I eventually found it hiding in some recessed pocket of my backpack and once cleared of having any felonies, we all laughed again. The deputy was a great guy. It turns out he was also a hiker and recently discharged from the mountain army base nearby. You just never know who is going to be a trail angel. This time it was a young deputy with a badge and gun.

Greyhound and I were back in the mountains south of Sonora Pass and hiking in elevations of almost 11,000 feet. We got to a notch on a steep wall, went through it and entered onto a landscape that, to me, resembled a barren planet. I thought, that I might be going into another daymare, then quickly dismissed the idea thinking that maybe we had walked through some type of time travel portal. Though neither were exactly true.

We were hiking on assorted scree of rocks and pebbles, the largest being no bigger than a football. We hiked like this for several miles on a knife's edge (a trail that runs along a ridgeline with cliff like sides falling hundreds of feet on either side) with no trees, no plants, in a void of all life forms. Exposed, we were lucky there were no high winds to blow us off the edge or thunderstorms to use us as lightning rods. And, the views looking back towards Sonora Pass were incredible. This was not just an ordinary mountain of solid rock. This

The V in the photograph is the notch

Krispykritter hiking the ridge

was a 10,000 foot mountain of rubble containing small rock and pebbles.

We finally dropped down into a glacier formed valley housing a forest. We hiked along Kennedy Canyon and its creek, passed several ponds, lakes and creeks and hiked over Dorothy Lake Pass, consisting of huge slabs of granite with an occasional tree. It was amazing how often the landscape changed. We called it "cowboy remote control." When went over a pass, saddle, or around a mountain it's like we heard a "click" and a whole new program of Mother Nature was before us. We dropped down from the pass and came to a sign that read "Yosemite Wilderness." We were officially in the famous Yosemite National Park!

We were the audience to a lightning/thunderstorm light show. It woke me up as the drops started hitting my tarp tent and the flash indicated that the thunder was 6 miles away. After several more flashes and low boomers, it became evident the storm was moving away from us. Showtime was over so I snuggled back into my sleeping bag and drifted off to sleep as I was thinking of a John Muir quote.

"Nature is ever at work building and pulling down, creating and destroying, keeping everything whirling and flowing, allowing no rest but in rhythmical motion, chasing everything in endless song out of one beautiful form into another."

The next morning the sun was breaking over Dorothy Lake. Greyhound and I broke camp and we continued our journey. The morning hike was fantastic through Grace Meadow and Jack Main Canyon. A stream stayed to our left, meandered through the meadows, and in the canyon held large granite boulders on its shoreline which gave us a playground for bouldering during our breaks. We stopped to look at a particular pool in the stream when suddenly a bush in front of us exploded and out ran a little fawn with white spots on its back. It galloped away from us quickly, probably looking for its mother.

Then with the click of our cowboy remote, the afternoon was a completely different landscape. Huge gray granite mountain-walls towered over us as we climbed up one wall to scramble down another.

Greyhound and I, just after going thru Malcomb Ridge Pass, entered a section of terrain comprising of several canyons. Access to the first canyon, called Stubblefield Canyon was attained by hiking over a small plateau. The arduous incline down the canyon west wall was made over small rocky switchbacks to the canyon floor. Hiking along the rocky floor we found a pleasant surprise - a cold water stream with a fine sandy beach and a swimming hole. This was a great place for lunch and relief from the sun, as well as my "Mid-day Meltdown". We couldn't stay as long as I would have liked, because according to the map, we had to climb out of the canyon via more switchbacks up the east wall, through a notch and then descend into the steep Kerrick Canyon. The life of a long distance hiker is never boring.

Since entering the boundaries of Yosemite National Park we were hiking in sections of the park that 95% of the people don't usually visit. However, bear confrontation with humans can occur anywhere within the park. Through years of bear research, park authorities have placed stringent regulations to lessen the human/bear interactions. These precautions are necessary to protect park visitors, as well as the bears. In the backcountry, we do not eat or cook in camp. All foods and products (like soap, toothpaste, gum etc. that are fragrant) go into a bear canister. We set the canisters 150-200 feet away from camp and in sight of our tarp tents. We fully trust our bear canisters and honestly, would enjoy having a bear visit us for a bit. Having a canister marked up with scratches would be like a badge of courage that we could show our grandchildren. Throughout that night and every night after, we woke up and checked our canisters in the hopes of seeing a battle between bear and canister. I am sad to report that the only thing we saw was the canister standing upright and alone, as our camp sentry.

We continued to walk through the forest that opened up to a landscape of large slabs of undulating granite interspersed with pine trees. I looked up and down the slabs and found trees rooted in cracks trying to sustain life in that harsh environment. The trail then started a slow descent from the top of Cold Canyon. A large stream entered into the canyon giving us fantastic views of sparkling cascades and clear pools. What sounded like large motors running was coming from the valley below. However, the sound was constant and did not diminish or get louder like a close-moving vehicle. Because I knew there was not a road around; I checked the map and realized the sounds we were hearing were coming from Tuolumne Falls and the White Cascades. Sound usually carries pretty far outdoors, but I knew this was still a good indication that we were going to see an excellent display of Mother Nature's energy at work.

We hiked into Glen Aulin, one of the High Sierra Camps in Yosemite that is supplied by mule train, a little after dawn. The only way tourists can get to these High Sierra camps is by mule train or foot. This particular camp consisted of white canvas cabin tents with an assortment of people standing around sporting their new outdoor clothes and spotless equipment. A campground for backpackers and the Boy Scouts was located behind the tents. Tuolumne Falls was located in front of the camp with a large pool below the falls. Suddenly, an air horn shattered the monotone roar of the waterfall. I looked in the direction of the sound and saw people filing in line like cattle, to enter a big cabin tent, that I later learned was the mess hall. This was the beginning of my experience of people taking to the wilderness of Yosemite - on trails that become the interstate of the woods. We left Glen Aulin and started a climb through the woods. We curved with the winding trail and caught a glimpse of a bear. However, 'city slicker backpacker' ahead of us started clicking his aluminum hiking poles and scared the bear away. What 'city slicker backpacker' didn't know was the bear had already smelled the scent of humans and was walking away to avoid us.

At the top of the climb the trail took us alongside the White Cascades. The sights and sounds of awesome water flows over granite slabs mesmerized our senses. Greyhound and I went off trail and scrambled on the rocks along the water's edge. I was in sheer delight imagining myself as a mountain man traveling up an unknown water source, possibly the first white man to see these wonders...maybe even the first man. Completing my sensory overload, all around me were huge granite monolithic mountains reaching skyward in sculptured rounded formations.

The trail followed the Tuolumne River, flowing over, around, and through slabs of granite. Greyhound and I decided to stop on top of a slab, drop our backpacks and get lost in the world of nature around us. Laying on my side and looking down towards the river, I noticed brown movement on the river bank. I woke Greyhound up just in time to watch a mule deer doe walking skittishly into the river, before freezing in its tracks. Nervously, she looked back towards the direction she came, then turned back around and took a few more steps. Again, she stopped dead in her tracks; turned back like before, then quickly left the openness of the river and disappeared. Greyhound and I watched the scene develop before us and considered what may have caused the doe's concern. We concluded the logical reason was maybe the doe was trying to coerce her fawn to come across the river, or that maybe a predator was nearby.

With the excitement over, Greyhound and I went back to our individual thoughts. Minutes later another golden brown movement across the river caught my eye. I studied the landscape and focused in on the color. Out of the trees a golden brown color wandered slowly on top of a slab of granite along the opposite shoreline. The bear suddenly halted, pointed its nose high in the air, and probably getting a whiff of Greyhound and I (we hadn't showered in 4 days, and were particularly ripe!) It lowered its head and continued in its lazy, lumbering walk back into the woods. We weren't watching Cowboy

TV, but what Greyhound and I began to refer to as "Muirvision", (in honor of John Muir who said of the Yosemite bear:

"And there stood neighbor bruin within a stones throw...how well he played his part, harmonizing in bulk and color and shaggy hair with the trunks of the trees and lush vegetation."

The bear of "Muirvision"

We arrived in Tuolumne Meadows into a sea of people and automobiles who were stepping outside their confines of the city and into the world of Mother Nature. Our next stop was Yosemite Valley, affectionately referred to as the "LA (Los Angeles) in the Woods" by local hikers. In less than two hours we were with our friends, John and Ruth, who volunteer for the national park. They live in Yosemite Valley - where I finally saw the famous mountains Half Dome, El Capitan and Cathedral in full panoramic dimensions.

Yosemite Valley - Half Dome to the right

The North Face of Half Dome

After the grand tour of Yosemite Valley by John and Ruth, Greyhound and I set off on bicycles to explore the valley. I could not believe how well the trees hid buildings, people and vehicles. There were definitely a lot of people in the valley. In fact, the valley was actually a small town with stores, post office, museums, visitor center, police, jail and courthouse. The valley was truly an international mixture of people from all over the world. A lot of people came there for vacation from California and Nevada - which explains the hiker's nickname for the valley. Bears, deer and little squirrels roam the grounds at will - almost Disney-like. Yosemite Valley was also a Mecca for rock climbers who come from all over the world to climb the park's famous rock face. Camp 4, known as the climbers' campground, is where you can hear their special language echoing through the camp. During the day, climbers looked like mere little dots as they inched up the vertical walls of El Cap. John and Ruth brought us back to El Cap during the night to see the star-like twinkle of their lights inching up the wall in the dark. Most climbers take longer than a day to reach the top, while other climbers take advantage of climbing in the coolness of the night. I thought how beautiful it must be to hang on the wall and look up to see Mother Nature's light show above and the glowing man-made lights below.

John and Ruth took us to Mariposa Grove, a forest of Giant Sequoias, the largest living things on our planet. These beautiful trees grow over 300 feet tall and can weigh as much as 300 buses. One tree can produce enough lumber to equal an acre of northwest pine forest. The trees grow in girth about one foot every hundred years. It took many men to appreciate their beauty and to finally stop the cutting of these 3,000 year old majestic beauties. It was truly an honor to walk among those ancient giants.

CHAPTER 7
Getting Muired! Part III
The John Muir Trail

Two days in 'LA In The Woods' was enough for Greyhound and I. We had mountains to climb, rivers to cross and passes to go up and over. We said good-bye to our dear friends and ambassadors of the park and were up before sunrise the next day because we wanted to climb Half Dome and avoid the late morning rush of tourists who had the same idea. John drove us first to the historic Ahwahnee Hotel for the grand tour and my last cup of coffee before hitting the trail. The first rays of daylight were breaking over the mountain as Greyhound and I stepped on the northern terminus of the JMT in Yosemite Valley at a place called Happy Isles.

The trail ascended immediately after leaving the trailhead into a combination rock and asphalt path. We could see in the dim early light Mist and Nevada Falls. The trail crossed over Nevada Falls where nearby an overlook was located at the top of the falls. It was mesmerizing to watch the water rush over the ledge into streams of droplets raining into the pool below. Six miles from Happy Isles, Greyhound and I left the JMT and began our climb on the trail to Half Dome.

I was apprehensive about climbing the back of Half Dome and decided to have a wait-and-see attitude. Greyhound and I got to the base of the dome and we could already see people climbing up. The switchbacks were rocky and small as they rounded up the steep mountain side. Near the top of the switchbacks a sloping rock face brought you up to a small plateau where the next stage of the climb took place. Two cables were anchored into the rock at the far end and ran side by side up the granite wall.

Climbing Half Dome

Greyhound was patient as I sat on a rock and contemplated whether I was going up or not. Next to me were two girls from the Netherlands who were also indecisive. The three of us were in a motivation discussion when a father and his 12 year old son came up the switchbacks and approached the cables. The man and boy turned towards each other gave a high five and without hesitation began their climb. Inspired by the fearlessness of the 12 year old, I looked at the girls and told them, "If a 12 year old can do it, so can I." The girls looked at each other and said "Why not!?" and off they went towards the cables.

Greyhound and I converged at the base of the cables and found a pile of assorted gloves to protect hands from possible barbs on the braided steel cables.

The initial start was not bad, but the angle of the rock wall quickly sharpened and I had to dig my boots into the rock face and literally pull myself up using arm strength on the cables. Already, there was a line of people going up. The higher up we went, and the sharper the incline, the slower the flow of traffic became. Someone would freak out from time to time and hold on to the cable for dear life and not move. This would stop the flow of traffic and there you are standing and hanging onto the cable waiting for the traffic jam of fearful climbers to move. I tried to pace myself so when the line stopped I would be at a wooden 2x4 that laid across the rock face where pipes were drilled into the granite to hold the cables. These were the only good places to get a good footing when standing still.

This was only half of the ordeal of going up. The other half involved dealing with people coming down, face forward, walking backwards, side stepping, or barging through with the attitude of, "Just get me off this rock. Halfway up, I thought KrispyKritter had really went too far this time. I was walking up the mountain's side on a seemingly almost impossible cable trail. I pictured myself like the old TV Batman and Robin series grabbing a rope hand over hand and climbing up the side of a vertical building. Finally, with heart and lungs ready to burst, I made it to the top. "Holy Granite, Batman" the views from the top were spectacular.

The Yosemite Valley below was very far away and small, the mountain views incredible, and my heart still hadn't stopped beating out of my chest. Then it was time to go down. This was when Greyhound gave me the good news/bad news routine. Good news - getting up was easy. Bad news - going down was much harder. Greyhound coached me how and where to step on the way down. My legs hadn't shaken that much since the day I said "I do" to Lady Kritter. Yet, we made it down with gusto. Greyhound and I high-fived each other at the bottom of Half Dome. We congratulated each other for surviving the climb without broken bones or scraped skin.

The rest of that first day was a steady climb up. I had spent my leg muscles on Half Dome and the afternoon was a bit painful for me. However, it did feel good to be in the higher elevations again. Our first camp on the JMT was at another condo camp called Sunrise High Sierra Camp, elevation 9,300 ft. I fell quickly to sleep as my worn out muscles pulsated irregularly - greatly needing a rest from the day's high adventure.

We were up with first light the next morning and by the time the sun rays are warming up the granite rocks, Greyhound and I had breakfast at Cathedral Pass. One particular peak in front of us resembled a fortress at the top. After breakfast we walked on a high plateau and noticed several more mountain peaks that were in the shape of cathedral spirals. One mountain peak had at least four to five spirals. Another had a high spiral on the left, a space, then another spiral with several rock columns extending upward. Greyhound figured the pass was named not for just one mountain peak but for all of them in this particular area. Further down the trail we came to the beautiful Cathedral Lake. The rest of the trail was a slow descent through forest towards Tuolumne Meadows.

Tuolumne Meadows was a beautiful and enormous meadow. The trail passed by Soda Springs - a favorite drinking spot for John Muir. It was only fitting that Greyhound and I stopped by, in honor of the great writer and environmentalist, to drink from the same spring. The water tasted just like soda water with an earthy flavor. We spent two leisurely hours at Tuolumne Meadows going to the store, post office and grill.

Greyhound and I left the sweet, soapy fragrance of the tourists, stepped off the asphalt and once again entered the 95% of the park not seen by tourists. We then followed Lyell Fork through Lyell Canyon, but I couldn't tell why they called it a canyon, because it has a large green meadow with a river running through it, surrounded by mountains. That was a valley to me.

The trail skirted along the side of the meadow for 10 miles. Several miles into the meadow, Greyhound and I were walking along the river and possibly found the best swimming pool we had encountered so far. The river ran into a deep pool that was surrounded on one side by a 30 foot high granite wall. Cool, sparkling, crystal clear water flowed into the pool flanked by sandy beaches on the other three sides. Greyhound came up with a great idea for me to beat my "Mid-day Meltdown". Our shoes, socks and whatever was in our pockets couldn't come off and out fast enough, 'Splash', in dove Greyhound, and when he broke the surface exhaled with an 'Ahhhhh!' I was not so daring. Slowly, I entered and let the soothing cool water wash over me a little at a time, quenching my "Mid-day Meltdown". It was so refreshing and as an added bonus, we were able to wash and dry our clothes without even taking them off.

I had noticed from the beginning on the Tahoe Rim Trail, assorted size boulders (small as a football to bigger than houses) just sitting on top of granite slabs, as though someone intentionally placed them where they sat. At first I thought they broke away from the mountainside and rolled down to where they stopped. Some of the boulders had the most unusual shapes, others were found in the most ridiculous positions, and I would wonder, "How did that get there?" I am sure some of the activity was due to gravity, but I now know it was another force of Mother Nature that occurred tens of thousands of years ago. The boulders, rocks, smooth rock faces, fields of small rocks and sand called moraines, were all part of the glacier activity that once occurred in the High Sierras. The smooth rock was the result of glacier movement, grinding and sanding over the rock surface. The moraine garbage dumps consisting of rocks and sand were the remains of the glacier after meltdown. It was a wonderland for me to walk through the hard granite walls and see, both at eye level and high on the peaks of mountains, what the forces of nature did to the hard stone.

We then climbed Donohue Pass, our first real pass of the JMT. Greyhound called this pass "The Gateway to the John Muir Trail." We hiked up switchbacks and leveled off for some awesome views of Lyell Canyon and its meadow behind us. The sun reflected off the water of the river giving it a mirrored snake-like appearance. The mountains towering over us still wore sheets of snow, feeding streams that cascaded toward the valley. Another series of switchbacks brought us to an alpine meadow with a waterfall at the furthest end. Tents lined the stream running through it. Greyhound and I both agreed there were way too many people here and with plenty of afternoon daylight still burning, decided to continue the climb up and over Donohue Pass. Up and up we climbed, leaving the tree line, crossing over rocks and small streams cascading down the rocks of the trail. One last look back at the tents below and we could see people standing in the sunlight, shading their eyes as they looked up at us curious to see where the trail would take them tomorrow. At sundown, we finally reached the pass, elevation 11,056 ft. With just enough light to set up camp we - for several reasons - decided to stay on the pass. First, it was getting dark. Second, up to that point Donahue Pass would have been my highest campsite ever. And finally, a hiker had told us there would be a major meteor shower expected that night. Being on top of the pass would give us a clear sky. I could not think of a better place than on top of a mountain to watch the light show.

The night on Donahue Pass was exceptionally beautiful. The moon came out early in a three-quarter globe of illumination. Next to the moon and shining bright was Venus. The rocky landscape, devoid of any vegetation, was cloaked in a grayish white glow. It was eerie... so primordial. "What planet am I really on?" The moonlight was actually too overpowering to gaze at the night sky so I said goodnight to Greyhound and went to bed. The glow inside my tent was like a street light shining through the material. Greyhound cowboy camped (slept under the stars) and had to shield his eyes from the radiant moon beams. I woke up before dawn after the moon set in the west, to find a vivid night sky of stars and Milky Way. I felt I could reach up and grab a star. Within a blink of an eye a streak shattered the darkness of the sky. Several minutes later another streak, then another. I saw the meteor shower! There were so many falling stars I thought I was a punched out boxer going down for the count. I fell asleep and woke up refreshed and ready to click the Muirvision remote for today's journey.

During the early part of our hike, Greyhound and I began a daily routine we called, ""Morning Cafe"." We would break camp before sunrise then hiked until we found a sunny location to warm up from the morning chill, find a view of Mother Nature in action and eat our breakfast. We would pretend we were sitting at an open air cafe and ordered our breakfast of Cherry Pop-Tarts. One particular ""Morning Cafe"" Greyhound found a spot with just enough space for two and shouted ""Morning Cafe" for two." We took off our backpacks and sat on a gigantic granite boulder that overlooked a golden green meadow. A small ribbon of a stream meandered along the boundaries of the meadow that emptied into various pools. One particularly large pool with crystal clear water was directly below us. We watched trout glide effortlessly through the water looking for their morning breakfast.

One of the benefits of hiking for the first time on a new trail is not knowing what to expect. At any moment, a turn in the bend could bring a new adventure of excitement to a hike. The John Muir Trail in the High Sierras furnished, at almost every turn, intoxicating views. They were spectacular gifts from nature. One such present occurred as Greyhound and I rounded a bend coming down from a mountain pass and stopped us in our tracks. The jagged Minaret Mountains laid before us with patches of snow covered fields resting on her sides. A second view reflected this breathtaking mountain view off the clear mirror lake waters of Thousand Island Lakes. This spot was a favorite of the black and white landscape photographer Ansel Adams and now became one of my favorites. The views were stunning at first.

The Minaret Mountains and the Thousand Island Lake – one of a few spots without the mushroom-like tents

Then, as I got closer and scanned the shoreline, I noticed assorted colored mushrooms popping up all over the place. Tents were everywhere, eye pollution interrupting my wilderness experience.

The next day another endowment of nature's magnificence was placed upon Greyhound and I. We had seen some unusual and unique natural features as we hiked (earth touch) the trails of Mother Nature, but the rock formation called Devil's Postpile caused me to think that some type of trickery or fabrication was used to create that oddity. Discovered by a group of explorers on an expedition from Yosemite Valley to Mt. Whitney in 1875, the Devil's Postpile was another display of Mother Nature's amazing work.

I am sure both native Americans and visitors since 1875, have scratched their heads and say, "What in the heck is going on here?" At first glance, you'd see tall, post piles of rock sitting next to each other in several rows. Then you'd think an enterprising individual played a trick on man by pouring concrete into forms, creating the post piles as an attraction. Or, as Greyhound speculated, they were fuel rods left there by the Ancient Ones for their flying space ships.

The post pile is actually lava that has cooled into unusual 60 foot tall columns of basalt. The flat tops reveal cross sections which are seven sided, grooved and smoothed by glacial activity eons ago. At the base of the pile a mound of broken pieces littered the ground. The Greeks and Romans could not have created a more perfect column.

The Devil's Postpile.

Approximately a mile from the Devil's Postpile we walked into Reds Meadow, a famous stopping point for thru hikers on the PCT. Reds is a rustic resort with cabins, campground, store, small cafe and an animal pack station tucked into the mountains of the High Sierras. As we were walking into the resort, the last bus was leaving for the ski resort of Mammoth Lakes. Timing is everything, so instead of re-supplying at Reds Meadow we hopped on the bus and found our way into the town of Mammoth Lakes.

Tucked into the High Sierra Mountains, Mammoth Lakes is a great community that has everything there is to meet the needs of skiers, mountain bikers, backpackers and all lovers of Mother Nature. This was the last reliable trail town/re-supply point until we came back down from the summit of Mt. Whitney. Re-supply can be made at two other locations, Vermilion Valley Resort and Muir Trail Ranch, but at the time were not reliable. Greyhound and I decided during the logistic stage of our planning and based on our daily mileage, that we were better off carrying our food, instead of depending on food availability and mail drops - food mailed in advance to a location by the hiker.

The next section was going to be a true test of our abilities of surviving whatever the backcountry had in store for us. This stretch of trail, 130 miles, was the longest stretch into the wilderness without a decent re-supply or contact with the outside world. The main problem we faced was putting eight days of trail food into a bear canister no bigger than a three gallon bucket. There was little room for error on food amounts and caloric intake. If we ran out of food, unlike in the civilized world, we couldn't just hop in a vehicle and walk, or drive around the corner to the nearest neighborhood convenient store. Our nearest food would have been days away.

Up for the challenge, Greyhound and I left Mammoth Lakes with a healthy re-supply of food and rode the early morning bus back to Reds Meadows. At the small café we ate breakfast, our last town food for the next week. We walked around the grounds for awhile then heard the call of the trail. We walked through the horse and mule pack station of Reds, into the burn area from a fire in 1992 and into the mountains once again.

The terrain going out of Reds was very similar to the terrain going in, mounds of off-white sand with tiny pebbles, leftovers from the grinding glacier movement on the granite mountains. Tall Pine and Fir trees fought for survival in the porous sand containing very little other organic matter. The landscape changed several times a day, each change having to do with the type of glacier deposits. First, it was the sand. Next, little by little, round rocks and boulders began to appear scattered among the trees. Then, the remains of ancient volcanic cones could be seen sticking out of the sand, with volcanic rocks scattered throughout the white sand and trees. You could look across the valley to the other mountains and see the forest sticking out of a background of white. It really looked like a winter mountain scene without the cold temperatures.

We went over a pass and 'BAM', found a completely different terrain consisting of piles (more like small mountains) of (almost) smooth granite rocks that were surrounded by the sand that was covering the mountainside. After that there was a combination of all the different landscapes that we had hiked through since Reds, thrown about recklessly without rhyme or reason. We spent a good part of the day hiking in this random world of sand, rock, boulder and volcanic leftovers.

We went up and over Silver Pass and the scenery before us changed into a completely different picture once again. Below us was a green valley with a small stream flowing through. The waters of a lake to our right reflected mountains with the golden light of morning. I could picture a Native American village down below utilizing the resources at hand, always respecting, harmonizing and in balance with Mother Nature and her creatures.

Greyhound and I knew from reading the guidebook that we were going to miss the morning ferry to Vermilion Valley Resort (VVR). Instead of waiting around for the afternoon ferry we decided to hike the 6 miles to VVR on the Mono Creek Trail. Like Reds

Meadow, VVR is a rustic resort where people stay in white cabin tents, or in their own tent at the campground. The resort also had a pack station to take people on horseback into the mountains. There was a store, a small cafe with excellent food and folks at the resort who were especially friendly to JMT hikers. VVR is located on Lake Edison, which was very low due to drought conditions. I saw a sign above the counter that said, "If you don't like the level of the lake then stop watering your lawn."

Greyhound told me the hamburgers at the small café were legendary to the PCT hikers passing through. So in true hiker hunger fashion, we both devoured our massive hamburger and fries. The meal was complete with refill, after refill, of ice cold coke.

We left the resort on what they called a ferry, which was actually a 20 ft inboard V-hull boat that sped us to the floating dock at the other end of the lake. On the water, we could see the skies turn a dark blue/grey over the mountain. They opened up thirty minutes after we got off the ferry, with the clouds bumping one another enough to make some thunder. We had our first moderate rain since the trip began. It lasted only briefly and the plants showed their appreciation by giving off fresh earthy fragrances.

There were days on this *Summer Hike in the High Sierras* that our world was dominated by water. Greyhound and I were in such a day on the East Fork of Bear Creek, which was flowing down into the valley on our right. The water was a joy to watch cascading, swirling in pools and sliding down granite slabs. Our "Morning Cafe" was chosen on a slab of granite heated by the sun, overlooking the trail crossing of Bear Creek. A deer walked across the creek, up to where we were seated, then wandered towards the grass behind us. She never flinched when she looked our way or spooked when we moved. It was as if the deer trusted us and allowed us to be a part of her world.

The trail continued to climb as we headed for Selden Pass, elevation 10,900 ft. At the foot of the pass was a clear lake with several boulder islands breaking the water's surface. There were so many lakes there in the mountains, each one had its own personality with different features and color of water. We crossed over a pass and out came the Muirvision remote. The terrain drastically changed again. Below us, a mountain stream was running into a lake that was shaped like a heart, Heart Lake. At the bottom of the heart, the lake's outlet fell to lower elevations, feeding a stream that emptied into twin lakes called Sally Keyes Lakes. Lying side by side, the two lakes were divided by a narrow rocky strip of land covered in trees.

Greyhound and I began a long, dusty drop on switchbacks into a river canyon until we hit the trail junction for Muir Trail Ranch (MTR), another type of rustic resort truly out in the wilderness. We met several other hikers at the ranch picking through several 5 gallon buckets of abandoned hiker food. The ranch required that if a hiker sent a mail drop to themselves it had to be in a 5 gallon bucket. Many hikers, for whatever reason, did not pick up their mail drop, thus leaving a dry food buffet for those that did make it to the ranch. Greyhound and I joined in the food frenzy and found hearty meals and candy for dessert. In record time my stove was out of the backpack and lit. The food feast was on. The 83-year old caretaker, Pat was a riot to converse with and was hiker friendly. There was no cafe and only a very small store. The bathrooms were for the paying guests and off limits to the hikers. "Giggles" an AT thru hiker in 2003 explained how the resort's main business and allegiance was to its paying customers. The folks at MTR also wanted to maintain an area for the thru hikers. I found the folks there friendly, polite to the hikers as well as their customers. The hikers that came in demanding, without knowing the full details of how the ranch operates, deserved the treatment they got. I waddled out of MTR on a full stomach including some great spring water. I will always have fond memories of the ranch. I decided against using the hot springs nearby because it was too warm outside and way too many hikers had been there already soaking off their hiker funk.

Crossing the South Fork of San Joaquin River we entered the Sequoia Kings Canyon National Park and left behind the John Muir

Wilderness. The trail followed alongside the river with crystal clear water as it rolled and tumbled down cascades, ledges and huge rock slides through the canyon. The energy and sound of the water's flow was very impressive, especially since water levels were low at that time of year. I could only imagine what the sight and sounds were like when the water flowed, or should I say, barreled through at the height of the spring snowmelt.

Greyhound and I crossed the river canyon on a wooden bridge and camped for the night on the South Fork of the San Joaquin River. Sound asleep, my dream world was interrupted by the far distant sound of what I thought was boat bells ringing. In that place in between sleep and being conscious I asked myself, "Have I been out here too long? "Am I dreaming, or... No!" This time I heard the bell again and I knew I was awake. Then, I heard the distinct sound of shoed horse hoofs hitting rock next to my tent. I carefully unzipped my tarp tent and with adrenaline flooding my blood stream, poked my head out to meet the unknown creature. I looked straight ahead, about knee-level and was staring at the boney legs of a horse. Behind it were two other horses grazing next to my tent. All I could hope for was they thought my tarp tent was a boulder, thus avoiding a horseshoe imprint tattooed on my body. The lead horse (with the bell around its neck) guided the other two horses past my tent and then roamed past Greyhound's tent, disappearing in the darkness. As I drifted back into sleep I could hear the hoofs crossing over the wooden bridge to bother the other campers. Greyhound told me the next morning he thought for sure that he would wake up to find my tent trampled and shredded.

The last four days had started the real push into the mountains. The hiking we had been doing thus far was a training ground to acclimate my body to the altitudes of the high passes and the grand finale climb on Mt. Whitney. Greyhound and I, from this point forward, had to carefully plan our daily hiking schedule according to the high passes. Dangerous and unpredictable wind, rain, hail and lightning storms could occur on exposed ridges at 10,000 feet or higher anytime in the afternoon. Therefore, it was best to cross these passes in the morning when weather patterns are the most favorable.

Greyhound and I began our climb to the first major pass - Muir Pass, elevation 11,995 feet. We were hiking on switchbacks next to the roaring Evolution Creek. The creek, at that point, was flowing down a narrow mountain gorge creating waterfalls and large pools with deafening sound. The first test for the day was fording Evolution Creek above the gorge, at times a very dangerous crossing. On that day the water was low. I crossed the creek on a log using Greyhound as support as he walked along in the water. I stepped off onto a sandbar, then onto another log before jumping off, and safely landing on the far bank, dry.

We continued to follow the creek up the mountain until we were above tree line and found Evolution Lake. Huge, jagged 13,000 foot granite mountains surrounded us. Greyhound and I continued to climb and found more lakes with the deepest shades of blue. We walked in talus (rock rubble) fields of rock above the lakes, slowly hiking upward. I took my time so I didn't burst a lung, or cause my heart to explode out of my chest.

Finally, we reached the pass to find Muir Hut a structure built of stone in 1930 to protect hikers from exposure in extreme weather.

The trail's rocky descent south of Muir Pass involved more switchbacks down steep mountain walls. The Muirvision remote once again clicked and as we turned a corner on a switchback we viewed a mountain of black (metamorphic) rock that was devoid vegetation.

The next hurdle to get up and over was Mather Pass. The climb was steady until we hit a section of exposed switchbacks called the "Golden Staircase." This section was a 1,500 ft climb built into the side of a mountain. The trail leveled off around Lower and Upper Palisades Lakes with outstanding views of the mountain peaks surrounding the lakes. Another series of switchbacks over large talus began the final push up to the pass. Looking over my shoulders as I climbed, the first indication of wispy clouds breaking the blue skies could be seen over Muir Pass.

Krispykritter and Greyhound at Muir Hut

Greyhound approached me half way up and stated he did not like the way the clouds were building. I concurred. I was in the lead when I met two hikers who just came over Mather Pass. We talked about the clouds building and in the conversation they relayed a story from several hikers they passed who told them they encountered hail and lightning going over Mather. That was all the incentive I needed. In KrispyKritter record time, I made it to the notch of Mather Pass, elevation 12,100 ft, avoiding the lightning. The clouds swept over like an overcast winter's day and passed without incident.

On top of Mather's, Greyhound and I took the Muirvision remote, clicked it, and then looked south into Upper Basin. It looked like a plateau of sand, boulders and small lakes with a sandy white ribbon (the trail) running through it. It was mid afternoon by the time we descended into Upper Basin, and time to relieve my "Mid-day Meltdown" with a dunk in South Fork Kings River. Afterward, I laid on a granite slab next to the water in the semi-arid air. Within minutes I was completely dried and refreshed.

Greyhound and I were making great time as we descended from Mather Pass. At the speed we were traveling, we would reach Pinchot Pass in the early afternoon. Greyhound asked me, during our descent, how I felt about going over the pass if the weather held out. Already in sensory overload from the Muirvision of Upper Basin, I wanted more, and told him I would seriously consider it. The cloudy weather over Mather Pass disappeared and the afternoon developed into a beautiful sunny day. When decision time came at the bottom of Pinchot Pass it was clear to me I didn't want to waste hours of perfect daylight, sitting around camp thinking where we could have been if we had continued. So I said what they say at NASA, "All systems go!" We climbed over the orange colored rocks of Pinchot Pass, elevation 12,130 ft. (Note: This was the first time I made two passes in one day and didn't get slapped for it.)

Descending from Pinchot on switchbacks through talus, rocky outcroppings and sand the blending colors of the landscape and sky were exceptionally beautiful. The setting sun blazed stunning shades of orange on the clouds against the greens and blues of the western sky. At the same time the oranges and reds of the rock complimented the sky. I had never walked through a land whose hues matched the sky and I was in awe by the beauty surrounding me. We walked that night until the sun settled below the mountains and cowboy camped on a small plateau under pine trees at 11,420 ft. The stars came out with brilliant twinkles, satellites zipped by and meteorites streaked across the sky in a blaze of white.

I woke up during the night with a charlie horse in the muscles of my lower back. No matter what position I tried to get into, the pain would not go away. In fact, it was getting so bad it was affecting my breathing and I couldn't take a deep breath. I sat up clutching my sleeping bag around my chest to stay warm. Greyhound woke up because of my commotion and asked, "Are you OK?" I replied in a labored breath, "No." Not the answer he wanted to hear, Greyhound raised his head up and in the dim light saw me holding my chest. He told me later he immediately thought I was having a heart attack. His mind went into immediate first aid mode with thoughts of how screwed I was since this was the furthest point from the real world at any time in the entire hike. In another flash of thought he wondered how he was going to explain all this to Lady Kritter. Greyhound asked, "What's wrong?" as he started getting out of his sleeping bag. "I have a muscle spasm in my back", I replied. All noise in Greyhound's tent stopped. He told me, as he calmly laid back down, to lie down on my back and pull my knees into my chest. The stretch would loosen the muscles and the pain would go away. I did exactly what Greyhound said and within minutes the pain went away.

The next morning, as we were going through the "Leave No Trace" protocol while breaking camp, we talked and laughed about the faux heart attack. Suddenly, I stopped whatever it was I was doing and had a shiver run through my body as I realized how glad I was that it was not an actual heart attack.

Greyhound and I entered into the canyon of Woods Creek where we found our next "Morning Cafe" while sitting on a slab of granite large enough for two in the sunlight. Running alongside the trail and across from us, we watched the water's of Woods Creek slide and dance down granite slabs. Our entree' for the morning meal was oatmeal for me and PopTarts for Greyhound. We arrived shortly after breakfast to a narrow and bouncy suspension bridge that crossed Woods Creek, called by some "The Golden Gate of the Sierras."

Greyhound and I came to a series of beautiful mountain lakes just below Glen Pass, consisting of the Lower, Middle and Upper Rae Lakes, a very popular camping area. To overcome my "Mid-day Meltdown", Greyhound and I stopped on the isthmus between the Middle and Upper Rae Lakes to have lunch and cool off in the crystal clear water. After playtime was over, we climbed up switchbacks taking us to Glen Pass, elevation 11,978 ft. The south side of Glen Pass was a steep walled cirque containing switchbacks descending into a plateau of rocks and sand. The trail entered the tree line and continued on a long and uneventful journey towards Forester Pass.

The timing and location of our camps the previous days had been crucial for an early ascent over the higher passes and to coordinate our last day on top of Mt. Whitney, the southern terminus of the JMT. Greyhound and I were ahead of schedule and averaging 20+ miles a day. The good weather stayed with us and we decided to use it to our advantage. Greyhound figured out that if we camped at the highest possible elevation below Forrester Pass, this would afford us the opportunity for an early passage over the pass, and more importantly, we would be very close to Mt. Whitney in the evening. Greyhound in fact came up with two possible scenarios, each depending on how many miles we traveled. The first scenario would have us camp at Guitar Lake and leave at 2:00 a.m. for a night hike up Mt. Whitney for an early morning summit. The second scenario would have us go beyond Guitar Lake, hike up the north side of Mt. Whitney, and spend the night near Trail Crest, elevation 13,650 feet. In this scenario we would still leave at 2 am, but would be at the summit for the sunrise. To tell you the truth, I was a little apprehensive on spending a night close to 14,000 ft. When I explained this to Greyhound he asked if I had any trouble breathing during the hike. "No", I said. "Then the problem is?" he said. "Good point! Then we have a plan." I replied.

I noticed as another hike was ending how Mother Nature was slowly putting her creatures to sleep. The vibrant petal colors of the wildflowers were gone. Seed heads were dispersing their seeds for the next generation to continue their colorful display. Mosquitoes were still around, but seemed to be out of energy. They would land on us and try sticking us, but were so weak that nothing happened. Chipmunks and picas were running around talus and rock formations with vegetation in their mouth to store for winter food. The days got shorter and lake water levels low in preparation for next spring's snow run off. These were subtle changes and I was sure as the summer came to a close and fall approached, the activities quickened in preparation for winter.

People would ask Greyhound and I, throughout our journey, how far are we going for the day. The answer was hard to give because we do not measure the day by distance, or increments of time from a clock. We measured the time and energy we had from sun-up to sun-down. We have a saying between us that is a simple answer to the question. "We wake up and start hiking with the sun and when the sun goes to bed so do we." On many occasions, we would find a piece of Mother Earth to either cowboy camp or set up our tents as the last rays of sunlight vanished. Time and distance are not important features in my hike. What is important is my rhythm with nature. Weather and nature's topography dictates how far I go each day. Greyhound and I both like the schedule from sun-up to sundown for several reasons. One, I can hike for longer periods in the coolness of the morning and late afternoon. Second, the prime time to watch Mother Earth's creatures foraging for food and water is in the early morning/late afternoon.. And third, I can escape the heat of day by having lunch somewhere in shade, near water, or in the cool mountain breeze of an overlook.

Greyhound and I decided to get as close to Forester Pass as we could for an early ascent. Climbing in elevation towards Forester Pass we passed hikers already tenting on sandy, pine-covered knobs along Bubbs Creek. There was still several hours of daylight left so in Greyhound/KrispyKritter fashion we leisurely continued on. Talus fields became more abundant and alpine meadows plentiful. The tree line was far below us, and as the sun was setting, we found camp on a small leveled bench in a stony, 12,000 something ft, cirque.

During the second week of the hike, I found myself deep in thought, and came up with the idea of finding a how many different ways I could say goodnight to Lady Kritter each night as I signed off in my journal. It became a challenge towards the end of the hike, to find unique and humorous ways to sign off. I wrote for example on the night on Wolf Creek Lake as the cold wind was howling outside my tent, "I settled in for the night higher than most folks in the lower 48, then, turned to the southeast and over the wind I too was howling, "Good Night Lady Kritter." I remembered another sign off occurred on the climb up the base of Forester Pass. I wrote, "A pika, sort of like a rabbit with Mickey Mouse ears, jetted out of the rocks carrying a small purple flower in its mouth. Suddenly he saw me and stopped at my feet. My first reaction was 'how cute, he's bringing a flower to his lady friend'. The pika then dropped the flower and looked up at me and began to squeak. The animal looked down at the flower, back at me and squeaked again. I nodded and said, "OK, I will." The mouse picked up the flower and scurried back into its hole. What was the pika saying to me? I'm pretty sure he told me, "Say goodnight to Lady Kritter." And so I did, "GOOD NIGHT, LADY KRITTER."

Excited about the potential of sleeping on Mt. Whitney, Greyhound and I were up before dawn, and on trail before first light. My trail legs were now strong and Forester Pass was quickly within my sights. The first thing to hit me on top of Forester Pass was the window and steep chute of talus looking south. And then, the incredible views from Forester Pass. At 13,100 feet the pass was the highest elevation on the PCT (not so for the JMT). We both agreed this had to be a "Morning Cafe" moment. Seating arrangements were very small so we sat right on the trail, and while eating our Pop-Tarts looked south and gazed below at the undulating tundra-like landscape. We could see below, closer to the pass, the ribbon of trail built on top of rock walls consisting of exposed switchbacks. The steepness of this side of the pass was incredible. I was sure dynamite had a part in building this part of the JMT. Mother Earth was naked, barren and incredibly beautiful. This entire sensory overload was less than an hour from breaking camp. However, we still had 20+ miles to go to before reaching reach Mt. Whitney.

The Muirvision remote constantly changed the landscape during that day towards Mt. Whitney. The trail, after descending from Forester Pass, wandered down a broad valley for many miles. The sandy valley floor was littered with boulders and contained numerous mountain lakes with a rocky shorelines. Click, we entered back into tree line and came to Tyndall Creek. Greyhound was bubbling with excitement as he re-lived the night he spent here on his PCT thru hike. The creek's water was refreshing and made a good spot for a break. Click, we entered an area called Tawny Point and walked along a sandy landscape covered with gnarly pine trees. The trees' bark was a canvas of twisted and knotty wood with brilliant colors of light and dark browns. Click, we came out of the forest and entered onto Bighorn Plateau, a landscape devoid of vegetation, barren and sandy, with panoramic views of the Great Western Divide mountain range.

I looked around me and I just knew that the weather in this area made it a harsh environment to live in. It was also on Bighorn Plateau that we saw our first official look at Mt. Whitney.

Krispykritter on the Bighorn Plateau

Click, Greyhound and I continued on the trail and wandered up and down the mountains, going in and out of forests and crossing streams. We came to a trail intersection that separated the JMT from the PCT. The JMT headed east towards Crabtree Ranger Station and the PCT continued south towards the Mexican border. We of course stayed on the JMT and at a box near the campsites of Crabtree Meadows, picked up our green human waste bags that hikers must use in "The Whitney Zone".

"The Whitney Zone" extends east from Crabtree Meadows, includes all of Mt. Whitney, continues down the eastern slope of the mountain into Trail Camp, Outpost Camp, and officially ends at Whitney Portal, where the waste bags are deposited in special containers. "The Whitney Zone" is a fragile ecosystem and its popularity/overuse has had an adverse effect to the alpine environment. All primitive toilets have been removed due to the fact human waste was not decomposing fast enough, resulting in the use of human waste bags.

Greyhound and I, on and off the trails, share a common bond for our reverence of Mother Nature. We have shared many magical moments together as we walked the footpaths of this planet. There are times we individually walk alone and are blessed with an entertaining moment, made only for that person, and for the most part is kept to ourselves. Greyhound decided to share with me one particular moment he had in "The Whitney Zone" because it lasted throughout the day and was hilarious. We call this moment "Shit-in-a-Bag." Even today we still break out in solid laughter when we talk about this event.

We were in "The Whitney Zone", climbing up endless switchbacks of increasingly barren talus towards Mt. Whitney. The day was ending in a magnificent sunset over rugged peaks and created reflections of sparkling fire colors on the mountain lakes below. We found in the twilight near the trail junction called Trail Crest, a small piece of flat land consisting of sand surrounded by a rock wall jetting out into the void just below the summit at 13,500 feet. Constructed by unknown hikers over the years, the wall was built by hand as a barrier against the fierce mountain winds. We decided to set up camp, cowboy style (sleeping under the stars without tents) so we could be up at 4:00 am for an early ascent to the summit.

The alarms rang out at 3:45 am and I woke up under a brilliant twinkling night sky. We broke camp and left behind the gear we were not going to use for the climb. 'Nature called' during this time and Greyhound took time out to take a poop. At first this was a good thing for him since he was irregular and had skipped yesterday's deposit. Off he went, disappearing into the night carrying his human waste bag.

To understand the humor of this comical moment you have to understand Greyhound's style of hiking. He is a very proficient ultralight hiker. A minimalist backpacker with a base weight (minus food and water) of less than 7 pounds. So when he returned carrying a steamy bag of shit the size of a loaf a bread that, according to him, weighed "at least 4 pounds," Greyhound was amazed how much two days of shit weighed. It then dawned on him he had to carry this bag of human waste down the mountain for most of the day.

We climbed Mt. Whitney and were greeted by the sunrise on the summit. (More about the summit later).

After our time at the top, we made our way back to the campsite, picked up our gear and Greyhound's bag of poop. As he picked up his kit to put on his shoulders I thought I could see a slight grimace on Greyhound's face and said, "What's the matter, too much shit?" I didn't let him off easy and the jokes then started. "Hey Greyhound why are you slowing down, carrying too much shit?" or knowing the bag is sitting on top of his gear inside the backpack and the rays of the sun microwaving the bag's contents I would turn to Greyhound and ask "Is it stew yet?" Throughout the day he would state how the weight was affecting his hiking style and couldn't believe how much two days of poop weighed.

Part two of the story ends at Whitney Portal and if you want to know what happened, you must continue reading.

Crabtree Meadow is the beginning ascent up Mt. Whitney to the south boundary on the JMT. Greyhound and I took a break in the shade of the trees and while snacking reminisced on the highlights thus far of our High Sierra adventure. Greyhound kept saying over and over "Was I wrong, didn't I tell you!" referring to the beauty of the JMT. He wasn't wrong. However, we still had a mountain to climb. Greyhound got serious and wanted to make sure I was ready mentally and physically for the next day's challenge. He kept firing positive energy towards me, building my confidence with phrases like, "This is what we worked for since setting foot on the trail, building our trail legs and getting our lungs use to the altitude." or "When we summit Mt. Whitney we will be the highest people in the lower 48 states." I appreciated his outlook, and I was ready to go even before we talked. I only had one thing to face...being on a sheer wall of rock without safety gear.

Greyhound and I left Crabtree Meadows and initiated our ascent. We hiked past Timberline Lake (11,070 ft.), crossed an alpine meadow and continued towards Guitar Lake. We reached Guitar Lake with plenty of daylight left, if we decided to push higher. I was really hungry at this point and wanted to eat supper first, and then make a decision on whether to go forward or not. Greyhound and I finished our meals and with a good rest still had at least two hours of daylight left. I hesitated in my decision to go forward, because I was now face to face with my fear. The mind game one plays can be very detrimental to one's health. I couldn't go back, which meant I had to climb sooner or later. "Hell, let's get it over with," I thought and said to Greyhound, "Let's go for it!" Greyhound and I slung our backpacks and started walking. We passed several hikers camped along the lake. The looks we got as we walked by and waved still makes Greyhound and I laugh when we talk about it. They could not believe hikers would start at such a late hour to go up the mountain. We climbed up boulder slopes and reached a small bench at around 12,000 ft. We would periodically look back down the mountain and still see the small stick figured hikers looking up to see if we were still moving, and more importantly, to see where they would be going in the morning. The views were fantastic and the climb steeper as we gained altitude in the golden glow just before dusk. I did let my mind get the best of me when I started not liking the steepness and the vastness of the void at my back. Greyhound, however, kept me occupied by talking to me as we climbed switchback after switchback. Before I knew it, we were just below the Mt. Whitney Trail Junction (13,560 ft.) and to my surprise found a sandy campsite, empty. A wall of loose rocks approximately 2 ½ feet high was constructed to block the blustery high mountain winds. Overlooking the rock wall, I could see below the outline of several lakes including Guitar Lake (sure enough, Guitar Lake does look like a guitar). The sky had an orangery glow from the setting sun. Greyhound and I cowboy camped under the blackest blanket of sky I'd yet seen, punctuated by the most fantastic display of bright stars and Milky Way I had ever witnessed.

I had one of the most peaceful night's sleeps I could remember. I woke up repeatedly in the middle of the night and star gazed until I fell back to sleep. I was already awake, star gazing when I heard Greyhound's alarm go off. Greyhound and I wanted to be on trail by 4:00 a.m. so we could be on the summit for the morning sunrise. We left the majority of our gear at our mini base camp and took only essential survival gear.

The morning was clear, crisp and cold. We were preparing our kits when a group of five hikers came up the trail from Guitar Lake. The piercing beams from their headlamps made them look like one eyed cyclops aliens piercing the darkness to and fro. We talked briefly when they passed our campsite. They started below at 1:00 a.m. and also wanted to be at the top for sunrise. The five lights went ahead of us and were five faint twinkles of light showing us the trail we were about to follow. We passed several notches and windows and gazed into openings of darkness. We passed several needles and spirals of rock pointing skyward. The trail slowly leveled off to a rock slab plateau and then came to a stone building with a metal roof. Greyhound and I passed the hut and reached the summit designated by the largest boulder on the plateau. We hopped on top of the boulder and with arms outstretched and legs far apart at 14,505 ft Greyhound turned his head towards me and said, "Do you realized we are overlooking the population of the lower 48 states as it sleeps."

I instantly had a daymare that we were lords protecting the people as they slept. Then I thought, "Would they actually be sleeping if they knew Krispykritter and Greyhound were their guardians?" Greyhound's voice interrupted my thought. He told me to crouch down. I looked at him, puzzled and he said again, "Crouch down." I brought my hands down and crouched. Greyhound stayed standing and yelled, "NOW I AM THE HIGHEST PERSON IN THE LOWER 48 STATES!" Then he told me, "Stand up." I looked at him as I stood up, and as I went up, he crouched down and yelled, "NOW YOU ARE THE HIGHEST PERSON IN THE LOWER 48 STATES. How does that feel?" Then we took turns going up and down like merry-go-round horses. We were laughing so hard.

Our morning wasn't over. Greyhound and I walked to the furthest point east on the plateau and watched, with the other five hikers, the orange-red ball break the horizon and wake up the earth for a new day.

Greyhound and Krispykritter on top of Mt. Whitney

The morning light brought with it unbelievable panoramic views of mountain peaks, valleys and ridges as far as the eye could see. We signed the registry at the hut and were about to leave when one, then two, and then two more men came up and over the boulders in front of us wearing mountaineering gear and rope. The guys told us they took the mountain climbing route to get there. "No thanks," I thought, "Not for me! I'll stick to the trails."

The hike back to our mini base camp was a completely different perspective then coming up. The dark windows and chutes were lit up by the sun and had an empty depth to them with very deep sides. One side of the trail was the rock of the mountain and straight out the other side blue sky and a long way down. We broke our mini-camp and I was kicking myself for having let my fear take over. The thrill of being on top of the world, with the beauty of the world waking up, was extraordinary.

We reached Trail Crest and started our descent on the eastern side of Mt. Whitney. We started passing hikers, who camped at Trail Camp on the other side of the mountain for an early ascent. The hike down the mountain was 11 miles to Whitney Portal. The trail continued after Trail Crest as a series of switchbacks going down (99 of them, in fact). We passed more hikers coming up from Whitney Portal as the morning continued. The descent was brutal on the knees, constantly going down, through canyons and narrow valleys. Finally, we reached Whitney Portal.

The end of the funny story, "Shit in a Bag", occurred as we entered Whitney Portal. No, Greyhound didn't break the bag in his pack, but at the sight of the first restroom he made a mad dash for it to unload his waste bag. It reminded me of someone who actually needed to go and was running for the door before an accident happened. Exhausted from his run, Greyhound and I sat down at the cafe and inhaled the most beautiful hamburger we'd ever seen.

The John Muir Trail is probably one of the finest mountain scenery trails in the United States. The northern terminus is located in Yosemite Valley at the base of Glacier Point in Happy Isles.

Mt. Whitney from Whitney Portal

The trail's southern terminus is 220 miles away on Mt. Whitney with an 11 mile hike to Whitney Portal. Greyhound and I walked through Yosemite, Kings Canyon and Sequoia National Parks, Ansel Adams Wilderness, and the Sierra and Inyo National Forests. Most of the trail was above 9,000 ft. On it, we climbed across 9 major passes above 10,000 feet, walked along towering granite cliffs, into canyons 5,000 ft deep, passed thousands of sparkling alpine lakes, epic waterfalls and mountain meadows emitting sweet fragrances chemical companies wish they could produce, and went up and over and alongside mountain peaks of 13,000 to 14,000 ft. In my opinion the John Muir Trail is another long distance trail that should be on the top ten trails to-do list for a long distance hiker.

Men of the mountains – Krispykritter, John Muir and Greyhound

CHAPTER 9
Magical Moments

Every time I've gone into the wonderment of nature, I have been gifted with an awe-inspiring moment that - at the end of the day - puts a smile on my face. I call these events Magical Moments. I describe magical moments as mysterious, brief periods of time that produce unaccountable or baffling effects or, quite simply, enchant me: flowers in bloom, panoramic views of mountains disappearing to the horizon, sunsets splashing magnificent colors across the sky, encounters with wild animals, crystal clear mountain streams cascading over rocks on its way to the ocean, majestic tree limbs denude of autumn leaves reaching up into the vastness of a deep blue sky. As quickly as these moments appear, they're gone. And you're left breathless, weak in the knees and wondering what in the hell just happened. It is an experience that only you can fathom, because you are there, in the "Now", experiencing that moment. Later, if you try to explain your incredible episode to others, they'll likely be able to understand the energy you felt or the euphoric feeling you had. And the only thing you have to say is, "You had to be there! It was awesome!" And, for you it was, and still is.

One of the reasons I travel in the wilderness is to experience these moments of enchantment, to be given this gift that only myself, or those around me will appreciate. And when that extraordinary magical moment appears, OH MY GOD! It is amazing.

One such extraordinary magical moment happened to Greyhound and I in England on the Pennine Way. In fact, we were blessed with two extraordinary magical moments. The first one occurred on a 2,349 ft major hill massif called Great Shunner Fell. Well rested and re-supplied, Greyhound and I left at sunrise and walked along the deserted cobbled streets of the busy market village, Hawes. The majority of our early British mornings consisted of gray clouds heavy with moisture that would take until early afternoon to burn off. The morning we left Hawes was no exception. After leaving the Victorian stone buildings of the village, we did a steady 5 mile climb up to Great Shunner Fell in strong wind, which had been our constant companion since we started in Edale. The closer we got to the summit the more vividly we saw dark clouds that looked like they were going to unleash their fury on us at any moment. Just before reaching the summit of Shunner Fell, the temperature dropped and we were covered in a heavy fog with a light drizzle. Hiking on top of the slick stone slabs encased in peat was an accidental slip waiting to happen.

We took refuge at the summit shelter - built of stone in the shape of a plus sign (+) with no roof. Whatever side had the least wind was the protected side, and that was the side we had chosen for breakfast. When Greyhound sat his kit down he noticed a light frost on its back. We ate our solid, refrigerated cold candy bars in silence as the wind whistled over the stone wall. The cold, damp wind was stealing our body-heat generated on the hike up. As if Greyhound and I had communicated by thought, without saying a word, we each secured our kits, placed them on our backs and continued our journey in order to stay warm. That's when the magic happened.

Greyhound and I were less than a quarter of mile from the summit, working our way down in the heavy fog. Suddenly, clear as day, a hole opened up in the thick fog bank, revealing ahead of us, the deep peat beds, the tussocky grass and the slabs of stone used to mark the way. We stopped in our tracks to watch the shroud of dancing clouds encircle us. I looked up, poked Greyhound to get his attention, and pointed up so he too could see the churning clouds directly overhead. Abruptly, the hole began to move away from us. I had the sensation of being in a car rapidly traveling forward through fog and looking out the back window watching the swirls of aerodynamic white threads of cotton clouds twirling by. It felt like we were being sucked into this hole. Then suddenly, the hole grew bigger, the sun came out and below us was this green (and I mean green!) patches of pasture land separated by stone walls. The scene contained multiple shades of green and resembled a large hand-made rectangular quilt.

Greyhound and I stood there not saying a word, mystified. Time stood still for us and we remained motionless with mouths wide open. For how long? I couldn't tell you. Finally, Greyhound said to me, "Dude did you see that?" I was about to ask him the same question. We were using incomplete sentences as a form of expression. "What the hell just...", "I am sooooo stoked that...."

Greyhound overlooking the village of Thwaite

Greyhound summed it up best when he exuberantly raised his arm, forcefully pointed in the direction of the valley and yelled, "That's why I go hiking!" Once again, Greyhound had verbalized what I had been thinking. The mist, like a force field, never surrounded us again as we descended from the fell. The heather seemed crisper in color, a brighter purple. Everything was alive, we even felt more alive, and Greyhound and I kept stopping to look at the valley in amazement. An hour or two later, we were in that valley in a small hamlet called Thwaite. The enormous energy that Greyhound and I felt tingled our senses for several hours.

North of Thwaite, the Pennine Way began to look like the trails of home (in the United States) meandering through the wilds of nature. Again, we started climbing. This time we were hiking the west rim of a deep, narrow valley with the River Swale running along the bottom. We stopped to have lunch on a ledge overlooking the valley. I could see two waterfalls on the other side, echoing their cascading music as we ate. Greyhound and I, excitedly talked about what each of us felt, sometimes repeating ourselves, relating to our experience coming down Great Shunner Fell. The aroused energy faded after lunch, and with only memories to cherish, we walked into another hamlet, Keld.

The second extraordinary magical moment on the Pennine Way occurred three days later, after crossing Great Shunner Fell. Greyhound and I were walking along the River Tees in the Pennines of Northern England., The trail ran alongside the river north of Middleton-in-Teesdale through cliffs and trees on both shores. The further up-river we went, the wilder the river became with rapids and waterfalls. Finally, after ten days of purple heather moorlands and farms deep in animal poop, The Pennine Way was finally becoming the wild Mother Nature trail that Greyhound and I like to travel. The low roar of a waterfall could be heard and soon we came across a magnificent fall called, Low Force. We actually entered into a forest and were greeted with the sweet smell of pines and juniper. Then, from a distance, we heard the sound of another low roar, and as we

High Force Waterfall

approached, the sound became thunderous. At the height of this auditory sound of energy we followed a path that led to an open area and the top of this great waterfall dropping 70 feet in-between rock cliffs called High Force. Along with the moorlands, Greyhound and I were beginning to see the wild natural beauty of England

The energy level intensified as the day progressed. The Pennine Way entered into a farming valley and Greyhound and I followed the River Tees' ragged rock and boulder shoreline until we were at the foot of several large crags (cliffs). We looked up and saw other hikers above us scrambling over the rocks. The rocky trail climbed and we were greeted by a roaring multiple waterfall called Cauldron Snout that dropped over a rocky cataract. Tremendous volumes of water were cascading down several ledges giving a powerful demonstration of fluid motion. I got as close as safely possible in several locations to witness the sights and sounds of the raw dynamic energy of water.

Krispykritter standing in front of Cauldron Snout

Leaving Cauldron Snout behind we were back in the moors, but they were different, higher with more ruggedness. The trail, or lack thereof pushed through tall grass and mud following Maite Beck a small stream.

Greyhound and I found an awesome ravine cutting through the grass floor of the valley. We climbed into it and scrambled over rocks exploring all the nooks and crannies we could find. We finally climbed out and crossed a bridge. The footpath from the bridge continued rising into the rocky moorland. Dark, ominous clouds were building behind us into menacing deep purple rain clouds, accompanied with heavy winds trying to blow us off the tablelands. The temperature was quickly dropping. Suddenly, I stopped dead in my tracks and my breath was taken away. The land before me disappeared into this enormous abyss of a u-shaped valley.

It looked as if the land had suddenly collapsed to the center of the earth (This natural amphitheater was carved out by glacial ice and is named, High Cup Nick). Heavy rains began to pelt our rain gear as the clouds encircled us. The wind was howling. Greyhound stood on the edge of the cliff, facing out; his clothes rippling from the force of the wind. He raised his hands in ecstasy and greeted the intensity of Mother Nature with a yell. I saw his mouth open and move, but couldn't hear anything because of the howling wind. Greyhound turned to me and motioned me to come where he was standing. "No FRIGGIN' WAY! Are you nuts?" I said to myself. Not taking no for answer, Greyhound motioned for me to walk forward. Slowly, I inched my foot forward (like I was entering a minefield) until I was standing just behind and to the side of him. The view in front of me was spectacular with sheets of slanted rain falling to the valley floor below. Off to my right, on top of the mountain, some movement caught my eye. I stood, mystified, as I watched a herd of dark colored horses, silhouetted against the gray sky and running at a gallop along the ridge. Mud and grass flew from their hoofs, muscles ripped and glistening with sweat. Their manes flowing like flags in the wind. The cadence of the horses hooves quickened as each horse in order to gain more speed, stretched out its neck, slightly bobbing its head up and down.

I knew, because of the howling wind and large rain drops hitting my rain jacket hood, that I couldn't hear a thing. But I swear to this day, that I could hear their thunderous hooves striking the ground. In unison the herd followed the lead horse as they disappeared over the ridge.

Talk about an energy rush! From Mother Earth, Father Sky and the free flowing spirits of the animals - Greyhound and I had been baptized in raw energy.

We left when we felt the time was right, completely buzzing. I don't remember much of the wet and cold walk into Dufton. Greyhound walked ahead of me. Each of us was lost in thought about what we'd just experienced. At one point I was wondering if maybe I had walked into the filming of a television beer commercial. I will never forget those incredible moments at High Cup Nick and will end this story with WOW!

MAGIC ON THE APPALACHIAN TRAIL

During my first thru-hike on the Appalachian Trail, there were so many incredible magical moments that came across my path. I think living in nature for an extended period of time only enhanced the opportunities for such occurrences. For instance, I was serenaded at night near Bly Gap, Georgia by two coyotes howling somewhere up the dark mountain behind my tent. I had front row seats under a magnificent diamond studded sky, listening to Mother Nature giving a live duet in concert. Now that was entertainment!

Or, witnessing millions of baby frogs indiscriminately hopping along the trail in Virginia. The land was alive with tiny jumping frogs everywhere. The ground would erupt like popcorn as my boots hit the mud of the trail.

Or, having butterflies all around me in Virginia. I wrote in my journal dated March 23, 2004:

"The weirdest thing happened to me this morning. While walking along the path, little butterflies began to follow me, dancing in the air all around me, while others would fly in front of me, showing me the way. It brought back memories of 'New Age' posters I had seen of a beautiful goddess dressed in a flowing gown, flowers in her hair, walking with little fairies floating about. By now you are saying, "Save Krispy! He's been in the woods too long. Now he's seeing fairies." Yes, I have, and I will stick to my story of butterflies, but do butterflies have human faces and giggle in a high pitch?"

However, there are two magical moments that stand out in my mind of my Appalachian Trail 2004 thru-hike that will forever remind me what magical moments are all about.

The first one occurred just north of the Nantahala Outdoor Center early into my hike. The fourteenth night on the trail was a cold and wet night at Sassafras Shelter. I woke up that morning wishing Lady Kritter's hot flashes were next to me for warmth. The temperature was still dropping after the darkness of night turned into daylight. Out of the 15 hikers who stayed at the shelter I was the last to leave. I just could not get myself in gear. I was not happy with the way I packed the backpack, which in turn did not sit right on my back. I packed and re-packed my kit.

It was just one of those days nothing seemed to be going right. Mentally, I was fine; I was just having a down day and couldn't figure out why. I was determined to overcome this funk that was hanging over me like the gray clouds above. So, I sat myself down, had a heart to heart talk with myself and bombarded myself with positive attitude. Looking back at it now, I wish I was a squirrel in a tree looking down on this grown up man talking, gesturing and pacing up and down the shelter, talking with no one but himself. It had to be a bizarre sight indeed. Definitely, the first stages of trail insanity you would say. I picked up my kit, looked north and stepped back on the trail. I finally left the shelter late, at 9:40 in the morning - as the rain turned to sleet. Even on the trail I was not comfortable, something was holding me back, causing me to stop, readjust, start again, stop, and start, over and over again. I was feeling out of sync, out of rhythm.

Climbing up the mountain the sleet turned into small wet snowflakes. Within minutes a blanket of falling snow quickly covered the landscape in a white, wintery wonderland. The air was crisp and fresh. The only sound I could hear was my breathing, my heartbeat and the crunching sound of my boots as I walked on the snow. I found myself dancing and skipping in jubilation down the trail. When hiking, I often turn around to pick out landmarks in case I need to go back down the trail (the trail definitely looks different going the opposite way). I did this maneuver and saw the only set of footprints outlined in the snow leading up to my boots. I looked up and had snowflakes land softly on my lips. It made me think of my Lady Kritter's kisses, not cold kisses, but moist, soft, delicate and fresh kisses. People say, "things happen for a reason and sometimes you never know why." On this day I knew why I was being delayed, Mother Nature wanted me to have a private show, a symphony of snowflakes, KrispyKritter style. I was so happy, so moved, I walked the rest of the day in snowflakes. Cold and wet, I reached the next shelter for the night in sheer delight.

Footprints in the snow north of Sassafras Shelter

The second magical moment, one of my all time favorites, is actually two events that occurred within the same 24 hour period.

The first occurred during a rainstorm on top of the ridges of New Jersey's Kittatinny Mountain. The weather report for the day was not promising. NOAA reported widespread rain for the area with 1 to 2 inches of rain. I weather-proofed my pack and left the shelter at 6:30 a.m. Two miles into my hike a light rain started that quickly turned into a heavy downpour so thick that frogs and ducks were probably using umbrellas to protect themselves. A chilly wind accompanied the rain. Running water amidst the rocks and boulders became a new challenge in ridge walking along with the slick rocks. The rain continued and the views at High Point State Park were masked by rain clouds.

I was walking past a small flat section of mountain rock about thigh high late in the afternoon. Sometimes, I do things in the woods and I don't know why (as if I was guided by the Spirit-That-Moves-Through-All-Things). I suddenly stopped, looked at as rock formation and for no apparent reason, sat down in the pouring rain. My immediate impression was how comfortable I felt, like a seat in a movie theater. I looked up and across from me was a large rock formation protruding out of the ground and slightly higher than me. The top was flat and angled in my direction. Trees surrounded the outskirts of the formation almost like a backdrop. "Could I be looking at a stage?" I thought. I had this weird feeling I was going to be involved in some type of play and I was the audience. Sheets of low moving clouds of white fog rolled across the rock formation in front of me, from right to left, obscuring my view of the stage, similar to the opening and closing of a curtain. The stage was now set.

I had the sensation of being in a dream-like state with a clear view of the empty rock formation. Another fast moving sheet of fog completely obstructed the stage. Within seconds the fog lifted, and before me, on the stage, stood the most beautiful deer with a fawn by her side. The doe's body was large and muscular with a bright brown coat. The fawn, smaller in stature, was the same color with white spots on its back. Both mother and child were looking, no, staring at me. Our gazes were locked and though I couldn't tell you how, we communicated. The fawn nervously fidgeted and shifted its feet. Its muscles were tense as it was looking at me, then back at its mother, back at me, ready to take flight on its mother's command. The mother was steady, her body language calming the fawn. Minutes went by. A sheet of fog rolled in that enveloped both me and the stage, as if a white cotton sheet was pulled over my head. I couldn't see anything in front of me. Within seconds the fog cleared and so was the stage, empty of actors. I sat in the pouring rain stunned at what just happened. Just as quickly as the mother and fawn appeared, they disappeared. At that moment, all the pain and suffering of walking on boulders, the ridges and in the heavy downpours were washed away and cleansed by a natural high. I got up from my rock seat, thanked Mother Nature for the afternoon matinée that I entitled "A Mother's Love" and continued my northbound hike in a mild state of euphoria.

The next morning, I left the shelter in a light rain still refreshed from yesterday's matinée. Less than twenty minutes into the hike, another magical moment occurred in the form of a comedy I call, "A Comedy of Clowns." I was walking down the trail not far from the High Point Shelter when I saw movement to my left. Frozen in my footsteps I saw a turkey hen waddle across the trail with her head and neck bobbing forward in-between footsteps. It reminded me of a Charlie Chaplin walk. Immediately following the hen was a baby chick, then another, and another, all in unison doing the same Charlie Chaplin walk. I lost count of how many because I was laughing so hard at the mother and 6-8 chicks that followed. When the mother turkey turned in either direction, so did the chicks. I stood in the middle of the trail and watched this parade through the woods until the last chick's tail feathers disappeared down the hill. I was totally in a trance from the events of the last 12 hours. It may seem small, but to me, these things are the accents that give character to any trip into the wild. And as Greyhound says, "That's why I go hiking!"

MOMENTS THAT MAKE YOU LAUGH

I see things in nature that make me laugh; whimsical events that are like the "Comedy of Clowns." Some of the funniest moments materialize when you least expect it.

One of the many that occurred on my 2004 Appalachian Trail thru-hike was in the Susquehanna Valley, north of Boiling Springs, Pennsylvania. This portion of the Appalachian Trail is flat with high grass on either side. Out of nowhere, an adolescent skunk came out of the grass and was walking directly in front of me, heading down the trail. Its speed was slower than mine, so I had to slow down. At first, I tried to scare it off by making noise. The animal never broke its trot. I then tried to overtake the skunk. That didn't work either. Just as I started to invade its space the little critter arched its back and raised its tail. It's was as if I could almost hear it say, "That's close enough. This is a warning. The next time, spray will follow." He immediately had my attention. I knew who was in charge, so I backed off and both the skunk and I continued down the trail. We played this game for some time until it finally got tired of messing with me, turned and disappeared into the tall grass. I thought for sure that he was going to ambush me at the spot he disappeared in the grass. I ran past the ambush site as quickly as possible with a backpack on my back. If I would have listened hard enough, I probably could have heard giggles emitting from the grass.

I was hiking on the John Muir Trail, gazed into the woods and came to an abrupt stop frozen in fear. You can almost hear the howl in this magical moment. I then laughed at the joke Mother Nature played on me after regaining my normal heart rate and breath

On another occasion on the Appalachian Trail, I was walking through the forest in New York near Shenandoah Mountain when off to my right a fast moving object was cresting a small hill and heading directly towards me. I could see, as the animal closed in, that it was a yearling deer with faded spots, flying at a full gallop. I quickly looked around for the mother, who was nowhere in sight. I looked back at the deer and just as it was along side of me, the yearling turned its head in my direction without breaking its stride, looked at me for a second and I heard in my head, "Not now, KrispyKritter. I'm late for dinner and mom's going to be upset!" The yearling's muscles were taut - the body streamlined - as it turned its bobbing head forward with its gait like a thoroughbred horse. It disappeared down the hill and I stood in silence as I thought to myself, "Ahhhh, the wonders of nature."

One of the funniest stories actually happened involving an argument with a squirrel. When I told this to people later, some folks believed I was nuts for wanting to walk a continuous 2100 mile trek in the first place, and others thought it was a good idea - but that I had been in the mountains far too long. The story began two hours into my day's hike somewhere in Connecticut, when Quest and CatDog wanted to take a break. The timing was excellent because I needed to go to the bathroom (so to speak). I trotted off trail, out of sight from the others, and found a fallen tree close to the ground. I was sitting on the tree minding my own business, doing my business, when a commotion occurred over my head in the tree that was next to me. I saw a squirrel, who started chirping at me, berating me. I didn't know if he was angry because I invaded his space, or was it because he could smell me. In a loud, intimidating voice I said, "Hey buddy, I was here first (even though it was probably his tree and he was likely there first).

The squirrel, was not intimidated easily. He ran back down the tree and read me the riot act in squirrelese. I looked at him and replied out loud, "Leave me alone, let me finish taking a shit and I'll be gone." The squirrel ran up the tree and suddenly started knocking off pine cones that were landing around me. I WAS BEING BOMBARDED BY A FRIGGIN' SQUIRREL! I looked up at him and said, "I am not Chicken Little, and I don't scare easy!" The squirrel then ran to the trunk of the tree and began scratching off bark. It was raining tree bark all around me. I finished, and as I was pulling up my pants the squirrel came down - and with a contorted face - appeared to be screaming at me. I flicked him the bird as I gave him a few words of my own. The squirrel turned around and flipped me off by lifting his tail, and then ran up the tree. I got back to where Quest and CatDog were sitting and they wanted to know who I had been talking to. I tried to explain my encounter. All I could see was their heads shaking back and forth as we continued up the trail and Quest saying, "Only you Krispy."

Another, hold my stomach, tears-in-my-eyes-from-laughing-so-hard encounter, occurred on the Foothills Trail, near the East Fork of the Chattooga River. Cole, a young man hiking with me, and I had been on trail for five days. Most of those days we were either wet from the rain, or sweating from the late summer temperatures and high humidity. In those five days, our clothes never dried. Our body odor was exceptionally pungent. Twice, we cooled down in the waterfall pools and hoped to wash some of the stink off of our bodies. Many times, I would take the lead just to be the first nose to breathe the fresh evergreen scent of the mountain air.

Cole and I were on a fairly level wooded trail and had just passed the power lines that service the Walhalla Fish Hatchery. We were walking on a portion of trail that curves around a bend and followed a level contour of a large hill. We were walking silently, each in our own thoughts, about to go around another bend of the hill. Suddenly, our quiet mountain world exploded in sounds of something crashing through vegetation. We stopped abruptly in our tracks and stood motionless. The colliding noise of beast and plant life was growing in intensity as the sounds closed in on us. Then we saw it off to our right and above us, a large black bear rounding the bend of the hill. Not moving a muscle, we watched from the trail as the bear lumbered through the ground cover heading right for us, less than 100 feet away. However, he appeared more interested in finding berries and following the path of least resistance along the same contour with his nose down. The only body movement from Cole and I was our heads following Ursus Americanus. I did not even want to move a muscle to reach for my camera.

We had several factors in our favor with this encounter. Black bears have poor eyesight, pretty good hearing and incredible smell. Cole and I were so rigid in our stance I am sure we were blending in with the surrounding trees. We were so quiet the only sound I was hearing was my heart beat. I am sure Cole was hearing his heartbeat, too. Scent, now that was different story. I hoped our special bouquet did not signal the dinner bell for the bear.

The bear was now passing us and heading downward towards the trail we had just come up. Unexpectedly, the bear skidded to a stop and lifted its nose, sniffing. I thought that the bear caught a nose full of Cole because it lowered its nose, reared on its hind legs, turned 90 degrees and in superman speed - faster than a speeding bullet - took off up the hill and over the crest. I immediately started laughing, bent over, slapping my leg, gasping for air, only to start laughing again. One, because of the bear's reaction to sniffing the air and second, it was a way to release my adrenaline rush. Infected, Cole started laughing then asked with a questioned face, "What's so funny?" Catching my breath again, I said, "Dude, don't you know what just happened? When the bear hit the trail behind us it got a good whiff of you. His brain registered SMELLY HUMAN, changed routes and ran away from your body odor." Between the two of us, he had the stronger smell, but since we both reeked, it was funny for us both. Cole started laughing again, which got me laughing all over again.

Scotland is noted for its beauty, its people and its mystical lore involving fairies, divas, unicorns and dragons. So of course, when Lady Kritter and I decided to hike the West Highland Way, we had fun discussing the possibilities of having magical encounters in the enchanted realm of fairyland.

Our first magical moment together occurred in the fading light of the second day on the West Highland Way. Things were not going well for Team Kritter. Lady Kritter had already fallen and twisted her knee. She was walking with a noticeable limp, and our pace had slowed drastically. Time was now becoming a factor. We were supposed to have a leisurely early afternoon arrival at the Rowardennan Youth Hostel, but now at the current pace were not going to get there until well after dark thirty. The only way to quicken our pace and relieve the pressure on Lady Kritter's knee was for me to carry her backpack. I placed Lady Kritter's pack on my chest with my arms through the shoulder harness. Next, I placed my pack on my back, hoping the shoulder harness would interlock with her pack's shoulder harness. It worked, and all we had to do was hike 6 miles to the hostel.

We had been walking for several hours and as the day's last rays of light faded we entered through a forest along the shores of Loch Lomond. Lady Kritter was mentally feeling down and needed a pick me up. I tried singing - which, if you have heard me sing, you would know that wouldn't work. I tried telling jokes - but Lady Kritter and I had been together for awhile so she already knew all my jokes.

All of a sudden my peripheral vision caught a glimpse of an animal poking out of the ground. "What the hell?" I said to myself. I was immediately startled by a unique beast. My senses were on alert and my adrenaline spiked. And then, I stopped and turned for a better look and started laughing. It was just a fallen log. A log that had looked suspiciously like a small dragon to us; with rough scale-like bark and wart-like fungi. Mother Nature had apparently heard my pleas to lighten Lady Kritter's spirit and presented us with a gift: laughter. I took several pictures of the dragon and Lady Kritter posing together. This quickly became a extraordinary magical moment for me as I watched my lady kiss a magic dragon.

The pain of the last few miles diminished as Lady Kritter and I talked about the magic dragon. Lady Kritter has often told me, as well as other people, that she had kissed a few frogs to find her prince. Now she wanted to know what did she get for kissing a magic dragon. I was too tired for a quick response.

Lady Kritter and the Magic Dragon

MOMENTS OF MYSTERY

Magical Moments can also involve moments of unexplained mystery. Such an occurrence happened to me while I was on the Appalachian Trail. Bear Tracks, Fire Marshal and I left Hot Springs, North Carolina in a drizzle with snow in the higher elevations. We crossed the French Broad River, began the ascent up the mountain and - for the type of weather we were having - had great views of Hot Springs and the river from the rock cliffs. Soon the drizzle turned into snow flurries and within an hour the ground was covered in 1-2 inches of snow.

We hiked in light snow throughout the day. Later in the afternoon, the trail snaked around the side of a mountain and entered into a small valley (what they call a holler in the southern Appalachians). A fog started rolling in towards us, adding to the serene dream-like world that was teeming with white. In the far off-distance, I became aware of a low droning sound. We continued hiking into the valley towards Rich Mountain and the humming grew louder. The density of the fog added to the mysterious eerie vibration that was echoing throughout the valley. At the intersection of the AT and a blue blaze trail that led to the Rich Mountain Fire Tower, the sound became a loud guttural sound that varied in pitch, coming close to me, then fading. The sound diminished as I hiked away from Rich Mountain. Two miles up the trail the sound was gone and I approached Spring Mountain Shelter. I was the first one at the shelter. One by one, as hikers came into the shelter, they dropped large rocks from their hands or pockets and asked about the Rich Mountain monster. "I heard it too," I said. Each hiker had a different interpretation on what was making the sound: bears or wild boars (sounding the dinner bell - "Meals in hiker boots approaching!") angry Bigfoot, or the wind was blowing through the cables holding the fire tower (which I called The Wind Monster). I thought it was someone at the fire tower twirling around their head an Australian aborigine instrument used to call the earth spirits.

Whatever the sound was, I hadn't been afraid. I thought it was beautiful. I felt safe and felt protected that I didn't have to walk in the Spirit World. Ironically, no one went to investigate the cries of the Rich Mountain monster. It will remain one of the unknown mysteries for those on their thru-hike of the AT in 2004.

DAYMARES

Bear Tracks, one of the guys I hiked with on the Appalachian Trail came up with phrase to describe a unique magical moment that he called, a daymare. One day on the trail, I caught up with Bear Tracks and told him a story about what just happened to me. After I was done with my story he said, "Oh, you just had a daymare!" "A WHAT?" I said. "A daymare," he repeated. We stop walking, turned to face each other and he described it as being similar to a nightmare but occurs when you are awake during the day. He said it happens during long periods of any type of activity where someone can get bored or let their mind wander. You become deep in thought and slip into a semi-conscious dream-state. Your mind can begin to play tricks on itself and think you actually see things that seem to be real. Walking day after day on a thru-hike, you have a lot of idle time looking at the scenery before you with nothing to do but think and play mind games with yourself. I've got to tell you, after he explained it to me, it made perfectly good sense. Especially since I have had several of them. The story I told "Bear Tracks" was my first confirmed daymare and went like this...

There was about 6-8 inches of fresh snow on the ground as we entered the higher elevations of the Smoky Mountain National Park. It was a bright sunny day and the temperatures were in the high thirties, which caused the snow to start melting. The trail - already eroded from so many hiker boots - was an ideal place for the snowmelt to runoff into streamlets. As I sloshed through the running water, I thought how similar it looked to a small river with rapids. I pictured a miniature kayak or canoe navigating through the chutes and eddies as the water flowed down the trail. I looked down again and in disbelief I saw a small canoe with one occupant in it shooting the rapids. I took a closer look at the face and it was a canoeing friend. He looked up at me and said, "Follow me and pick up the pace, you're as slow as molasses." Before I could answer, he looked down river, saw a water bar across the trail (a log or series of rocks that directs water flow down the mountain to stop erosion), and gave a 'yahoooo' as he disappeared over the waterfall and down the mountain. I shook my head. Now I know I was caught up in a daymare.

One of the scariest daymares happened to me during an October weekday section hike on the Florida Trail. I had arrived early at the River Junction Campground and set up a stealth camp (a campsite that is well hidden) on the banks of the Withlacoochee River. The campground was only open on the weekend so I had the whole place to myself. I decided to take a walk along the river bank and watch

Mother Nature at play. I sat on a large fallen oak log and looked out over the coffee colored water towards an island splitting the river in two. The whole scene had a wild primitive feel to it. A sunbeam of light poked through the trees and touched the water. Just then a fish jumped out of the water and into the beam attempting to catch a flying dragonfly. The insect at the last second made a sharp maneuver in mid-flight and escapes the fish's jaw. The fish dove back into the water - leaving concentric rings radiating out to the shoreline without his meal. This whole sequence of events reminded me of a spotlight illuminating two actors on a stage.

I got up from the log and continued to walk along the bank. The tranquil and untroubled surroundings lured me into an hypnotic state of mind. I found myself leaning against an old hickory tree whose canopy reached out over the water with Spanish Moss dangling down from its limbs. The river view was spectacular. I was off in lala land when suddenly a small column of water exploded in front of me with a "thoomph." Quickly following were several more "thoomp" sounds with more exploding columns of water. Each one was coming closer towards me. The television in my head turned on and I simultaneously envisioned thousands of shoot' em up gun battle scenes. Some of the scenes even spraying bullets into the water closer to the target. TARGET? Was I a target? My imagination took over and I swear I could hear the bullet casings hitting the ground. "Why are people shooting at me?" "Were there bad guys nearby?" I went into a defensive stance behind the tree, my heart racing. Now what do I do? There was a short period of silence and then again, "thoomph, thoomph, thoomph", bullets were dancing in the water - this time really close. I wanted to dig a hole to protect myself when suddenly, directly on top of my head I felt it, a "thrwarp"! I was hit. A second knock on the head woke me up. That is when I realized the wind gusting through the tree canopy had been releasing hickory nuts that fell into the water with a forceful, "thoomph." I looked around to see if anybody saw the scene, waiting to say "Wow, you are a dumbass."

SOUNDS THAT CREATE MAGIC

The sounds of the forest have intrigued me since my earliest days on the trail. When I arrive on any trail, one of the first things I try to do is filter out the sounds of mankind; airplanes from above, the mechanical noises from the rail and roadways on the ground and the sounds of civilization in the cities and towns. Initially, it takes awhile to get accustomed to the silence, but gradually I will begin to hear new sounds.

When I start walking, the first sound I concentrate on is my footfall. I'll listen to the crunching my boots make on leaves and twigs, and the slapping they make on rock and dirt. The cadence of my steps slowly becomes the baseline for a chorus of music that abounds around me.

I'll begin to hear the air rushing in and out of my lungs, faster and heavier as my body longs for more oxygen to fuel my body's furnace. I'll listen to the cadence of my exhaling as I begin to climb. The higher and steeper the climb, the shorter the breath. I'll think I can hear, almost simultaneously, my heart beat, ready to burst out of my chest, pumping the blood faster and faster into the capillaries of the lungs.

Once I become more accustomed to the sounds of my body, the sounds of nature began to be more clear. Leaves rustling, water cascading, insects buzzing. Songbirds break out into chorus of so many different songs! (I wish I knew the names of the birds by their song.) I love these walks in the mountains, through the forest, in the valleys. I am alive at the cacophony of sounds of life in the wilderness.

One time, Greyhound and I were on the Bartram Trail, near Russell Bridge. We were nine miles from the trailhead when we came to a blue blaze that led to Dicks Creek Falls. Greyhound and I looked at each other deciding whether or not to take trail. I don't remember who said it, but I am sure the thought was shared by the both of us. "We are here for adventure, right?" "So let's see what's at the end of this blaze!" After a short hike to the top of the falls, the trail dropped down and soon opened up to a 180-degree view of a scenic wonder-world of land, water and sound. In front of us was a river valley landscaped with massive boulders and rocks jutting out into the running Chattooga River. Water was cascading everywhere; over, under and around rocks in the river. I went off trail with the intention of playing leapfrog on the rocks surrounding pools of water, but Mother Nature's magic got even better. As I reached the water's edge and started out on the rocks, I looked over to my right and saw a large waterfall plummeting 65 feet over a bulging monolithic mound of rock in the river. The noise, view, and overall feeling was overwhelming.

Greyhound enjoying the surround sound of the Chattooga River

I found a comfortable viewing rock about 30 feet into the water and sat down. I was engulfed by the sound of water. I sat there, silent (not that you would have been able to hear me anyways), slowing my breathing and focusing on taking in as much as I could with all of my senses. I became part of the river. I watched the water roar over the cliff, mingle underneath, and disappear into distant trees. The water roared, babbled, whispered, shouted, lapped and echoed.

I had heard waterfalls before, but the sound on that day was truly incredible. After that day, all other water sounds seemed to be one dimensional. And on that rock, the sound was a natural 360-degree stereophonic sensation of energy. Greyhound and I each got lost in our own thoughts, took out food for lunch and spent well over an hour in Mother Nature's own symphonic hall. Few experiences can touch that one.

The wind, too, can add to the symphony. During one of my section hikes in the Great Smoky Mountain National Park, I was walking on the leeward side of a mountain with a slight breeze hitting my face. Up and over the ridge, I came to the windward side of the mountain. The blustery wind caught the tree tops like a sail and forced trees to rub against one another. Depending on the intensity of the wind, the rubbing created an assortment of human-like eerie sounds of crying. The next minute I'd heard the mournful, final cry of a wounded animal, or the creaking sounds heard from a wooden sailing ship riding out a storm on the high seas. Throughout the day, I knew I was in a bad weather front as the wind picked up momentum creating violent, deafening sounds as it whistled through the tree canopy.

Safety became an issue when I heard consecutive POPs and then a SNAP. Turning towards the noise, I watched the final act of a majestic tree lose its battle with the wind. Under my feet the earth shook as the tree hit the ground. I headed towards the nearest shelter possible as I looked up into the treetops for any dead branches that might come crashing down on me. We call these widowmakers. But, as fast as the wind was upon me, it was gone and all that remained was the regular noises of the forest. Within minutes birds started singing again, and then I knew Mother Nature was giving me the "all clear" signal.

THE VISION

I have often heard and read about Native Americans having visions/dreams when they were traveling in nature. I, too, had a vision - when I was on a section hike on the Appalachian Trail.

After almost 60 years of enjoying Mother Earth, I somehow abandoned my positive attitude and began a period in my life where everything around me (wife, family, work and most importantly me) felt out of sync. I would break down and cry for no apparent reason at the littlest notion concerning my life. Ridiculous, meaningless, comments threw my way would irritate me. I found that I was slowly spiraling into the depths of depression. I began to believe my problems were bigger than I could handle, and my age wasn't helping. I knew I had to do something to clear my mind. I decided that a section hike was what I needed to escape, cut the strings of depression, and rediscover myself.

Section hiking involves picking a section of a long distance trail and hiking that segment. I asked Greyhound if he wanted to go for a two-week section hike on the Appalachian Trail. He obviously agreed (anytime Greyhound has the chance to get on trail, he takes it). We planned to start at Fontana Dam, thru-hiking the Great Smoky Mountain National Park, and finishing near Erwin, Tennessee. I was counting down the days I would be in the mountains. I was so ready, I was packed a month before hitting the trail.

Greyhound and I left Florida in the late afternoon and by 2 o'clock the next day we were walking across Fontana Dam entering the national park under low, fast moving gray clouds and rain. Three days later, after a nasty fall (because I was not paying attention to my surroundings and I didn't have my trail legs yet) the depression began to creep back in. I started to make excuses why I should not be on the trail hiking. I told myself that I was a safety risk, I was letting my hiking partner down, I wanted to go home and crash in the comfort of the bed that Lady Kritter and I call, the nest. I started the uncontrollable crying that I left back home. One minute I wanted to continue, the next minute I wanted to do something I had never done before, go off trail and leave a hike early.

Greyhound and I arrived at Newfound Gap in a particularly heavy downpour. I looked up towards the heavens, arms stretched up to the skies and screamed - with rain, and tears, running down my face. Into the swirling wind and rain, I asked for Spirit to give me a sign. Then I thought, "That's stupid. In your state-of-mind, you wouldn't know a sign if it hit you. Did you think it would be so noticeable you would recognize it like a road sign along the side of the trail saying, 'Go Home.' Get a grip."

I normally would have found exhilaration in the strong winds, the fast moving swirling clouds, and the sheets of rain on top of Newfound Gap. Instead, I told Greyhound we needed to have a pow-wow. In the confines of that shelter, Greyhound heard for the first time where I stood mentally. I told him it was my decision to go off trail. Once the decision was made, so many unanswered questions arose. Where would I go? How would I get there? Would I go home, or just go off to disappear to be by myself for the remainder of my vacation? For the moment I didn't care to answer any of these questions. All I knew is that the reason I came to the mountains was not working out. I was still a mess.

I was also sad, because I knew Greyhound would be totally disappointed. A great warrior is always ready for battle, whatever that battle is, and whoever the enemy. In true warrior fashion, Greyhound put aside how he felt, showed me compassion and strength, and accompanied me back to the civilized world - to fight my enemy.

My magical moment occurred later that night in a dream and went like this:

I was lying on the side of a residential street, face up. A group of bystanders were standing around me looking down at my body. Lady Kritter and Greyhound were in the crowd, too. A siren wailed and an ambulance with a large crane on it turned a corner, stopping directly in front of me. The driver's door opened and out stepped a man dressed in a light-colored medical smock with long pants. He had

Native American features in his chiseled face; dark eyes, dark brown skin and long black hair pulled back in a ponytail. He walked over to me, bent at the waist and said "I'm a medicine man, what seems to be the problem?" I spilled my guts out, telling him everything that was flying around inside my head. At one point, as I was talking, he turned around, fiddled with something inside a leather looking shoulder bag, turned back to me and handed me a glass containing a white liquid similar to skim milk. "Drink it," he said. I could hear my mother saying, "Never take an unknown drink from a stranger", so I asked, "What's in it?" The medicine man said some word that sounded very earthy, and I, nevertheless, drank it. I handed him the empty glass and asked him "What's up" with the crane. He said it was a "man-crane" because the initial report involved, a "man down." However, he wasn't going to use it because he didn't see a man down. He turned away from me again, fidgeted for a few seconds and returned with another small vial containing a dark colored liquid saying, "This will make you sleepy."

I drank it and asked, "What 's wrong with me?" The medicine man replied, "You simply need to un-clutter!" "How do I un-clutter?" I asked. "When you wake up you will know!" He replied.

The medicine man then turned back to the opened driver's door, climbed in, and as I fell asleep, he drove off.

Then, I had a dream within a dream. I was standing on a street corner of some port city. I watched a large freighter speeding down a channel creating a huge wake. A man was standing next to me and I asked him why the freighter was moving so fast in the channel. He told me that in order for the freighter to clear the channel it must travel at this high rate of speed. I watched as the waves crashed over the seawall, wash into the city streets and regress back into the channel. The streets were then cleansed of garbage.

I woke up in the middle of the night. Refreshed. Greyhound was asleep in the hotel bed across from me. I laid awake in the darkness of the room and felt a new energy surrounding me. It was hard to describe, but I almost felt like I'd been reborn a completely different person from the one I was before I went to bed. I remembered what the medicine man had said about "un-cluttering." I immediately sat up in bed, and knew exactly what he meant, and what I had to do.

I woke up the next morning, and told Greyhound my hike was over. I was going off trail, with no regrets and going home. Greyhound and his wife helped me find a way home, So I could un-clutter.

I first thought going hiking into the mountains would cure my ills. Then, I thought I made a mistake and needed to be somewhere else. On top of that, I was putting people out of their way on this trip. I realize now I DID need to be in the mountains, just not hiking. It was also those very same people I thought I was putting out of their way (a great warrior and his wife), who were instrumental in helping me out of the abyss of gloom. I will be forever indebted, not only on that trip, but on every one. Thanks Greyhound and Lady Greyhound for helping e through an important magical moment in my life.

Things have a funny way of working out.

CHAPTER 10
Working at an Outfitter

During my time away from the trails and waterways of Mother Nature, I work for a retail outfitter store, Travel Country Outdoors (TCO for short), that specializes in backpacking and kayaking, sort of a home away from home. TCO is one of the most popular outdoor stores in the southeastern United States that regularly has a cast of characters that come in looking for equipment and advice on how to survive in the wilderness. These folks want to break out from the asphalt and concrete of mankind and become hikers and kayakers. The cast of customers include the new Boy Scouts, preparing for their first adventures in the outdoors under a tent, and the older Scouts looking for the newest, latest and greatest piece of outdoor gear. The father, bringing in his family to find a common bond away from the electronic world of civilization, hoping to open a new line of communication with each other through nature. The young adult who has just graduated and decided, before immersing themselves into the adult world, to embark on a backpacking journey to exotic lands across the big ponds to discover the mysteries of life. Women, young and old, breaking the chains of what females can, and cannot do, by going out alone exploring the world without a man. The retirees who want to travel to places they have read about in National Geographic Magazines. And the adventurer, who enjoys the adrenaline rush of pushing the limits of survivability in the outdoors. Really, there's no limit to the different types of people we often meet in that store.

I have a name that I give to each of these outdoor hiker and kayaker enthusiasts. Hikers can be day-hikers, weekend hikers, or long distance hikers. Each group is trying to find a corner of peace in a fast paced, concrete and asphalt world. I call them earth-touchers because they leave a soft imprint on the earth by leaving only footprints and taking only pictures (sound principles of the *Leave No Trace* Program. For more information on the ethics on how to enjoy the outdoors responsibly go to www.lnt.org).

Kayakers leave Terra Firma ("solid earth") and paddle the aqua world of blue seen covering the surface of the marble planet, circling the sun, called Earth. These folks, single and in groups also use Leave No Trace Principles, and find adventure and escape by paddling the waves of oceans, floating on ponds and lakes, or paddling down fast moving streams and rivers for an exhilarating roller coaster ride on sheets of bubbly current. I call them riders of liquid energy.

Snake Boots

Every so often, someone will walk into the store from these earth-touchers and riders of liquid energy and make an impression that lasts with me forever. One such group, made up of three individuals, came into the store on a rainy, cold morning and walked directly to the gear room up to the backpacks. The trio, one man and two women, were standing and looking up in awe at the assorted backpacks hanging on the wall. I greeted the trio and asked if I could help. The young man turned towards me full of excitement said "Yes." "We want the biggest backpacks you have!" he continued in a southern drawl. After hearing that eight word sentence, my mind started firing nano seconds of thought. "Are they going on an expedition? Do they know what they are doing? How big is BIG?!" The best way to find the answers to these and other questions is to qualify the customer (an integral part of customer service that makes a specialty store successful). So, I began. "Hello, my trail name is KrispyKritter, my birth name is Wayne."

In a strong handshake the young man replied, "Folks call me Bobby." (Note: names made up to protect identities and reputations of all parties involved). Based on his previous comments, I thought they might be going on an expedition, "How long is your trip, Bobby?" I was floored at the reply, "One week for the first trip and, after a couple of weeks off, out for another." I was puzzled because under normal circumstances one does not need a very large backpack for a one week trip.

"How big is big?" I asked. Bobby replied again, "The biggest backpack you have!" "The biggest backpack the store carries is a 110 liter," I said. "What's a liter?" Bobby wanted to know. I immediately knew something was awry. But, I still did not have enough information about their unique adventure, so I asked, "What type of equipment will you be carrying?"

Once again, I was floored by the response. "A 16 pound, 4 person tent, three meals a day of the civilian equivalent of the military MRE's (Meals Ready to Eat, a heavy food containing water) and zero-degree sleeping bags, bought at the department store on sale for $32 apiece, A bargain," he said. And, "Snake boots."

"SNAKE BOOTS?" I repeated with a raised voice and I am sure a look of bewilderment. "Where are you going?"

Bobby's body language matched his reply. Shoulders back, chest out and making eye contact with everyone in the room, Bobby proclaimed, "The Appalachian Trail!" Again, I was floored

My face did not betray the laughter within me. It was all I could do to keep a straight face. I tried to explain, as a former thru-hiker, that although there were rattlesnakes on the AT (as well as copperheads), there would be no need for snake boots. He'd simply need to be aware of where he placed his feet. The snakes generally avoid humans at all cost. Bobby disagreed with me and said he knew a lot from the military and that he knew what he was doing. Unruffled, I conceded (the customer is always right), and claimed to have the backpack he needed. "Oh no, not for me, I have a military pack. The backpack is for the girls." Bang! Hello floor.

My mind was doing pirouettes as I went upstairs to the back stock area to try to locate, according to the customer qualifying I'd just performed, the following: two of the largest woman backpacks that we have in stock, for a one week trip on the Appalachian Trail with a carrying weight of 60 to 70 pounds. From the visual information I'd gathered during their size-up, interchangeable shoulder harnesses and waist belts would be needed due to the unique body style of each lady. Within minutes, I was back in the gear room with two different colored backpacks that I thought would be the ex-soldier's requirements. I yelled out, "Who likes blue?" as I laid the other pack on the floor. "Oh, I do!" said one of the ladies, and so began my first pack fit, Amber Lynn.

Bobby was circling me like a hawk, watching every buckle strap I adjusted and listened attentively as I explained to Amber Lynn the function of each strap. A female sales associate by the name of Stephanie brought another customer to the loft for a pack fit during Amber Lynn's pack fit and both overheard the following conversation.

Bobby asked me, "Did I hear you say you hiked the Appalachian Trail?" "Yes." I said. "The whole trail?" "Yes." I said.

Bobby then approached me cockily, leaned towards my left ear and stated, "I want to bring a rifle with me on the Appalachian Trail. What do you think?"

I looked over to Bobby's two lady friends who were simultaneously gazing at him, placing Bobby on a pedestal with unspoken trust and awe. I then quickly looked over at Stephanie standing nearby to see if she heard him. What I saw on her face must have been the look on mine when my jaw hit the floor. My head cocked, neck extended, wide-eyed, mouth open with the look of "What in the hell did I just hear?"

My immediate reply was "No, the trail goes through National parks and forests and the rangers would have a problem with that." Then, I just had to ask, "Why do you need a rifle?" Standing proud, Bobby replied, "For the Grizzly."

I swear, I could hear the sound of heads snapping and the words "There are no Grizzly bears on the east coast!" coming towards Bobby and me from at least three different directions.

Bobby looked at me and stated "Well, maybe that wasn't a good idea." I gave him a nod of agreement.

Amber Lynn liked the way the backpack felt on her back and looked towards Bobby for approval as he circled pulling and pushing straps and buckles. "Not bad!" he said.

The other woman's fit went a little smoother. Her name was Cheri and I had to endure the story of how she and Bobby met, where they came from, and touched on their personal lives that I jokingly said was getting to be TMI (Too Much Information). During the fit, Cheri asked me (since I'd hiked the Appalachian Trail) if I thought she could do the 20 mile days Bobby had planned for them. I tried to be diplomatic in my response, noting the frequency all three were going outside for cigarette breaks and noting that they looked fairly out of shape. I explained that I thought 20 miles was a bit aggressive for the first couple days. The pack fit was completed and I finished the conversation by stating I thought a lower daily mileage would make the trip more enjoyable for them.

While Bobby was off on another part of the store with a female sales associate, Amber Lynn came back from a cigarette break and stood to my left while Cheri was sitting on a stool. Cheri looked over to Amber Lynn, then looked straight into my eyes and asked "Is it OK if we ask you a question?" "Sure" I said. "What do you do about the stank?" ("God, I hoped Cheri's not going where I think she is going.")

Assuming Cheri was talking about the body odor from not bathing (known to hikers as "hiker funk") I told her, "Everybody stinks on the trail." "NO" replied Cheri, "I'm not talkin' about that. I'm talkin' 'bout female stank, you know, the monthly." My jaw hit the floor again (it was really starting to hurt at that point).

Though I have knowledge of this subject through past experiences with the women in my life, I stumbled for words when

Cheri cut me off and stated, "I saw in another part of the store here, where certain underwear don't keep the smell. So, can I put those on first, then put my real undies over them. What'd you think?"

I was speechless. This group was throwing me for a loop. I was overcome with the sensation of being in a very bad dream, time was slowing down and I had no control over my lips or tongue. The next thing I remember is grabbing, with both hands, the hair of my beard and stating, "Look, there is hair on my chin, I am a man, I can't relate how a woman thinks about herself when it comes to the matter of womanhood." I'm not sure, but, I think I repeated that statement again. Then, I looked Cheri straight in the eyes and said, "There are several women that work here at the store, that have the experience of living/hiking in Mother Nature's Wilderness who will listen to your questions and be very happy to answer them."

Just as this conversation ended, in walked Bobby and Stephanie, and I thought, why do I have this sick feeling in my stomach that my jaw would be meeting Mr. Floor again. Bobby turned to Cheri and asked in a domineering voice, "What's goin' on?" Cheri quickly turned to Bobby and without hesitation stated "Nothin', masterboss, just talkin'."

Stephanie looked at me and silently mouthed the words "MASTERBOSS?" I nodded my head for two reasons: First, to acknowledge my agreement with Stephanie. And second, to clear my spinning head a bit after having just hit the floor, again.

Bobby, Cheri and Amber Lynn stayed in the store an additional 5 hours after my assistance, with help from additional sale associates. Let's just say, I heard stories of the hiking trio known as Snake Boots long after they'd left the store.

Sharktooth Springs

Working at Travel Country I try to help brand new employees learn what it means to be a "specialty store." Sure, you can teach technical information on the materials and construction, describe how it operates under optimum conditions, or explain how a particular item of clothing, or gear will perform. But, there are two things that people can't teach if they haven't experienced it. They can't explain what it is like being bathed in moonlight inside a tent, cowboy camp under the stars, or what it's is like to hike, or kayak, in the rain. Second, when asked, "Have you ever used this?" or, "How does this (customer holding up a particular piece of equipment) perform in the woods?" I don't want to see one of our sales associates have a blank look and state, "Well no, but I know someone who has and..." Or, will circumnavigate the question with BS, like I have witnessed in the past in other specialty stores. The experience can only be acquired through actual use in the outdoor environment. "Let's take the toys outside and play!" is a simple solution to the problem. What's the saying? "Experience is the best teacher." So I have been willing, at any time, to take new employees on a weekend backpacking, or kayak trip, to learn first-hand what it is like to be outdoors, with nothing but your kit on your back, a kayak under you, surrounded by nature, and learning the gear they are selling.

I tried to rally the new store employees on one occasion to a camp out behind the store during a major multi-day sales event. This was the perfect opportunity for those who didn't know how to do certain things outside to learn how to do so; set up and evaluate a tent; see how a sleeping bag performs, find out how to use and cook on a backpacking stove, how not to scratch insect bites, etc. That camp out was going to be in the safety of the store's backyard property behind a chain link fence.

Did I get any takers? One person showed up, set-up his tent, then left the area never to return until the sale event was over and we had to break camp. I confronted the individual each day why he didn't camp out and got a different excuse each time. A few folks from the store came after closing for a curiosity look, said "Hi", and then were off to someplace at the edge of pavement. The only person to stay with me that weekend was a semi-retired attorney by the nickname of Bump Bill, now a river rat paddling for the Nantahala Outdoor Center, who helps sell kayaks at the store during the off season of whitewater rafting. Bump Bill and I stayed up into the wee hours of the morning in front of a campfire and solved all the world problems (we got a reality check the next morning when we woke up with the world problems still on the radio). All-in-all, I was disappointed in the response and turnout from my co-workers.

Several months later, and with several more newbie employees, I wrote an e-mail to all store employees with an invitation for anyone interested in a weekend overnight hike to Sharktooth Springs to contact me. I was not expecting too many responses based on my last try. So, to my surprise, several individuals approached me with interest. Eight said they were definitely in, and ready to see Mother Nature up close and personal. Their spirit for adventure was strong for never having been in the woods longer than a day hike. I couldn't let them down now and my thought was, "I sure hope I am not biting off more than I can chew."

The master plan was simple: leave work on Saturday after closing at 6:00 pm, drop vehicles at my house and take two vehicles to the trailhead. We'd hike before dark thirty to the campsite and set up camp, and then kick back and enjoy the day Sunday. We would hike out Monday morning, drive back to my house to pick up the vehicles and then head off to work in the afternoon, telling everyone who did not go what a great time they missed.

Everything went according to plan until Murphy's Law decided to join the trip. One by one, five of the eight came up with a reason for not going and dropped out the day of the hike. The remaining three, Corey, Grant and Daniel left work with me (later than I wanted) at 6:45 that evening (thanks to Murphy). Next, since I was dealing with 18 to 21 year old young men, we had to stop and feed their constant hunger, which brought a 45 minute delay. Our feet did not hit the trailhead until way after dark thirty – 10:00 pm to be exact. Sometimes Murphy's interference has been a blessing. This hike took place in late July in Central Florida where the daytime temperatures tend to be around 95 degrees Fahrenheit with an extremely high humidity of drenching wet. So, a night hike saved us from the brutal summer heat. We left the trailhead and I could not find the orange blaze of the Florida Trail (FT), which meant we couldn't get to the campsite via the trail. However, I knew the road intersected the FT, but how far from the trailhead I couldn't remember. "Forget the blaze," I said. "We'll take the road and find the trail." Off we went into the Seminole State Forest down a road as three headlamps of concentrated beams of light nervously pierced the surrounding darkness of night. I did not have to use my headlamp with all their energy flashing around.

Ten minutes into the hike, the road opened up to pitch darkness. Crisscrossing beams of light bounced off a rolling hill of low prairie grass. One of boys pointed his column of light to the right along the tops of the knee-high grass. A gasp of warning alerted everyone. All eyes followed the length of his steady beam of light to where the brightness meets darkness. Glittering back at us was a pair of small, shining yellow-white circles of lights. Two more beams of light added to the intensity of light shining toward the unknown lights, piercing into the dark void, revealing another pair of twinkling lights, then another, and another. One of the pairs of lights rose up from the grass, and all the shining eyes were staring back at us, watching. Wild animals staring back at two legged aliens with one cycloped "eye" of light disturbing their nocturnal peace. I could sense twinges of fear surging through the guys. I envisioned so many scenarios of what might be going through their heads on their very first backpacking trip/first night hike into the wilds of Florida swamplands. Television has a lot to do with how we conjure up in our minds, unexplained occurrences in the real world. Picture these television scenarios for the lights gleaming back at us. Saliva dripping canine teeth from a pack of wild dogs, or any type of predatory animal, looking for their next meal, encircling and ready take down their prey. My Science Fiction version, Zombies rising and stiffly walking towards us with their rigid arms out, surrounding us, and closing in to convert us to their demonic underworld. Anyway, you get the picture. I calmed the boys down and told them that they were looking at a herd of deer bedded down for the night. Relieved, we moved on, found the orange blaze and entered the woods on the Florida Trail.

I love night hiking, and that night was a great example of why. It becomes such a different world, full of nature's surprises and beauty. As we passed through the forest on the narrow trail. Our lights splashed across the path to reveal concentric threads of thin, white silk, dripping with the night's dew, anchored to the trees. I turned my headlamp on and pointed it down the trail to discover yet another web just as beautiful. I explained to the boys that I wanted to disturb the webs as little as possible, so we could pass through and co-exist, becoming a part of Mother Nature rather than an intruder. Happy to be on the trail, we leap frogged from orange blaze to orange blaze, keeping everyone between the two known orange blazes. I would alternate the boys as scouts and send them into the dark abyss looking for the next blaze. I could feel the confidence level rise each time the young men went out.

The next wonder that transpired was when we came out to another prairie and observed a low glow on the eastern horizon. A magnificent, huge fire-orange moon, rose through the pine and oak forest. Exhilarated from the night's events we walked into the primitive campsite at Sharktooth Springs. We each chose our private spot of earth, pitched our tents, and pleasantly went to bed as the fire tinted moon cast hues of orange-yellow light into the night.

I was the first one up the next morning as the rays of sunlight broke through the morning clouds. I greeted the day with my usual blessings, thanking the Spirit-That-Moves-Through-All-Things for a safe journey and sharing Mother Nature and Father Sky I decided to stay inside my tarp tent to avoid the squadron of mosquitoes flying on the other side of my no-see-um netting. An hour and half later a bright sunrise broke over the campsite. I got up and walked in the morning's glow and started brewing a pot of coffee. The tranquil morning was abruptly shattered by a stereo playing the song "Cotton Eye Joe" from somewhere deep in the forest. For a few minutes at least, I thought I had escaped the vortex of civilization. I don't know if it was the smell of fresh coffee percolating or the revelry of country music echoing through the forest that greeted the guys, but one by one, they awoke to a new day of adventure.

The morning was spent exploring the campsite and surrounding area. Of course, one of the first locations to explore was the tiny spring. A gentle walk off of the Florida Trail, Sharktooth Springs is a petite spring emitting from the base of a hill nestled in green vegetation. The spring's run, with crystal water and sandy bottom, flows into another creek called Sulfur Run. The first thing one becomes aware of as they walk towards the spring is the light odor of matchstick heads – sulfur. I was sitting on a small wooden bridge that crossed the little run as the boys played in the water. One of boys wanted know why the spring was called Sharktooth Springs. I told them to carefully scoop up the sandy bottom in their hands and look inside. One by one, the boy's faces revealed wonderment as they held tiny, black shark's teeth scattered in the sand. "Touch and explore, but don't take," I said, as I used this opportunity to discuss with them the principles of Leave No Trace.

After lunch, I took the boys on a day hike heading south on the Florida Trail. Minute changes in topography brought the trail out of the woods and onto a shell rock road with swampland on either side. A short walk on the road and we arrived at our destination, Blackwater Creek. I told the boys that that was the genuine, primitive Florida you read about, or see in some old movies. Huge live oak trees with the gray colored Spanish Moss hanging from branches, reaching out over the coffee-colored tannin water. We scanned the water world before us as fish jumped out in an attempt to catch an insect flying low over the surface. An alligator lazily floated like a submarine below the water's surface, exposing only its nose and barely causing a wake. Long-legged wading birds on the shore carefully watched it pass by. We sat down on a picnic table where a canoe launch site was located and discussed the beauty that surrounded us. I then asked the boys to transform the scene before them. Replace the vegetation with concrete, the shell rock road with asphalt, rows of buildings replacing the majestic oaks with polluted water flowing by. I could see facial changes of amazement as they looked out at the beauty before them and replaced it with the materials of civilization. One of the guys then stated he now knew why preserves and parks were created - to protect these fragile ecological systems from the greedy hands of developers. I left the guys at the picnic table to ponder the words I had just spoken and walked away in my own Muir state of mind.

We returned to the campsite mid-afternoon to find the site without shade and the 90-degree heat and high humidity melting us. I told the boys I was spending the rest of the afternoon in Mother Nature's air conditioning unit – the bridge over the spring run. The air was cooler because of the shade from the trees and the cool wind whipping off the spring water. I bathed my skin by dipping my bandanna in the water and replaced the high humidity sweat with the coolness of spring water. Lying on the wooden bridge, I couldn't help but hear the words of a beer commercial in my head, "it doesn't get any better than this."

Throughout the day, I noticed the guys walking barefoot and laying in the grass without some type of ground barrier. The first time I observed one of them walking barefooted I explained this was not a good habit to follow due to the many biting insects in the Florida woods. But 'boys will be boys'. I didn't want to be the authoritarian adult always telling them what to do, so I only told them once. I felt it was a better learning experience to gain personal knowledge of why not to do something instead of just hearing the words. This particular event would be something not soon forgotten.

On cue, the squadrons of mosquitoes arrived with their constant buzzing as the sun settled in the western sky. Grant started a fire in the hopes the smoke would diminish the flying man-eaters. All the fire did was increase the ambient temperature from warm to steamy. After a quick dinner of freeze dried beef stroganoff and protein rich flying insects landing in our meals, I went to bed early - seeking relief from the blood sucking bugs and to cool off in the sauna night air by lying on top of my sleeping pad naked and perfectly still.

Monday morning we woke up early, broke camp and were on the trail by 7 o'clock, walking in grass soaked with dew. By 8:30, the four of us were in a restaurant eating a healthy breakfast and reminiscing about our hike. I noticed as we entered into the restaurant Corey was limping and I asked what was wrong. He told me he had blisters on his heals from his shoes being wet. I asked what kind of socks he wore. "Cotton", he said. "*Cotton*, COREY!" How many times a day do we tell customers in the store not to wear cotton in an outdoor environment?" I said. Corey replied, "Yeah, I know, but I didn't think..." Another Lesson learned. Next, I saw all three boys scratching their legs. "What's up with the scratching?" I said. "Let me see your legs." All three boys had numerous itchy red dots all over their legs. I then explained about chiggers. Grant had a particular nasty bite on his ankle and finally told us about a scorpion he saw by his bare foot. Another lesson learned, wear shoes. And yet, another lesson was learned when the guys got to the house. Each one, when it was time to take their shower, found seed ticks all over their body after the clothes came off. The lesson: lying in grass without a ground barrier can induce itchy bites from disease causing insects. I came away from this weekend adventure unscathed, bug free and very entertained, and in the process, taught some young men to better appreciate nature

Upon our return, I was glad to see each of the boys use the events of the hike as a sales tool when talking to customers. Those guys also came away with life lessons that I think will be with them throughout their stay in Mother Nature's playground.

Every day, I try to learn something new and therefore I, too, learned from that adventure. I learned Corey, Grant and Daniel are outstanding young men, who have a zest for adventure. More importantly, I learned that there are individuals in the next generation who are willing to embrace Mother Nature and Father Sky and protect them.

Finding Pirates

I learned to love boating when I was young, even if it was unconventional. Living in South Florida as a 10 year old boy, it was always a memorable occasion when one of our young family members celebrated a birthday. We knew there would be a birthday celebration on the first Saturday after the birthday involving my large family. The anticipated party would take place at a small amusement park with rides, cake and ice cream. Going to school on Friday was a long day that never ended. Often, I would daydream about the up and coming adventure only to have it shattered by the piercing voice of the classroom teacher, followed by the whizzing sound of the chalkboard eraser passing by my ear. After detention, the festive atmosphere would really kick-in during my parents Friday Family Night when we with talk about the party.

The next morning, family members of all ages would gather and, roll call was taken as we were assigned seating while we packed ourselves in several cars. A short prayer was said to protect us on our journey as the wheels started to turn. We didn't have the interstate back then, so any road taken with more than two lanes was considered the fastest line between two waypoints. Traveling down US Highway #1, past the city of Hallandale and south of the Gulf Stream Race Track, the road began its rhythmic sounds of a train's clickity-clack as the car passed over the expansion joints of the concrete highway. Gazing out the window, man-made objects would rush past me in a blur. The concrete colors of buildings turned into the colors of natural greens and browns as we passed Greynold's Park. Suddenly, my focus became clear and I saw trees, and I felt a bond with them and the peacefully serene area they lived in. I wanted to live in that type of outdoor world. The car would continue south to the next landmark, a major intersection with a sign showing a picture of a man with a white beard and the words, "Big Daddy's Lounge." This landmark told me we were close to the shopping center where the amusement park was located – our final destination.

It took (what felt like) an eternity to pull into the gigantic parking lot to find a parking space. Finally unloaded, we followed one another into a frenzy of people heading towards the shopping center like field ants trailing one another on an invisible line. Other convoys of family members had a pre-determined time to meet at the center of the complex. Sometimes we would go early just to walk up and down the outside walkway that connected all the stores. And then it took other kids forever to finally start walking to the location of the amusement park.

The amusement park was not big; in fact, it was pretty small. A miniature version of a passenger train circled it on a small track. The walkway into the park crossed the railroad tracks. If you entered at the right time you would hear the train's whistle, the red lights would blink above the white X on either side of the walkway, the gates would come down and a huge man in denim overalls and an engineer hat rode by in the engine with his knees up to his chest, followed by carloads of screaming kids. On one side of the park was the merry-go-round with carousel music emitting from speakers. At the other end of the park contained a ride called "Bimbo the Flying Elephant" consisting of gray flying elephants attached to a metal bar that went to a center spoke. You sat inside the elephant and traveled around in a circle while going up and down. Towards the back was my ride, "The Boats." The birthday party was held inside a building off to the side that contained a small room filled with colorful balloons, wrapped presents and the smell of sweets.

After the candles were blown out, presents unwrapped and the cake and ice cream eaten – it was time for the rides. This was the moment I had been waiting for all day. This was the only ride I wanted. The Boats!

The construction was simply a doughnut shaped metal tank filled with water and little motor boats floated on top of the water attached by metal rods. Like the spokes of a bicycle wheel, the rods were attached to a centered metal shaft, connected to a motor. One by one, children were placed in the boats. When the word was given, the motor coughed, the shaft turned, and my boat began to make a wake that smashed against the metal wall. I grabbed the steering wheel in the dashboard and pulled the string attached to a bell located on the bow in front of the clear windshield. It was then, at the sound of the bells clanging, that I lost the boat's metal rod and sailed off. No matter what boat I was in, it was the fastest. I would follow Errol Flynn and Ward Bond, sailing the open seas, free men, free for adventure. Pirates would loom on the horizon in tattered clothing, holding in one hand the rope of sail rigging, and in the other, flashing their sword. A battle plan in place, I would race towards the blue smoke of the cannon fire only to be interrupted by the ending of the ride. Throughout my time as a kid, I can tell you matey, that I experienced the salt on my face and the likes of the skull and crossbones many a time. I was a pirate.

Along the way I lost sight of the boats and became enthralled with hiking, and experiencing the land. Travel Country Outdoors had not only given me a job after retirement, but also the time and opportunity to enjoy what I like to do - play outdoors. For years, that meant on land, only.

Then, many years later, I was approached by a kayak sales rep, who told me there was an opening for a kayaker to participate in a week long, open water kayak trip in southwest Florida, and I heard, "Would you like to go?" Before the inflection was raised in his voice, I could hear my own voice replying, "Just tell me where to meet and the time. I'm In!"

Forty-five years after boating in my boyhood world of pirates, I looked over the bow of my kayak, and saw a line of 10 multi-colored kayaks and paddlers making a wake in the Gulf of Mexico. We were on a five day adventure in an area known as The Ten Thousand Island National Aquatic Preserve in Southwest Florida, an area steeped in the history of Spanish conquest and pirate folklore. I was a pirate, again.

Stopping for a break on the high seas, I looked at my fellow kayakers and suddenly saw, bobbing up and down in the gulf waters, not adults in kayaks but tiny speed boats carrying boys and girls within a metal doughnut, sailing on fantasy dreams. I heard from a distance a faint voice from deep within, getting louder, until I comprehended the words... "Let's make for White Horse Island for lunch." The mental image of my fantasy dream vanished with real bobbing kayakers bringing me back to reality. The break was over and one by one, we pointed our bows to a distant land mass, that was - according to my map - called White Horse Island, and began paddling again through the rolling waves. We arrived at White Horse and beached our boats on a sandy white shoreline that was covered in shells, driftwood and the floating debris of civilization. The other guys sat around their boats and ate lunch. Still fresh with forty-five year old memories, I set off to explore the island, look for treasure and to chase after other pirates. Away from the crowd of my fellow paddlers, I was walking on a footprint free beach, dreaming of possibly being the first human to visit this island. But my mental image was destroyed as I stared at the remains of a fire pit piled with charred wood, sand and the melted remains of aluminum beer cans.

Disgusted by the garbage of man, I picked up the debris and let Mother Nature sooth my anguish by gazing out into the crystal blue waters with floating white puffy clouds set off against a blue sky. I was further rewarded by several dorsal fins breaking the surface in the channel and hearing the exhale of the dolphins. I was asked by the group when I got back, "Did I find any treasure?" "Of course," I said.

Back on the water, thoughts and images flashed through my mind as the cadence of the paddles hitting the water once again put me in a trance. Memories of my boyhood Boat Rides made me realize that I gave up looking for pirates (bad guys) and plunder (evidence) when I retired from a past life as a fire investigator. But I was looking for adventure again. Seconds later I could feel myself smile as I realized I had freed myself from the metal rods that held my little speed boat and was now living a boyhood dream.

EPILOUGE

This is not the end, but just the beginning. There are so many trails for me yet to hike in the United States and in other countries of our world, that I have a perpetual Top Ten List. As I complete and check off one trail another comes to my attention. Part of my top ten list includes The Coast to Coast in England, The Wraith Way in Scotland, The Bruce Trail in Canada, The Beadford Track in New Zealand, The Inca Trail in Peru and in the United States: The Long Trail in Vermont, The Wonderland Trail in Washington, and a thru hike of the Florida National Scenic Trail . New trails are constantly being trail blazed adding to the list. What I am trying to say, is that no matter what your age, there is a lifetime of hiking waiting to be walked or what I call, earth touching.

It is always sad for me to say good-bye to a trail. Some trails you wish never ended, other trails you can't wait to end and others find a way to end at just the right moment. However, all trails can teach you lessons in life and nature. Time spent on a trail is a learning experience of oneself, of man's relationship, or lack of relationship with nature and how delicate the fulcrum of nature is balanced. It is a journey over a dirt path that leads to different challenges, magnificent scenery, and powerful spots of energy to recharge the spirit and soul.

To my hiking family (past, present and future), trail angels and readers of my writings: each of us has contributed to the other's journey and I thank you for being a part of mine. I sincerely hope each of you discover your own paradise, whether on the water, a long distance trail, a day hike, a city park, or just stepping outside of your home - it's only a footstep away.

KrispyKritter

APPENDIX I

KRISPYKRITTER'S TOP TEN ESSENTIAL ITEMS YOU SHOULD CARRY IN THE OUTDOORS

Once you open the door and step outside, your adventure adrenaline kicks in. You are either a beginner, or continue to be, an adventurer in nature. It does not matter what form of pursuit you take (hiking, paddling, biking, climbing outdoor snow activities, etc.), you *are* outdoors, and I believe it imperative that you carry a small kit of insurance just in case the adventure, becomes a misfortune.

There is a chance some type of injury, or other event, will delay your return safely, thus developing a survival situation. To better the odds in these events, many mainstream outdoor enthusiasts and organizations recommend carrying ten proven items to assist in such situations.

This proven list was created by a Seattle based organization for climbers and outdoor adventures called mountaineers. Members of the club got together in the early 1930's because their adventures continued year round. To ensure member's safety, they developed a top ten list of essential items to be carried by anyone going into the outdoors. The purpose of the list, according to the authors:

"Has always been to answer two basic questions, first, can you respond positively to an accident and emergency? Second, can you safely spend a night – or more – out?"

The following, is the original list by the group and is referred to as *"The Ten Essentials"*:

1 Map
2 Compass
3 Sunglasses/sunscreen
4 Extra clothing
5 Headlamp/flashlight (also known as torch)
6 First-aid kit

7   Firestarter
8   Windproof and waterproof matches
9   Knife
10 Extra Food

Today, the industrial world has given the consumer large selections to choose from. Changing with the times, some outdoor enthusiasts (including KrispyKritter) have upgraded the *The Ten Essentials* to create categories instead of items. The following is a list of categories I use. Some of them may incorporate several of the classic items into one category:

1   Navigation
2   Sun Protection
3   Extra Clothing/Emergency Shelter
4   Illumination
5   First-aid kit
6   Fire
7   Repair kit and mini tools
8   Nutrition
9   Hydration
10 Signaling Device

NAVIGATION – Involves all the tools (map, compass, altimeter, GPS) needed to know where you are and, more importantly, how to get out of an emergency. A map and compass should always be carried. The map (hand-made or professionally done) incorporates details of the area used as navigation points. The compass should be liquid filled, have 2-degree increments with a range of 0 to 360-degree, and a base plate with a straight edge for map bearings and determining distance. Most importantly learn to properly use the map and compass, together and separately.

Anything with a battery is subject to failure due to breakage and loss of energy. The GPS (Global Positioning System) is a great tool to use in conjunction with the map and compass, but should never replace them for navigation. For further information on GPS there are many websites describing its use and function. Try www.rei.com/learn/expert-advice/gps-receiver-howto.html www8.garmin.com/manuals/GPSGuideforBeginners_Manual.pdf.

Another useful electronic tool is the cell phone. However, this is not a dependable piece of equipment due to loss of reception, batteries going dead, and being damaged through dropping, soaking or being lost.

SUN PROTECTION – Clothing and sunscreen are the two best systems for protection from the sun. Use light colored clothing to cover exposed layers of skin. Wear a hat to shade sensitive areas of the head (ears, nose and neck).

Sunscreen is rated as SPF (Sun Protection Factor) numbers and is applied to the skin as a liquid or balm-stick. SPF is a measure of protection from ultraviolet radiation (invisible light waves called UVA and UVB) produced by the sun. Both UVA and UVB penetrate the atmosphere and play an important role in conditions such as premature skin aging, eye damage (including cataracts), and skin cancers. Protection is rated from 1 to 45 or above. For example, a sunscreen with an SPF of 15 filters 92% of the UVB. SPF 15 will delay the onset of sunburn in a person, who would burn in 10 minutes would now burn in 150 minutes. The SPF 15 sunscreen allows a person to stay out in the sun 15 times longer. The bottom line is to protection your skin.

Sunglasses are another important sun protector. Elevation gains increases the intensity of ultraviolet rays that can damage your eyes. Compound this with light reflection from water and snow and you are asking for disaster. Look for glasses that have the highest UV protection.

ILLUMINATION – Is a form of temporary lighting using a battery as an energy source. Lighting is important for night time activities especially when confronted with an unexpected overnight stay, for those times when the activity takes longer than planned and getting back to the starting point is after dark. In today's market, there are three types to consider: the flashlight, headlamp and what I call the 'pinch light', that can be easily carried in the essential kit:

- Flashlights have gotten smaller and lighter, but still bulky for a small carrying kit.
- Headlamps are great when worn on the head because it follows the direction where one is looking. However, this also can be bulky.
- The 'pinch light' contains a small coin battery with one LED bulb and by squeezing the light between the forefinger and thumb will turn it on and the illumination is bright enough for walking in the dark. Some lights have an on/off switch. Pinch lights are small and ideal for a kit, or as a backup to your main light source.

Regardless, remember to always carry spare batteries.

FIRST AID KIT – Is a small kit that carries supplies for minor injuries (band-aids, antibiotic ointment, disposable gloves, CPR mask, small syringe for irrigation and tweezers). A variety of kits can be bought on the internet or in stores, or you can make your own to fit your needs and knowledge. Remember to include prescribed medication.

I highly recommend taking some type of first aid training to learn how to handle potential life threatening situations and medical emergencies.

Three very good organizations to learn more about first aid and CPR: the American Red Cross www.redcross.org/take-a-class, Wilderness Medical Associates www.wildmed.com and the National Outdoor Leadership School, Wilderness Medical Institute www.nols.edu/wmi.

FIRE – This category includes cigarette lighters, matches, and firestarters. The first source of ignition is the cigarette lighter. However, this mechanical tool can fail for various reasons. A backup supply of waterproof/windproof matches should be included in the kit.

Firestarters can be any type of material used to quickly ignite and maintain a fire for a short period of time. They can be homemade or store bought, and are useful in emergency situations, especially igniting wet wood. There are many variations of store bought firestarters, composed of magnesium blocks with strikers, chemically-treated fire sticks, or cotton material. Homemade devices can be found in survival books and on the internet. There are too many to list, so find the easiest to make and use, then before going out, try it out. Through trial and error a confident decisions will be made that the firestarter will work.

REPAIR KIT AND TOOLS – This is a small, essential kit used to repair clothing and gear. Items should include, 6 ft. of rolled duct tape, cable ties, needle and thread, assorted size safety pins, medium sized buttons, and 15 ft. of accessory cord.

At one time, tools referred only to a knife. Today, there are multi-use tools that can cut, saw, screw, and ply. The majority of these products do contain a small knife blade, one of the most useful tools in a survival situation.

NUTRITION – Your extra food depends on the time period spent outdoors. As a rule of thumb, the extra food is not considered a part of the day's snack and should maintain a person for a 24 hour period. It is best if this extra food is 'cold food', meaning it does not require cooking.

HYDRATION – The human body needs daily intake of water - differing in amounts based upon the size of the person. The body needs more water in strenuous activity and hot weather. Lack of water can cause dehydration. Carry a container of water of at least one liter for hydration. More will depend on length of stay and climate conditions. Also carry reliable water purification consisting of either a filter (eliminates a variety of bacteria, parasites and protozoa) or some form of purifier system (eliminates viruses along with a variety of bacteria, parasites and protozoa).

EXTRA CLOTHING/EMERGENCY SHELTER – Knowing the area where you will be in and the expected weather conditions are important factors to consider when wearing and bringing extra clothing. Besides the basic layers, clothing with insulation qualities can make an unexpected overnight, pleasant.

There are two important components to consider when choosing clothing for protection from the cold. Air and moisture will use improper clothing to steal body heat, creating a life threatening situation called hypothermia.

In cold conditions, it is important for clothing material to stop the wind from penetrating to the skin. The insulation, either manmade or natural, is constructed to contain small pockets of air that are warmed up by the warm air close to the body.

Water is a good conductor of heat and with improper clothing could replace the warm air surrounding the body with cold air. Heat loss may occur if clothing is wet from rain, immersion, or dampness from sweat.

Outdoor enthusiasts recommend layering your clothing into three layers (base, thermal and hard shell) for the best protection from the cold.

Base layer - the layer that remains in contact with the skin and its main function is to move water vapor away from the body and expel it to the outside air.

Hard shell - the exterior piece of clothing that makes contact with the outside environment. It is the final layer in keeping warm air in, so the material is both waterproof and windproof. Also, look for a material that is breathable to release the escaping water vapor into the outside air.

Thermal layer – the piece in between the base layer and the hard shell. This thick layer traps the air for warmth. It is o.k. to use multiple thinner layers so that if the body begins to produce excessive water vapor (sweat), a layer can be removed to cool down the body. Remember, the whole purpose of the layering system is to prevent sweat buildup. This can also apply the other way. If the body begins to feel cold add another thermal layer.

I cannot stress enough how important it is to have updated weather information before setting out into the outdoors. Being prepared with the proper extra clothing could make the difference.

In this category the discussion is about protecting the body from the elements of nature. Therefore, I have included emergency shelters. You never know when a day outing, even one for a few hours, will turn into an unexpected overnight stay in the outdoors. To prepare for such an event, carry an emergency shelter that is waterproof and windproof. It can be a tube tent, emergency space blanket, or as little as a large, plastic lawn trash bag that can be set up to crawl into and be protected from the elements.

SIGNALING DEVICE – A whistle is a good signaling device to carry in the case of you are lost, someone else is lost, or you are immobile due to an injury. A whistle can be heard farther than voice and doesn't require as much energy as shouting. The best whistle to use is the one used on PFD's (personal floatation device) approved by the United States Coast Guard.

In the search and rescue community the universal sign for distress occurs in threes. For example, three fires in a row, three columns of smoke, or in the case of a whistle, three distinct, separate blows of the whistle. The response back to let the whistle blower know they have been heard is two distinct whistles back.

Another type of signaling device called a PLD (personal locator device), uses technology and is activated by acquiring your exact GPS coordinates through satellites and then sends that location along with a distress message to International Emergency Response Centers. There are several on the market that are lightweight and easy to use. One of the most popular companies is called SPOT. For further information on SPOT, go to http://www.findmespot.com/en. With any type of electronic device, make sure before you step outdoors, it is fully charged, and you have spare batteries.

I always carry 20 ft. or more, bright color (usually orange) surveying flagging tape and a small permanent marker. The tape helps mark routes when temporarily leaving a camp in rough terrain (going to the bathroom, getting water, exploring, etc.). The tape can also help mark the unexpected overnight campsite and help alert rescuers to your location. I use the tape to mark routes for a return trip, picking up the tape as I go. Also, if you are lost and the situation warrants that you have to move the tape is great to leave notes on and to leave a cookie-crumb trail. (name/date/time/direction of travel and pertinent information rescuers might need (how many in group, any injuries, etc.)

Having the right gear is only part of the equation of survival. The number one tool on any survival list is *common sense* and using your ability to think. It is generally the lack of good judgment and inexperience that gets people into trouble. Knowing when and how to use your equipment, combined with using your head, may mean the difference in a struggle for life in the outdoors.

Practice, Practice, Practice.

APPENDIX II
KRISPYKRITTER'S TOP TEN SAFETY RULES FOR OUTDOOR RECREATION

If you go on the internet or reads 'how-to' books and articles on particular forms of outdoor recreation - hiking, paddling, biking, climbing, outdoor snow activity, etc. - you will find rules and tips on how to be safe in those particular activities. But I wanted to create a generic top ten list of safety rules for any type of outdoor recreation. This does not mean you ignore other rules not listed. Each is unique and will have additional safety tips that should be applied. The benefit of being outdoors in nature energizes our mind, body and spirit and KrispyKritter wants everyone to safely return home, and then prepare for the next adventure.

1. Have a plan – Before stepping outdoors develop a plan to where you are going. Research the location to make sure it is within the abilities to all who are going. Check on the latest weather forecast and make sure everyone knows the proper dress for the activity. Include:

- Time of departure
- Names, addresses and phone numbers of everyone in the group
- Medical condition of group members
- Vehicle's make, model, color and tag number
- Expected route of travel, information on start location, camp locations (if it applies)
- Final destination and expected time of return

2. Let Someone Know the Plan – Leave the plan with a family member, or friend. Make sure they know when you are coming back and notify them of your return. Designate a time interval between your expected time of return and when authorities' should be called upon failure of your return.

3. Stick to the Plan – Once you are out the door and out of communication with the person who has your plan, do not deviate from your itinerary. If you change the plan and you get lost, or injured, SAR (Search and Rescue) Units will be following your plan and make locating you more difficult.

4. Carry Your Ten Essential Items – For whatever the reason, even the experienced outdoor recreationist can have an unexpected delay on returning home. Being prepared will increase your chances of surviving the unexpected.

5. Physical Abilities – Be aware of what your limitations are both physically and mentally. Never go alone as a novice. If you attempting to go beyond your experience, or physical ability, take *someone who is knowledgeable* and can monitor your movements. Your body will tell you when something is wrong. Listen to it. Rest, hydrate and take care of the need before an emergency situation develops.

6. Hydrate – The human body can go without food for weeks. However, water is a different matter. Every cell, tissue and organ needs water to maintain temperature, remove waste and lubricate joints. Water is essential for good health, become dehydrated and the muscles begin to build up with lactic acid, that may cause cramping. If you become thirsty during an outdoor recreation you are already in the first stage of dehydration. Other systems are:

- Headaches
- Weakness
- Fatigue
- Problems thinking
- Decrease in sweat
- Muscle cramping
- Dry mouth

7. Carry ID and medical history – In the event you are found unconscious, information about you may be critical in saving your life. Include your name, next of kin, medication you currently are taking and medical history.

8. Be Alert – Look where you are in relation to landmarks and maps. Also, when walking, biking, climbing, paddling, etc., look for things that may cause you to lose your balance and fall, or cause you to stray off track.

9. Be Back Before Dark – Unless it is a planned overnight stay in the outdoors, plan your adventure to conclude before nightfall. Traveling after dark increases the chances of injury and getting lost.

10. Bring Some Type of Communication – The advancement of electronics and coverage make it advisable to take a fully charged cell phone with you. Just know, depending on your location, a signal may not get out, the battery fail, or the phone dropped and damaged. Also, if you have a Personal Location Device, like the SPOT, bring it.

APPENDIX III
KRISPYKRITTER 10 MOST COMMON MISTAKES IN OUTDOOR RECREATION

Being involved in the SAR (Search and Rescue) community, we have found that many mistakes made by lost individuals during an outdoor recreation were due to:

- not following the outdoor safety rules
- not carrying the ten essential items kit
- not following what to do in the case if lost
- not paying attention to surroundings

The ten most common mistakes made by both the beginner as well as the experienced outdoors person are:

1 Not telling anyone about a plan
2 Straying from the plan
3 Failure to bring the proper clothing due to lack of preparation for terrain or weather
4 Not bringing the "Top Ten Essential Items for Outdoor Recreation"
5 Not staying hydrated
6 Losing track of time and staying out unexpectedly after dark
7 Wandering off, not paying attention, and forgetting where you are in relation to the landmarks
8 Not knowing when to turn back
9 Going into dangerous terrain alone (unless you are experienced and have given your plan to someone)
10 Separating when in a group.

APPENDIX IV
WHAT TO DO IF LOST

You've done everything right, you planned, prepared the right gear, and followed the safety rules for outdoor recreation, and yet - you get lost. Now what?

By remembering the simple acronym – **STOP** - your chances of being found safe are greatly enhanced. Already in your favor , you gave the plan of your outdoor excursion to a family member or friend. Second, you did not deviate from the plan and third, the person with the plan, followed your instructions, because you did not return within specified time period.

Now you are alone or, in a group, and/or injured, and have no idea where you are, and how to get out of the situation.

STOP will help you assess your predicament.

S – stop – The instant you feel that you are lost:

- stop moving – to continue moving as a lost person will only get you deeper into trouble,
- stay put, If your location is not safe, find one close by
- stay calm

T – think - use the number one tool in any survival situation - your mind.

- Sit down, drink some water and/or eat something – this will help you relax
- By thinking things over you may solve the problem and get out of your predicament.
  - o In your mind retrace your movements
  - o What was the last known landmark you can remember
  - o Can you re-trace your footprints to that landmark
  - o What do you have that can help you in the situation
  - o Do not move at all until you have a specific reason to take a step. Walking around while thinking is not a great idea.

O – observe – Look around you
- If you do not know –find the cardinal directions
- Do prominent landmarks correspond to landmarks on the map? If you can orient the map to landmarks, this may be enough to re-orient yourself. You can now consider yourself misplaced – not lost.
- How much daylight is left
- Are you prepared for weather
- How much water do you have and is there any nearby
- If there are other hikers involved what is their condition and assess their equipment

P – plan – if you have not re-oriented, or can't move due to injury – what is the   plan
- By taking into account what you observed and your thought process prioritize your actions
  - What type of signals are you using to be found
  - Shelter
  - Water
  - Fire – for light at night, boiling water, heat from the cold, and the feeling of comfort
- If you move, mark your route in case you need to get back to your last known location
-

WHEN IN DOUBT, STAY PUT!
By staying put there will be threats to overcome while waiting for rescue.
- ❖ Loneliness
  - Being alone
  - Stay busy by completing tasks of your plan.

- ❖ Fear
  - Wild animals.
    - Not getting found
    - Use fear as moviation to complete tasks (ex. shelter, fire water, type of signaling devices)

❖ Getting hurt

It is your choice, fear can paralyze you and lower your survival chances or, control your fear through action and increase your chances.

❖ Thirst – Dehydration affects the body and mind - hydrate, hydrate, hydrate

❖ Exhaustion

- Rest whenever possible. Exhaustion lowers the body and mind's effectiveness
- Increases the possibility of injury
- Complete tasks of shelter and warmth early in your situation makes life of being lost more comfortable and somewhat restful –eliminating threats.

❖ Hot/Cold

- Staying dry and warm are two of the most important tasks you have when lost.
- Know the signs of hypothermia and heat illness

❖ Injury

- Immediate treat any injury promptly
- Keep all wounds no matter how small, clean and treated. Infection is a serious threat that will be hard to overcome, was the infection starts.

❖ Hunger

- Every day of not eating is another day you are consuming your body's stores and becoming weaker. You can go many days without food, but each day without food makes a weaker body.
- Complete priorized task early when body is stronger.

APPENDIX V
SEVEN PRINCIPLES OF LEAVE NO TRACE

The member-driven Leave No Trace Center for Outdoor Ethics teaches people how to enjoy the outdoors responsibly. This copyrighted information has been reprinted with permission from the Leave No Trace Center for Outdoor Ethics: www.LNT.org . The Leave No Trace Seven Principles are also available for various environments and activities.

1. Plan Ahead and Prepare
- Know the regulations and special concerns for the area you'll visit.
- Prepare for extreme weather, hazards, and emergencies.
- Schedule your trip to avoid times of high use.
- Visit in small groups when possible. Consider splitting larger groups into smaller groups.
- Repackage food to minimize waste.
- Use a map and compass to eliminate the use of marking paint, rock cairns or flagging.

2. Travel and Camp on Durable Surfaces
- Durable surfaces include established trails and campsites, rock, gravel, dry grasses or snow.
- Protect riparian areas by camping at least 200 feet from lakes and streams.
- Good campsites are found, not made. Altering a site is not necessary.
- In popular areas:
  * Concentrate use on existing trails and campsites.
  * Walk single file in the middle of the trail, even when wet or muddy.
  * Keep campsites small. Focus activity in areas where vegetation is absent.
  * In pristine areas: Disperse use to prevent the creation of campsites and trails.

*Avoid places where impacts are just beginning.

3. Dispose of Waste Properly

- Pack it in, pack it out. Inspect your campsite and rest areas for trash or spilled foods. Pack out all trash, leftover food and litter.
- Deposit solid human waste in catholes dug 6 to 8 inches deep, at least 200 ft from water, camp and trails. Cover and disguise the cathole when finished.
- Pack out toilet paper and hygiene products.
- To wash yourself or your dishes, carry water 200 feet away from streams or lakes and use small amounts of biodegradable soap. Scatter strained dishwater.

4. Leave What You Find

- Preserve the past: examine, but do not touch cultural or historic structures and artifacts.
- Leave rocks, plants and other natural objects as you find them.
- Avoid introducing or transporting non-native species.
- Do not build structures, furniture, or dig trenches.

5. Minimize Campfire Impacts

- Campfires can cause lasting impacts to the backcountry. Use a lightweight stove for cooking and enjoy a candle lantern for light.
- Where fires are permitted, use established fire rings, fire pans, or mound fires.
- Keep fires small. Only use sticks from the ground that can be broken by hand.
- Burn all wood and coals to ash, put out campfires completely, then scatter cool ashes.

6. Respect Wildlife

- Observe wildlife from a distance. Do not follow or approach them.

- Never feed animals. Feeding wildlife damages their health, alters natural behaviors, and exposes them to predators and other dangers.
- Protect wildlife and your food by storing rations and trash securely.
- Control pets at all times, or leave them at home.
- Avoid wildlife during sensitive times: mating, nesting, raising young, or winter.

7. Be Considerate of Other Visitors

- Respect other visitors and protect the quality of their experience.
- Be courteous. Yield to other users on the trail.
- Step to the downhill side of the trail when encountering pack stock.
- Take breaks and camp away from trails and other visitors.
- Let nature's sounds prevail. Avoid loud voices and noises.

ABOUT THE AUTHOR

Wayne "KrispyKritter" Petrovich grew up in Florida, then spent 33 years with the fire service as a firefighter/medic. He concluded his career as a fire investigator for the Florida State Fire Marshal's Office. Wayne became a Search and Rescue Technician and organized the State Fire Marshal's Office Emergency Response Team who responded to natural and/or manmade disasters and assisted governmental agencies in the search and rescue of lost individuals in the wilderness. As a fire investigator, Wayne authored *A Fire Investigator's Handbook: Technical Skills for Entering, Documenting and Testifying in a Fire Scene Investigation.*

Wayne's first backpacking trip was in 1976 and has yet to stop hiking. Throughout his firefighting career he backpacked when he could on weekends and annual vacation time. Unsatisfied with letting the embers of life smolder after retirement, Wayne fueled his passion for the outdoors and found a second life as a long distance hiker. Beginning with a six month communion with nature on the 2,172 mile Appalachian Trail in 2004. Wayne, also known by his trail name KrispyKritter, currently has over 8,000 trail miles under his boots, and counting.

"Krispy" or "Kritter" as his friends call him, has completed thru hikes on The Appalachian Trail, Bartram Trail, Foothills Trail, Tahoe Rim Trail, John Muir Trail, Ocala Trail, West Highland Way in Scotland and the Pennine Way in England. He currently works for an outfitter store in Central Florida helping others enjoy the rewards of Mother Nature.